Arms Trade and Economic Development

ARMS TRADE AND ECONOMIC DEVELOPMENT

EMERGING SCENARIO

Brig. (Retd.) P.V. Mann

PRASHANT PUBLISHING HOUSE

DELHI-110094

Published by :

Prashant Publishing House

C-34, 28 Foota Road, Gali-3,

West Karwal Nagar, Delhi-110094

Phone : 011-22963970, Mob. : 9810396373

Arms Trade And Economic Development

Emerging Scenario

First Pubished 2011

ISBN 978-93-80565-20-0

PRINTED IN INDIA

Published by Mr. R.K. Jha M/s Prashant Publishing House and Published at H.S. Offset House Press, Delhi.

Preface

The movement of arms across the world is a huge threat to human security. Around 8 million new small arms are manufactured every year, but far more significant is the movement of second-hand guns from one user to another. They last-and remain lethal-for decades. At present, it is impossible to monitor or interrupt this deadly flow of weapons. This is because there are no agreed global standards for governments when authorising exports or transfers. The proliferation and misuse of small arms and light weapons is one of the most pressing security threats of the 21st century. From Sudanese refugees hunted by gun-toting militias to air passengers targeted by shoulder-fired missiles, no one is safe from this deadly scourge. Providing a gripping overview of these cheap and easily obtainable weapons, the threat they pose in the wrong hands, and strategies for reining them in, this Beginner's Guide is required reading for anyone wishing to fully understand one of today's key threats to international peace.

The combined arms sales of the top 100 largest arms producing companies amounted to an estimated $315 billion in 2006. In 2004 over $30 billion were spent in the international arms trade (a figure that excludes domestic sales of arms). The arms trade has also been one of the sectors impacted by the credit crunch, with total deal value in the market halving from US$32.9bn to US$14.3bn in 2008. Many industrialized countries have a domestic arms industry to supply their own military forces. Some countries also have a substantial legal or illegal domestic trade in weapons for use by its citizens. An illegal trade in small arms is prevalent in many countries and regions affected by political instability.

—Editor

Contents

1

The Arms Trade, Debt and Economic Development

INTRODUCTION

Poverty is one of the root causes of violence. Many of the most heavily indebted poor countries (HIPCs) in the world are currently engaged in, or emerging from conflict. Protracted conflict inevitably leads to highly militarised societies, reflected in above average levels of military expenditures and large numbers of combatants under arms. Conflict provides lucrative markets for arms dealers, of both a licit and illicit nature. In order to purchase arms poor countries cut public expenditures in health and education and borrow foreign exchange from international creditors. The poor become poorer and conflict becomes more widespread. This sets up a vicious cycle of debt, underdevelopment and conflict, which can only be broken if radical action is taken by the international community to confront the systemic nature of poverty and underdevelopment.

A fundamental starting point for comprehending these issues is to explore the complexities of the damaging relationship between poverty and conflict on the one hand, and the positive relationship between sustainable development and security on the other. These are the structural elements that contribute to the problem of debt and underdevelopment. Arms transfers and militarism are the triggering factors that exacerbate debt, poverty and conflict. These issues are examined in detail in the first part of the chapter. The second section examines some of the existing contradictions in the UK's policies towards development, debt and the arms trade. The final section provides case studies which explore the relationship between development, debt and the arms trade in two HIPC countries-Sierra Leone and Kenya, and two middle income countries-Indonesia and South Africa.

Sustainable Development and Security

The international community concerned with peace and security has been slow to recognise the importance of sustainable development to security, but as the United Nations Development Programme (UNDP) has observed 'it is not possible for the community of nations to achieve any of its major goals-not peace, not environmental protection, not human rights or democratisation, not fertility reduction nor social integration-except in the context of sustainable development that leads to human security.

Sustainable development is a wide-ranging concept referring to a simultaneous improvement in the environmentally supportable economic output of a country, the advancement of employment opportunities, the promotion of social well-being and the eradication of poverty. Sustainable human development as advocated by the UNDP is intrinsically related to the creation of social stability by virtue of the fact that it seeks to remove discriminatory factors within an economy (sources of conflict) by providing opportunities for all members of society to enrich their socio-economic potential.

Poverty and Conflict

Despite the significant development gains which have been made in the last three decades there are still an estimated 1.3 billion people who live in abject poverty, whose economic circumstances have deteriorated over the last ten years. According to the World Bank, the minimum requirement for a basic standard of living is an annual income of $370 ('$' are 'US$' unless otherwise indicated). In 1997 average per capita income in low income countries in Sub-Saharan Africa was $350 per annum, life expectancy at birth was 59 years, infant mortality was 78 per 1,000 live births and illiteracy was 47% of the population over the age of 15. The average annual growth of real gross domestic product (GDP) in Sub-Saharan Africa-the poorest region in the world-has fallen from 2.5% between 1985-1989 to 1.9% between 1990-1997.

Table 1: Average Annual % Rate of Growth In Selected Sub-Saharan African Countries

	1975-84	*1985-89*	*1990-97*
Angola	-	4.7	-1.6
Burundi	3.8	5.1	-2.8
Cameroon	8.5	-0.1	-0.9
Congo	-0.3	1.7	-6.7
Ethiopia	-	4.1	3.5
Gambia	4.3	3.3	2.4
Kenya	4.7	5.9	2.1
Liberia	0.1	-1.2	-
Mozambique	-	6.0	4.2
Rwanda	6.8	2.9	-5.5
Sierra Leone	2.0	0.8	-3.3
Sudan	2.6	0.9	-
Zambia	0.2	2.3	-0.4

Source: World Bank Data 1998

The widespread economic collapse of many sub-Saharan states has undermined the social cohesion of societies and exposed the inability of the state to extend basic security to its citizens, reflected in the widespread proliferation of humanitarian emergencies and conflict on the continent. In many cases this has led to the loss of political legitimacy and the subsequent collapse of states. Collapsing states are defined by Zartman as 'a situation where the structure, authority (legitimate power), law, and political order have fallen apart'. Throughout the African continent, the collapse of states is reflected in a general deterioration in central authority, a disintegration of social cohesion, corruption, ethnic strife, widespread militarism, large numbers of non-state actors under arms and the proliferation of light weapons and intra-state conflict.

The enduring nature of conflict, debt and underdevelopment in certain regions of the developing world can trace their origins to the Cold War. At the height of bi-polar confrontation in the

1970s and 1980s a number of the world's poorest regions, such as Central America, the Horn of Africa, Southern Africa and Indo-China, were drawn into the superpowers' wars of proxy. The escalation of localised conflicts through superpower intervention led to rapid regional militarisation, reflected in high levels of military expenditures and conventional weapons' proliferation. According to World Bank figures, in 1985 Nicaragua allocated 26.2% of government spending to military expenditures, Mozambique spent 38%, El Salvador 29.1%, Ethiopia 28.9%, Iran 34.1%. In most of these cases arms purchases were a significant factor in placing upward pressure on military expenditure budgets. With the end of the Cold War many of these conflicts have been resolved, but the debt of war remains as a debilitating factor inhibiting sustainable development and the ability of these countries to establish a durable stability.

Military Expenditure, Debt and Development

In most developing countries government revenues are insufficiently elastic to be able to accommodate rising military expenditures. In this situation a government has three options; it can reallocate expenditures from other government expenditure headings such as health and education; it can borrow foreign exchange in the international financial markets; or it could do a combination of these. In all three situations there is an opportunity cost in terms of development. Opportunity costs can be defined as the benefits foregone by selecting one option at the expense of another or several others. In a world where resources are scarce, choice implies sacrificing something. The benefit that could have been derived from the alternative, not chosen, is the opportunity cost of the option actually selected.

The UNDP has for some time utilised opportunity cost analysis in an attempt to understand the effect of military expenditures on sustainable development. In its Human Development Report 1994 it argued that the allocation of scarce national resources to military expenditures had incurred a huge loss of potential spending on human development, observing that 'some of the poorest African countries now spend more on defence than they do on their populations' education and health.' Military expenditure influences growth and development in a number of direct and indirect ways. By redirecting government expenditures away from education and health it has an indirect effect on human capital formation. Excessive military expenditure affects the balance of payments situation and levels of infrastructural investment, while large purchases of military equipment from foreign suppliers can distort the balance of trade situation.

Current Military Expenditure Trends in Developing Countries

In general, measuring military expenditures in developing countries is difficult, and in some cases impossible, because of the general lack of transparency and accountability in government accounting procedures and the resistance of authoritarian regimes to revealing their military expenditure accounts. For instance in 1996 no African country reported its military expenditures to the UN under the Reporting Military Expenditures programme. The IMF's latest audit of government finances, published in late 1997, gave 1996 figures on the military budgets of only Burundi, Madagascar, Mauritius, Tunisia and Zambia.

Nevertheless, considerable effort has been made by organisations such as the International Institute for Strategic Studies (IISS) to provide some sort of statistical account of military expenditure trends within the developing world. According to the IISS Military Balance in 1997 Sub-Saharan African expenditure was $8.8bn, a slight increase over the 1996 level, and accounted for around 3.3% of regional GDP. In Southern Africa and East Africa military expenditure has been on the increase largely as a result of recent acquisitions of weapon systems. Botswana's 1998 security budget was $323m, accounting for 11.5% of government expenditure. The armed forces accounted for about two thirds of the budget, with the rest being allocated to policing expenditure. Namibia's 1998 military budget was N$443m ($89m), up from N$416m in 1997. Botswana and Namibia are involved in a border dispute over Kasikili-Sedudu and Sintungu islands in the Caprivi strip of the Linyanti-Chobe river, so their recent arms acquisitions have raised concern within the region.

The Angolan government had an estimated budget of $380m in 1998, about 10% of government spending, although final outlays will probably be higher due to the continuing conflict with UNITA. Military and police spending in Mozambique continues to decline, although it still consumes 19.4% of government expenditure, down from about 38% of government expenditure during the height of the war in the 1980s. Zimbabwe's military expenditure of $456m in 1997/98 dramatically increased because of a one-off disbursement of $210m to war veterans, and is certain to increase because of its involvement in the Congo conflict.

Within the Southern African region, South Africa's military expenditure and budgets, at around R11bn ($1.9bn) for each of the years 1996 to 1999, dwarfs all other military budgets. Current plans to purchase $4.8bn worth of military equipment will reinforce its overwhelming balance of military power within the region and contribute to neighbouring countries' growing concerns over South Africa's hegemonic intentions. In East Africa, military expenditure continues to grow in Uganda, which is engaged in war with the Democratic Republic of Congo and is contending with guerrilla insurgency operations in the north of the country. The 1998 budget was $153m, 26% higher than in 1997. In Tanzania the combined military and police budget of $311m accounted for 23% of the government budget. In Sudan, where civil war wages on relentlessly, the military budget is thought to account for 80% of government expenditure.

In addition to the formal military expenditures, there is a high degree of off-budget funding of military activity in many sub-Saharan African countries, most notably in the procurement of military equipment and the funding and expenditures of armed opposition groups and mercenaries. In the Middle East and North Africa, regional military expenditures increased between 1996-1997 by some 5% in real terms despite declining oil revenues. At an average of 7%-8% of GDP, the region continues to spend significantly more than any other region of the developing world. Countries increasing their military expenditure include Algeria, which is engaged in a vicious civil war, Iran, where rising expenditure is covering a number of expensively produced indigenous weapon systems and Saudi Arabia, UAE and Qatar, which are all involved in importing expensive state of the art weapon systems. Israel has a military budget of $7bn, accounting for between 10%-12% of GDP, and is a major market for US weapon systems. The region remains the largest and most lucrative arms market in the world for sales of advanced weapon systems. Regional arms deliveries in 1997 were estimated at $17bn.

Military spending in Central and South Asia showed a growth of 3% in real terms in 1997, from $18.7bn in 1996 to $19.2bn in 1997. India and Pakistan account for over 80% of regional military expenditures. Military expenditure as a proportion of GDP was around 5% in 1997, higher than anywhere else except the Middle East. In East Asia and Australasia military expenditures have been significantly affected by the financial crisis and fell by about 5% in real terms in 1997, from $149bn in 1996 to $142bn in 1997 (1997 prices). The depreciation of East Asian currencies against the dollar increased the cost of foreign imports forcing some countries to cancel orders for expensive weapon systems.

High levels of state and non-state military expenditure and the purchase of arms have done little to enhance the security of the majority of citizens in the developing world. Since 1945 more than 20 million people have died in wars and internal conflicts, a large proportion of these in the developing world. The UNDP maintains that 'countries spending very little on defence and much more on human development have been much more successful at defending their national sovereignty than those spending heavily on arms'. By way of illustration it compares the relatively peaceful experiences of Botswana, Costa Rica and Mauritius with the conflicts afflicting Iraq, Myanmar and Somalia.

Arms Sales

The reliability of data on arms sales to the world's poorest countries is even less conclusive than the information on military expenditures. Since 1994, statistical records of most government to government transfers of major conventional weapons are recorded by the UN Register of Conventional Arms Transfers. Of the 44 countries in Sub-Saharan Africa only Ethiopia, Mauritius, Namibia, Seychelles, South Africa and Tanzania reported their arms transfers, military holdings and domestic procurement to the UN Register on Conventional Arms in 1997.

The figures below on the regional distribution of arms transfers to the developing world produced by the IISS should only be taken as trend indicators as much of the data available only provides a partial picture of the actual scale of transfers.

Table: Regional Distribution of International Arms Transfers 1987 and 1997

	1987 ($m)	*% of world market*	*1997 ($m)*	*% of world market*
Middle East/& N. Africa	33,232	37.5	15,629	33.7
East Asia	10,531	11.9	14,693	31.7
South Asia	6,534	7.4	1,669	3.6
Latin America	5,319	6.0	1,982	4.3
Sub-Saharan Africa	6,791	7.7	991	2.1

Source: IISS Military Balance 1999

Arms sales to Sub-Saharan Africa are particularly difficult to quantify as the majority of transfers go unreported, particularly as the categories of light weapons and ammunition, which constitute a significant proportion of arms procurement in the region, are not currently included in any of the existing data bases on arms transfers. Light weapons and ammunition are supplied by local industries as well as by international suppliers, but more significantly there is a large trade in recycled weaponry from past conflicts for personal use, as well as for use by statutory and non-statutory forces. This latter form of trade is particularly hard to track and thus to quantify. Under these conditions it is very difficult, if not impossible, to measure in any statistical way the scale of transfers into conflict zones in the developing world.

The main sources of supply for conventional arms are from a handful of industrialised states which comprise the Permanent Members of the UN Security Council-the US, France, UK, Russia, China. In addition there are a number of newly industrialising countries such as Israel, Brazil and South Africa which have become recent entrants into the international arms market. Since the end of the Cold War, a huge second hand market in weapon systems has also emerged with large supplies coming from former Warsaw Pact countries. Developing countries continue to be the primary focus of foreign arms sales activity by the major weapons suppliers. According to Grimmett, during the years 1989-1996 the value of arms transfer agreements with developing nations comprised on average 67.5% of all such agreements worldwide. The value of all arms transfer agreements with developing nations in 1996 was some $19.4bn, which represented the first increase in arms sales since 1992. In 1996 the United States was the biggest exporter, having sales agreements worth $11.3bn, the UK with agreements worth $4.8 was in second place, and Russia with sales agreements worth $4.6bn ranked third.

The influence wielded by military industrial elites of the supplier states and their drive to export, created by the need to maintain employment in domestic military industries and generate returns from large outlays incurred on domestic weapons procurement projects, ensures that certain violent and repressive regimes such as Indonesia, Nigeria and Pakistan have been able to acquire weapons with relative ease. In part, these patterns of transfers derive from patronage relations established during the Cold War which have endured despite expectations of a new and positive world order.

Patronage not withstanding, a contradictory trend is discernible amongst those Northern states which support the principles of conflict prevention, development and good governance, yet place little if any unilateral restraint on the export of arms to developing countries. There are some signs that measures are being taken to rectify this anomaly in the international community's dealings with post-conflict and conflict-prone societies. The recent adoption of a 'security first' approach, for instance, is based on the notion that security should no longer be considered discrete and unrelated to other spheres of foreign policy, but should instead form part of an integrated approach by donors.

One cannot conceive of an effective conflict prevention policy that does not tackle the problem of arms supplies. At present no multilateral system for controlling sources of supply of major weapons systems exists, as there is for nuclear, chemical, biological and intercontinental ballistic missiles. Even less control exists for light weapons which have caused most of the casualties in war in the developing world since the end of the Cold War. Nevertheless there are a number of initiatives that are likely to come to fruition in the next few years that may rectify this hiatus.

Spurred on by the success of the global campaign to outlaw anti-personnel mines which resulted in the signing of the Ottawa Treaty in December 1997 by more than 120 states, a number of interesting initiatives have been advanced with a view to controlling the flow of light weapons. Support has been gaining momentum for a convention on the prevention of the illegal use of light weapons, aimed principally at establishing strict criteria to govern the export, collection and destruction of surplus armaments and at promoting more transparent international co-operation. In this spirit the UN Panel of Governmental Experts on Small Arms has recommended a number of practical measures to reduce the quantity of weapons in circulation and to curb future acquisitions of small arms, including establishing a regional information-sharing network: providing assistance for democratic internal security forces and assisting post-conflict initiatives related to disarming and demobilising regular and irregular forces. In May 1998, a UK-government-sponsored conference entitled 'Developing Controls on Arms and Illicit Trafficking in Southern Africa' examined ways of developing a regional action plan for Southern Africa, aimed at controlling light weapons proliferation and diffusion. The programme is to be supported by the European Union (EU). Other initiatives by the EU, including the establishment in 1997 of its Programme for preventing and combating illicit trafficking in conventional arms and the adoption of an EU Code of Conduct in June 1998, are a step in the right direction. But it is important to recognise that current initiatives remain inadequately developed and in need of sufficient resources and greater co-ordination at regional and international levels. In the coming decade the challenge will be to enhance and empower these initiatives so that they become the foundations of a new multilateral arms control regime.

Debt and Conflict

Sub-Saharan Africa may only account for a small share of the global arms market but nowhere else is the relationship between debt, development and the arms trade so stark. The profligate policies of military regimes and the widespread proliferation of conflict on the continent have contributed to a high incidence of HIPCs on the continent. In fact 31 of a total of 41 HIPCs are located on the African continent. Moreover, of the countries identified by the World Bank as HIPCs over half are involved in, or have recently emerged from, conflict situations. Those countries currently engaged in either interstate or intra-state conflicts include Angola, Central African Republic, Chad, Republic of Congo-Brazzaville, Democratic Republic of Congo, Ethiopia, Guinea-Bissau, Guinea, Liberia, Sierra Leone, Senegal, Somalia, Sudan and Uganda. Note that all of the above are located in sub-Saharan Africa.

Five countries-Burundi, Mozambique, Nicaragua, Rwanda, and Yemen-are undergoing the fragile process of transition from war to peace, while Vietnam and Lao are still suffering from the effects of conflict which ended over 20 years ago, not least because of the large presence of mines, which affects agricultural production and the return of displaced peoples. Other severely indebted countries such as Nigeria, Kenya and Myanmar are experiencing serious internal instability. In other words, 23 of the 41 HIPC countries, that is over half of the world's poorest, most indebted countries are, or have recently experienced conflict. Many HIPCs are currently ruled, or have been ruled in the recent past, by highly militarised, authoritarian regimes. These include Bolivia, Central African Republic, Chad, Democratic Republic of Congo (formerly Zaire), Kenya, Liberia, Mali, Myanmar, Uganda and Zambia. A report produced by Jubilee 2000, entitled Dictators and Debt, has drawn attention to the fact that one fifth of all developing country debt consists of loans that were given to compliant dictators.

The Cost of Conflict

The cost of conflict to development has been systematically analysed in recent years. The economic consequences of war are multiple and complex. They can be divided into immediate human costs and the longer-term development costs. This division is somewhat artificial because human costs such as the deterioration in nutrition and education, the loss of life and depletion of skills constitute development costs, while developmental costs such as destroyed infrastructure and negative growth are among the causes of human suffering and deprivation. In Southern Africa the sustained costs incurred through the destabilisation campaign waged by apartheid South Africa on its neighbouring states has been estimated to total $115bn. With the end of the Cold War the Southern African region has witnessed the withdrawal of superpower intervention, the end of apartheid, the termination of conflict in Namibia and Mozambique, a thirty percent decline in regional military expenditure and the demobilisation of tens of thousands of soldiers. However, the debts and cost of destruction that accumulated during the Cold War will remain a burden for generations to come. Children not yet born will have to pay the price of debt for wars they did not fight, for ideas they do not hold, for a regional and global system that no longer exists and for decisions made by regional and world leaders no longer in power.

Conflict contributes to debt, but by the same token unsustainable debt poses an ongoing and insidious threat to the well-being and security of millions of people in the developing world. Scarce national resources are siphoned away from poverty alleviation to service debt, enriching the creditors of the affluent Western world. At least 20 of the most heavily indebted poor countries (HIPCs) transfer more than one-fifth of their revenues to creditors in the developed world. In 1995 Africa's external debt amounted to $328bn of which approximately 45% was owed to official bilateral sources, 30% to official multilateral sources, and 25% to commercial lenders. In order to service this debt fully, African countries paid Western governments and external commercial lenders more than 60% ($86.3bn) of the $142.3bn in revenues generated from their exports. In fact, African countries paid more than 17% ($25.4bn) of their total export earnings to these creditors, but this still left a total of $60.9bn in unpaid arrears.

HIPC Debt Initiative

In recognition of the unsustainability of the accumulated debt burden of many poor countries, the World Bank and IMF launched the HIPC Debt Initiative in 1996, which gave some hope to developing countries that they might get some relief from their debt burdens. The identified heavily indebted poor countries include those countries which are unable to generate sufficient foreign exchange through the export of commodities to be able to pay the interest on their loans. The main aim of the World Bank's Debt Initiative for the HIPCs is to bring a country's debt burden to sustainable levels in terms of debt to export earnings ratios, subject to satisfactory policy performance, so as to ensure that adjustment and reform efforts are not put at risk by continued high debt and debt service burdens.

So far the Debt Initiative has proved disappointing. Of the 41 countries identified as HIPCs, so far only three countries have received debt relief, Uganda, Bolivia and Guyana. In all three countries debt relief has been subject to meeting stringent conditionalities imposed by the IMF over a six year qualifying period. In development terms these countries have benefited very little from the initiative, as debt relief has proved to be far too little, far too late. In the case of Mozambique, for instance, which qualifies for debt relief later this year, it will save only $11m on a total debt service bill of more than $108m. Debt repayments will continue to absorb more budgetary resources than health and primary education combined. As Kevin Watkins of Oxfam's Policy Unit has observed 'Defining such a state of affairs as 'debt sustainability' as the framework does, is as absurd in economic terms as it is unacceptable in moral terms'. Critics of the HIPC Debt Initiative argue that the terms and conditionalities that HIPCs are expected to meet are too stringent. According to Jubilee 2000, ratios for measuring debt unsustainability need to be lowered, made more realistic and brought into line with historical precedents. Currently debt sustainability is measured solely in terms of debt-to-export ratios rather than in terms of budgetary burden. This reflects the IMF's insistence on prioritising monetary targets over human development goals, contributing to reduced spending on health and education and creating unemployment and increased levels of household poverty in the process. In order to give some protection to poor countries' development needs, Oxfam has argued for the introduction of a fiscal cap into the debt relief framework, limiting debt repayments to 10% of government revenues.

On a more progressive note, the IMF has introduced caps on military expenditure levels since the end of the Cold War-an initiative supported by the OECD (Organisation for Economic Cooperation and Development) that has argued for the reallocation of military savings to sustainable development goals. But so far few savings from military budgets find their way into development priorities, as the IMF insists on redirecting them towards debt serving. This state of affairs makes a mockery of the IMF and World Bank's publicly-acclaimed commitment to strengthen the linkages between debt relief, poverty reduction and conflict prevention. Kevin Watkins of Oxfam's Policy Unit argues that instead of insisting on compliance with IMF programmes, creditors should offer pro-poor incentives for countries willing to transfer savings from debt relief into schools, clinics and water supplies that will make a qualitative difference to poor peoples' lives. The benefits of converting debt liabilities into investment for poverty reduction are enormous. Not only would it create a platform for social and economic recovery but it would create the conditions for greater social and political stability.

Odious Debt

The heavily indebted poor countries must accept some of the responsibility for their present debt situation, but as UN Secretary General Kofi Annan has argued 'the international community needs to acknowledge its own role in creating this problem. During the Cold War bilateral and multilateral loans were often linked mainly to geopolitical priorities, purchasing political peace and stability in areas of interest to the super-powers or their principal allies. In many cases bilateral loans provided funds for extensive military expenditures by African countries. Across Africa, governments were sometimes pressurised into accepting a wide range of loans which they did not need and could not productively utilise. In many cases little or no effort was made to ensure accountability for expenditures, despite clear reasons for lenders to expect that substantial sums were likely to be diverted or misappropriated.'

Since the end of the Cold War many former dictators have been removed from power and replaced with democratically-elected governments. The tragedy of this otherwise welcome development is that the democratically-elected successors are expected to repay those debts. As the Jubilee 2000 report points out, the lenders and not the borrowers should be responsible for the loans to dictators. There are two compelling reasons why these debts should be forgiven:

- First they are 'odious debts' as defined in international law, and cannot be the responsibility of those who did not incur them and who suffered as a result of those loans.
- Second, there is the issue of 'moral hazard'. By forcing repayment of these loans, the international community signals an acceptance of lending to corrupt and oppressive dictators. If lending is to embody a level of integrity compliant with universal norms then creditors must accept that such lending is morally unacceptable and economically unsound.

All too often the international financial community links the issue of 'moral hazard' to debtor irresponsibility rather than accepting its own share of responsibility for the build up of odious debt. Currently, the IMF acting as a lender of last resort provides a safety net for lenders against the high risks of lending to authoritarian and corrupt regimes. This is the ultimate form of 'moral hazard' and one that has come under close scrutiny since the advent of the East Asian financial crisis that has caused so much suffering and instability throughout East Asia, but most particularly in Indonesia. Only if lenders are forced to take the full risks of their loans will the uneconomic nature of odious loans be made apparent.

A classic case of odious debt and moral hazard is that of the debts of apartheid. The apartheid regime is recognised throughout the world to have denied basic human rights and to have used its security forces for internal repression and external wars with neighbouring states in Southern Africa. During the 1980s its external debt accumulated as the society became increasingly militarised. At the height of militarisation, South Africa officially spent 5% of GDP on military expenditure. This did not include sizeable hidden expenditures on its expensive nuclear weapons programme and its chemical and biological warfare projects. Since the end of the apartheid regime, South Africa has been at peace with its neighbours, and its military expenditure has been cut by over 50% since 1989, yet the debts incurred by the apartheid war machine continue to undermine the alleviation of poverty in the new South Africa.

The archbishop of Cape Town, Njongonkulu Ndungane, has made a strong case for writing off the odious debts of the apartheid era, 'as we approach the new millennium, the time has come to invoke the Doctrine of Odious debt. In the case of South Africa, its foreign and domestic debt was incurred, by and large under the apartheid regime, and should be declared odious and written off.'

Post-Conflict Societies and Debt

At the best of times, meeting the challenge of IMF and World Bank economic reform and structural adjustment-a precondition for debt relief-is onerous, but for those countries emerging from conflict it is nigh on impossible. Kofi Annan has argued that 'where a country's capacity to develop and implement a comprehensive programme has been disrupted by conflict, consideration must be given to relaxing the normally strict financial conditions imposed by international lending institutions. Conflict prevention, including post-conflict peace-building, may require an urgent infusion of funds to support a fragile state during a delicate political transition. It is particularly necessary to avoid situations in which conditionalities are imposed that are antithetical to a peace process, or in which international financial institutions and the donor community cut off funds from a weak government making, in good faith, a popularly-supported effort to pursue reconciliation or implement peace agreements. Where economic reform is needed it is necessary to consider how best to provide for a peace-friendly structural adjustment programme while easing the conditionality that normally accompanies multilateral loans.'

Post-war countries are faced with the immense task of (re)integrating into the global world economy. Peace being settled, they have to strive to become gradually able to compete effectively in world markets and promote their interests in the economic and trading system. This is more arduous now than it was decades ago, as the process of world-wide liberalisation and technological progress has accelerated. While many war-torn societies have fallen prey to the internationalisation of criminal and purely speculative activities, they are in a much more difficult situation to seize potential benefits from the current global economic context, commonly referred to as 'globalisation'.

There is a strong case for debt forgiveness in post-conflict societies to be linked to an insistence on fundamental political change, i.e. a transition from authoritarian military rule to democratic pluralism. In this vein Boyce and Pastor suggest that external actors must formulate appropriate conditionalities if aid is to support the peace process and attract or 'crowd in' domestic resources for peace-related requirements. They argue that in cases such as El Salvador, the international community failed to exert effective peace conditionality but pressed forcefully for macroeconomic reforms.

In so doing the international financial institutions weakened the consolidation of peace by being both too rigorous on public expenditure reduction and not rigorous enough on the reallocation of domestic resources from military to the new democratic institutions. For these authors, the reinforcement of power sharing and democracy is a priority in the wake of a negotiated settlement to a civil war. There is also a strong case for some sort of Marshall Plan approach to economic reconstruction in post-conflict societies, particularly where foreign intervention was responsible for the escalation of militarism and conflict within a region.

UK POLICY TOWARDS THE ARMS TRADE, DEBT AND DEVELOPMENT

As a leading OECD economy with a strong presence in the UN Security Council, the G8, the Paris Club and the EU, the UK government is highly influential in setting the international climate on issues concerning debt, development and the arms trade. Although there have been many progressive reforms in certain aspects of the UK's foreign policies towards the developing world, as this section attempts to show, there is a lack of coherence in the Labour government's current policies towards debt, development and the arms trade.

Development Policy

In November 1997 the Department for International Development (DfID) published the first White Paper on Development to be produced by a UK government for 22 years. The White Paper defined DfID's central mission to support the internationally agreed target to halve the proportion of the world's population living in abject poverty by the year 2015. To achieve this goal, DfID quickly realised that it would have to address one of the major obstacles to development, namely conflict and the highly militarised regimes that dominate many of the world's poorest countries. The DfID Departmental Report 1999 states that 'A major obstacle to the eradication of poverty is the persistence of violent conflict, or its legacy, in many of the poorest countries. Reducing the incidence, duration and effect of armed conflict is essential. DfID's policy for conflict reduction seeks to strengthen political and social systems to enable disputes and grievances to be resolved without recourse to violence.'

As part of this programme DfID has identified security sector reform as a priority for its development agenda. Given the controversial policies of the ODA (DfID's former incarnation) in supplying aid to sweeten arms trade deals, Clare Short, the Secretary of State for International Development, has been emphatic that no UK development assistance should be used to reinforce the role of the military or support arms sales, 'There is obviously no question ...of development resources being used to strengthen the aggressive capability of military forces or being linked to arms sales. Our interest is in helping to secure a security sector of appropriate scale that is properly accountable to democratic, civilian authorities.' A central objective of security sector reform is to reallocate military resources to social need. In the words of Clare Short 'In too many countries, a bloated security sector soaks up resources that would be better used elsewhere. And resources spent on excessive procurement and perks for the military mean the denial of essential public services for the poor.'

In pursuit of these objectives Clare Short has emphasised the importance of co-ordinating DfID's efforts with other government programmes such as the Foreign and Commonwealth Office programme of Assistance to Support

Stability with In-Service Training (ASSIST) and the Ministry of Defence's (MoD's) Defence Diplomacy Programme. She stressed that 'Co-operation is essential in this area of policy, as in others such as trade or debt, to ensure that our Government's influence is used coherently in international affairs.' A problem that DfID is likely to encounter, however, is that the coherence in international affairs so necessary to the success of security sector reform simply does not exist between or even within Whitehall departments.

The UK Government and its Debtors

The UK government has been at the forefront of arguing the need for reform of the HIPC Initiative, and it has initiated debt cancellation in a number of cases on a bilateral basis. Yet the UK government has a track record of providing financial support to facilitate arms sales to unsavoury regimes, and as yet this pattern does not appear.to have been altered. More than one third of all debt owed to the UK government is owed by Nigeria, which amounts to £3bn. Loans were extended to Nigeria while it was under a military dictatorship. Sudan, which is fraught with conflict, is the UK's fourth largest debtor owing £382m. The military regime in Algeria owes the UK £166m which was lent by the UK after the results of the democratic election were annulled. The Democratic Republic of Congo with its history of authoritarianism, human rights violations, corruption and cronyism owes £134m to the UK government.

A large percentage of UK bilateral debts have been incurred through the Export Credits Guarantee Department (ECGD). The ECGD is an independent department under the responsibility of the Secretary of State for Trade and Industry. Its main function is to promote UK exports abroad by guaranteeing payment to UK exporters in the case of a default by foreign customers. It takes on risk that the private sector is not prepared to accept. For the exporter this is an insurance policy. If an importing country does not pay, then the ECGD pays the supplier. A significant percentage of ECGD credit is made available to underwrite UK arms exporters. Between 1994-97, 20% of UK export credits were allocated to cover arms sales.

Many of the existing loans to unsavoury dictators were made under the former Conservative administration whose foreign policy practices came under considerable public scrutiny towards the end of its term. On taking power Robin Cook, the Secretary of State for Foreign Affairs, announced a new mission statement for the Foreign and Commonwealth Office which stated that 'Our foreign policy must have an ethical dimension and must support the demands of other peoples for the democratic rights on which we insist for ourselves. The Labour Government will put human rights at the heart of our foreign policy'. Many areas of foreign policy are undergoing a process of reform to reflect this new ethical commitment, but in the area of the ECGD continuity rather than change appears to characterise current practices.

Some of the most controversial ECGD decisions to have been made under the Labour government are those to cover recent arms sales to the incumbent Indonesian regime, currently facing financial crisis. There are of course strong moral and ethical issues for not exporting arms to Indonesia, which have been elaborated elsewhere. But there are also strong reasons to question the sagacity of the Labour government's decision not to withdraw ECGD cover to Indonesia given the endemic corruption within the former Suharto regime and the Golkar Party which remains in power. A recent World Bank internal document revealed the corruption which resulted in the embezzlement of vast loans meant for Indonesian development since 1997. One third of the loans worth $24bn, intended for infrastructure projects, disappeared into the pockets of the Suharto regime. By extending cover to the current regime the UK government confers a high degree of legitimacy on a regime with a track record of heavy-handed militarism, corruption and human rights abuse, and which does not conform to DfID's policies on conflict resolution, humanitarian assistance and development.

UK Arms Trade Policy

Nowhere is the contradiction between the UK government's development goals and foreign policy objectives more at odds than in its arms trade policy. In July 1997 Robin Cook committed the FCO to a 'responsible' arms trade policy. He pledged to introduce tougher restrictions on arms exports and to play a constructive and leading role in pressing for a European Code of Conduct on arms exports. In theory at least, the Labour government has committed itself to restricting the sale of weapons to regimes that might use them for internal repression or external aggression, and is attempting to increase accountability and transparency in decisions on export licences. In addition the government has undertaken to reform existing legislation on strategic export controls and was instrumental in setting up the EU Code of Conduct which includes a set of eight Common Criteria for Arms Exports that EU governments must take into consideration. One of these is 'the respect of human rights in the country of final destination'.

Complementing the Foreign Office's 'ethical policy' on the arms trade, DfID has adopted a policy which links the arms trade to development. In its 1999 Departmental Report it has categorically recognised the relationship between arms supplies and conflict: 'The supply of weapons, particularly small arms, continues to fan the flames of conflict. In parallel with the FCO's work on developing a Code of Conduct for Arms Exports, we have tried to help developing countries and regions deal with the problem of illicit trafficking. We have supported seminars in central and Southern Africa to agree measures for tackling arms proliferation'.

In reality, however, the improvements in the government's unilateral and multilateral approaches to arms control appear to have done little to stem the flow of weapons systems to developing countries. According to IISS estimates, the arms trade grew by some 12% in 1997, bringing real growth between 1995 and 1997 to some 36%. In 1994 the UK exported $5bn worth of arms, by 1997 this had increased to $8bn. This contrasts with the general decline in arms export values that were sustained from 1987 to the early 1990s. The UK was the second largest exporter of arms in 1997, accounting for 18.5% of the global market and has in no small way contributed to the growth in arms deliveries particularly to the developing world.

The surge in arms exports reflects deliveries to the Gulf States-particularly Saudi Arabia's $11bn military imports which included the delivery of 36 Tornados and 20 Hawk trainer aircraft built by British Aerospace. Arms deliveries to East

Asia also peaked in 1997. Whether primarily pursuing geostrategic interests or propelled by the profit motive, as a supplier state the UK has indirectly supported highly militarised regimes such as the Suharto regime in Indonesia, the Saudi family in Saudi Arabia, the military dictatorship in Nigeria. All these countries have been condemned for human rights abuses by Human Rights Watch and Amnesty International. Apart from conferring a high degree of political legitimisation to these repressive regimes, UK arms sales encourage regimes to spend scarce national resources on weapon systems rather than on development objectives. In this way arms sales promoted by the Defence Export Services Organisation of the MoD undermine the development objectives of DfID. Detailed illustration of the contradiction in the government's policy towards arms transfers, debt and development are to be found in their policies towards to Sierra Leone, Kenya, Indonesia and South Africa.

CASE STUDIES

The four case studies that have been chosen have been selected to reflect a broad spectrum of developing countries facing diverse debt, development and security challenges. They are all countries that the UK has recently transferred arms to. In the case of Sierra Leone, a poor war-torn society with HIPC status, the UK government has been implicated in supporting the illicit transfer of small arms, in the case of Kenya, also a HIPC economy, the UK has recently exported riot control equipment. In both these cases, weapons transfers are relatively small in terms of value, but have significant political and development implications. In the cases of Indonesia and South Africa the weapons being transferred are major weapon systems and the values are much more significant. These two countries are more highly developed than the first two, but face severe debt, development and internal security problems. The differing individual experiences of each country reflect the complex interaction of development, debt and arms transfers.

Sierra Leone

Sierra Leone is a small highly indebted, impoverished and war torn West Africa state with a population of 4.7 million. In 1997 the World Bank estimated that it had a GDP of only

$0.76bn and a total debt to GDP ratio of 164.6%. The World Bank recognises Sierra Leone as a heavily indebted poor country. The civil war in Sierra Leone began in 1991 when the Revolutionary Unified Front (RUF), supported by Liberia, overthrew the then President and imposed military rule in 1992. Following considerable international pressure to reinstate democracy, elections were held on March 29th 1996 which gave the Sierra Leone Peoples Party (SLPP) headed by Ahmad Tejan Kabbah, 60% of the popular vote. The principal rebel group (RUF) signed a peace agreement with the new government, but in May 1997 the RUF backed a military coup led by Major General Paul Koroma. President Kabbah fled to Conakry in Guinea. The international community was determined to dislodge the illegal junta from power. To this end neighbouring African states and the United Nations imposed sanctions including an embargo on the supply of arms and military related equipment. The UN arms embargo required Member States to 'prohibit the supply of arms to any person or legal entity, for the purpose of any business carried out in or operated from the Republic of Sierra Leone, or any activities by their nationals or in their territories which promote or are calculated to promote such sale or supply'.

In 1993 the Economic Community of West African States (ECOWAS) had sent a mainly Nigerian force known as ECOMOG to help suppress the rebels. Nigerian troops were still in the country when, in February 1998, after a week of intense fighting, they recaptured the capital Freetown from the junta. The return of President Kabbah did not bring the violence to an end, however. The RUF nearly captured Freetown in December 1998 and still control more than half the country. Horrific violations of human rights have been committed by both sides in this destructive and persistent war.

Economic Performance and Development

Sierra Leone is a desperately poor country. In 1996 its gross national product (GNP) per capita was $200 and male life expectancy was 37 years. Since then the economy has deteriorated dramatically because of the effect of the war. According to World Bank figures GDP growth declined by 21.1% in 1997 and per capita income declined by 23.1%. A quick glance at the figures below will reveal a process of dramatic decline in exports, a depletion of national savings and growing current account deficit and a dramatic increase in debt since the 1970s.

Table: Sierra Leone Economic and Social Indicators

Key Economic Indicators	*1976*	*1986*	*1996*	*1997*
GDP, $bn	0.67	0.41	0.86	0.76
Exports/GDP	26.6	19.8	11.8	11.3
Gross domestic savings/GDP	5.4	8.2	-11.3	-10.3
Current account balance/GDP	-13.3	-10.8	-18.0	-21.2
Interest payments/GDP	0.8	0.5	1.6	1.6
Total debt/GDP	28.4	210.6	134.4	164.6
Total debt service/exports	16.9	32.7	61.0	46.4
Poverty and Social indicators, 1997				
Population, millions		4.7		
Population growth, annual %		2.5		
Life expectancy at birth		38		
Infant mortality per 1,000 live births		169		
Child malnutrition, % children under 5		29		
Illiteracy, % of population age 15+		69		

Source: World Bank Development Data 1999

These somewhat depressing indicators of poverty and economic decline disguise the fact that Sierra Leone is one of the world's principal diamond producers. The diamond mines have attracted many foreigners with an eye to quick profits, and they are at the root of the internal struggle for power. The diamond trade has also attracted a considerable mercenary presence in the country who insist on payment in lucrative mining concessions. Since the fighting resumed in 1997, the economic situation has deteriorated as civil war has wreaked destruction and chaos across the country. The social disruption and the economic costs of war have been enormous. The conflict has claimed the lives of an estimated 10,000 citizens, over two million people have been internally displaced and a further 450,000 are refugees in neighbouring countries. Substantial damage has been caused to the productive sectors, in particular agriculture and mining, thereby greatly reducing the government's revenue earning capacity. Significant infrastructure has been destroyed or has deteriorated due to the lack of maintenance, and the delivery of basic social services has largely ceased. The violence and destruction in Sierra Leone during 1998-99 has been relentless. According to a report released from Refugee International in March 1999, between 65% to 85% of the capital, Freetown, has been destroyed. More than half the internally displaced are cut off from international assistance because of the fighting. By April 1999 the humanitarian crisis in Sierra Leone was catastrophic, at least equal to the humanitarian crisis in Kosovo. In April 1999 The World Food Programme warned of an imminent food crisis and of insufficient medical aid even to treat the ever growing number of amputees. Apart from the internally displaced there are some 95,000 refugees in neighbouring Liberia and approximately 350,000 Sierra Leonean refugees in Guinea. Refugees fleeing into Guinea have not necessarily found sanctuary from rebel violence-in March rebel troops raided the Guinean town of Pamelap where 5,000 refugees had fled.

UK Policy Towards Sierra Leone

Sierra Leone has been an independent member of the British Commonwealth since 1961 and has long standing links with the UK. The UK government contributed £2m to fund the election which put President Kabbah in office. Since then the UK has provided bilateral aid to support projects that nurture democracy and the rule of law and that provide humanitarian aid to the poor. After the military coup in 1997 the UK government announced that their policy was to support the peaceful restoration of President Kabbah's democratically elected government. However, as the Legg report has revealed the UK government played a highly controversial and clandestine role in the Sierra Leonean crisis.

The Legg report found that certain Foreign Office officials actively supported the role of the mercenary organisation, Sandline, in overthrowing the military junta. Sandline, who describe themselves as 'military consultants', were reported to have bought £6m worth of arms in Bulgaria to supply Mr Kabbah's forces in a counter-coup in 1998, with the implicit blessing of the UK government. The arms supplied by Sandline were destined for the Kamajors, a tribal militia who are among

Mr Kabbah's most loyal supporters and sworn enemies of the RUF. In the event, the military action planned by Sandline in collusion with the Kamajors was pre-empted by the military intervention of the ECOMOG forces. Sandline's arms purchases were conducted in the full knowledge of certain Foreign Office officials and the High Commissioner of Sierra Leone, Mr Penfold. The Legg report found that no Ministers gave encouragement or approval to Sandline's plans to ship arms to Sierra Leone.

In its defence, the Labour government argued that it took the moral high ground in the crisis in Sierra Leone by helping to re-establishing the rightful and democratically-elected government, but many ambiguities remain about the UK's role in the crisis. Following the findings of the Legg Inquiry, public debate on the UK's role in Sierra Leone focused mainly on legal and procedural matters – i.e. to what extent did UK officials collude in the breach of a UN embargo. In terms of reform, focus has been placed on the banning of arms brokerage. While this is a welcome development for those concerned with stemming the supply of light weapons, insufficient attention has been given to the more substantial issue about the willingness to engage and arm irregular forces and what this means for long-term political stability and sustainable development.

Meddling in the affairs of another country through clandestine means sets a dubious and problematic precedent, particularly when the supply of illegal arms are involved and where military operations are sub-contracted to mercenary groups. Recent African history, such as the war in Angola, shows us that the use of mercenaries and the provision of arms encourages elites to seek military rather than diplomatic or political solutions to conflict resolution. It reinforces a winner takes all approach to political power which is at the root of the problems of income inequality and corruption in Africa. There are few, if any, cases where mercenaries have been used and conflict has been resolved. Yet the influence of mercenary groups on conflict and development is harmful and expanding. National resources such as diamond and other mining concessions handed over to mercenary groups in exchange for their services represents a loss of development potential and a loss of control over national resources. Such rich rewards provide little if any incentive to mercenary groups to bring conflict to a close. In many cases, the relationship between mercenary groups and military and political elites is corrupt and the clandestine nature of their operations undermines the principle of transparency and accountability in security sector activity.

Finally, as mentioned by Tony Lloyd (UK Foreign Minister), dealing with mercenaries can have an adverse impact on the implementation of the government's foreign policy objectives and its standing in international circles. This observation also applies to support for the clandestine supply of arms. For example in an article in Sierra Leone's national newspaper The Progress, on the 9th April 1999, the UK's role in the crisis and in particular the supply of arms to ECOMOG have been questioned, 'We believe that providing more arms and ammunition to ECOMOG to fight the rebels will all go on to prolong what seems to be a seemingly unending nightmare. In fact providing more arms to ECOMOG may also mean indirectly providing arms to the rebels since the possibility for arms reaching the rebels is likely'. The article then goes on to cite an incident in which the RUF ambushed and captured a large consignment of arms destined for ECOMOG.

The article also raises the important question of the UK's funding priorities in seeking to fund a solution to the civil war; 'Britain like other members of the international community claim that they support the two-track approach forwarded by the government. Now if Britain is honest in her support for this approach, how many pounds has she donated towards solving the crisis peacefully rather than (through) the use of force'. So far UK actions far from improving the situation have, if anything, helped to escalate the conflict and the UK's role in it. Meanwhile the victims of the conflict have been all but ignored by the international community.

Kenya

Kenya was a British colony and protectorate from the 1890s until independence in December 1963. It is a member of the British Commonwealth and has enjoyed close relations with the UK since independence. Jomo Kenyatta transformed Kenya into a de facto one party state centred on the Kenya Africa

National Union (KANU) party which has dominated Kenyan politics ever since. The current President, Daniel Arap Moi, succeeded Kenyatta in 1973. In 1992, under international pressure, more parties were allowed to form and take part in national elections. Nevertheless KANU sustained election victories in 1992 and 1997 amidst considerable controversy about election rigging and localised violence.

Economic Performance and Development

In 1997 Kenya had a population of 28 million and a GDP of $10.2bn. GNP per capita is $330 per annum. Kenya has a relatively diversified economy but most employment is dependent on agriculture which contributes 29% of GDP. Kenya enjoyed steady economic growth from independence until the late 1970s.

Table: Kenyan Social and Economic Indicators

Key Economic Indicators	***1976***	***1986***	***1996***	***1997***
GDP, $bn	3.5	7.2	9.2	10.2
Exports/GDP	32.5	25.8	32.9	29.2
Current account balance/GDP	-3.6	-6.6	-2.4	-3.3
Interest payments/GDP	1.5	2.6	2.6	1.8
Total debt/GDP	43.0	63.4	74.4	63.4
Total debt service/exports	14.8	36.1	28.0	19.7
Poverty and Social indicators, 1997				
Population, millions		28		
GNP per capita, $		330		
Population growth, annual %		2.6		
Poverty, % of pop below poverty line		42		
Life expectancy at birth		58		
Infant mortality per 1,000 live births		56		
Child malnutrition, % children under 5		23		
Illiteracy, % of population age 15+		22		

Source: World Bank Development Data 1999

The average GDP growth rate has declined from 6.5% in the 1970s to 2.2% in 1990-97, below the rate of population growth at 2.6%. The Kenyan economy was badly affected by the oil crises in 1973 and 1979. Following these external shocks

Kenya began to descend into debt. Kenya's foreign debt is high, amounting to 63.4% of GDP in 1997, although debt servicing, at 28% of foreign exchange receipts, is fairly low by Sub-Saharan standards. This is because a large proportion of Kenya's debts are domestic debt. Interest payments on domestic debt are, however, a serious burden accounting for 25% of government revenues. In the early 1980s, Kenya had distinctly more favourable social indicators than most countries in Sub-Saharan Africa. But, as the country's economic performance began to deteriorate, sustained per capita income growth became an elusive goal. By the early 1990s social indicators began to show that gains made in poverty eradication were in reverse. In certain regions of the country child malnutrition is on the rise. Some 47% of the rural population remain in poverty and experience chronic food insecurity. Furthermore, the difference between the minimum required consumption and the actual consumption of the poor has increased and the distribution of consumption has worsened. In the 1980s Kenya was among the major aid recipients in Africa, but the 1990s have witnessed a steady decline in development assistance, occasioned by a perception of poor governance and mismanagement of public resources and development assistance by the Moi regime.

Security

By African standards Kenya is not a highly militarised state. In 1997, military expenditure amounted to $198m or 1.9% of GDP and remains lower than state expenditure on education. There are, however, some alarming trends within Kenya which should raise concerns for those concerned with conflict prevention. The Moi regime, in conjunction with the Belgium company Fabrique Nationale Herstal, has built a £6m munitions factory which was completed in 1997. The factory is reputed to have supplied arms to Rwanda in violation of the UN arms embargo. This development has given rise to concerns about Kenya's role in light weapons proliferation in the Great Lakes region. Moreover this investment has been made despite the fact that Kenya is experiencing a deteriorating economic situation.

Kenya is also facing a deteriorating internal security situation. There are for instance low intensity ethnic conflicts involving the Turkana and Samburu peoples in the north. Ethnic clashes in the early 1990s resulted in hundreds of dead and thousands being displaced. There are also reliable reports of widespread human rights violations committed by the police on behalf of the increasingly isolated and ruthless Moi regime. Political opposition to the Moi regime has been growing and during the 1997 general election there was violent political conflict in Mombasa.

Despite Kenya's growing internal instability and the authoritarian nature of the Moi regime, the UK has exported military equipment to Kenya, albeit in small quantities by UK export standards. Between January 1992 and January 1998, 380 standard individual licences were issued for the export to end users in Kenya of goods described under the Export Control Organisation's Military List, including licences for tear gas and plastic baton rounds. Since the Labour administration has come to power it has attempted to tighten restrictions in line with the criteria set out by the Foreign Secretary in July 1997. Under these criteria equipment that might be used for internal repression is restricted. In 1997 the government rejected applications for licences for riot control equipment worth an estimated £1.5m. In addition the government has removed Kenya from the coverage of several Open Individual Export Licences. The Moi regime is unlikely to last long into the next century, yet there is no guarantee that there will be a smooth transition from a one party state to a functioning democracy. Even if democracy does assert itself, it will face a legacy of debt that will restrict the ability of the government to implement a sustainable development programme that will reverse the deteriorating social conditions and rising poverty. The failure to address poverty and the growing inequalities that have come to characterise the Kenyan economy in recent times will exacerbate the underlying tensions within Kenyan society. The early warning signs of impending conflict are visible to those that want to see. Now is the time to take action on debt and development assistance to prevent the sort of humanitarian crisis that has become all too common on the African continent. It is also time to remain vigilant on arms sales restrictions to Kenya to prevent the flow of arms which will only act to intensify the potential levels of conflict and human rights abuses.

Indonesia

Indonesia with a population of 200 million is the fourth largest country in the world. It is a middle-income developing country with a GNP per capita income of $1,080 in 1996. However, within the space of a year, from 1997 to 98, the Indonesian economy contracted rapidly due to the effects of the East Asian financial crisis. In 1998 after years of successful poverty eradication the proportion of population in extreme poverty was estimated to be 16.3% and rising.

For over 35 years Indonesia was ruled by the corrupt and authoritarian Suharto regime which relied upon the military to impose social order through brutal and repressive means. Despite the widespread repression and corruption the Indonesian economy grew at a healthy and sustained rate for over two decades and great strides were made in reducing the levels of poverty and income inequality within Indonesian society. While economic conditions remained buoyant the malpractices of the Suharto regime were tolerated. The economic crisis which began in 1997 has however, dramatically transformed the political climate. The economic hardship tearing at the fabric of society, caused people to protest and increasingly riot against the corruption, cronyism and nepotism of the Suharto regime. In the face of mounting opposition and political turmoil Suharto resigned in May 1998. Dr. Habibie, Suharto's right-hand-man, now presides over a regime that remains military-dominated, undemocratic and repressive, and continues to commit atrocities in East Timor, Aceh and Irian Jaya. The death toll from the widespread violence rises every week. Indonesia's chaotic internal political situation shows little sign of stabilising at the time of writing in May 1999.

Economic Performance and Development

Before late 1997, Indonesia was a middle income country. Its extraordinary progress in poverty reduction from 60 percent of the population in the 1960s to 15 percent in 1996 has been well-documented. Gains in the health and education sectors were equally remarkable and much progress was made in improving the gender gap. These gains are now in jeopardy as the socio-economic effects of the East Asian financial crisis takes their toll.

Table: Indonesian Economic and Social Indicators

Key Economic Indicators	*1976*	*1986*	*1996*	*1997*
GDP, $bn	39.3	79.9	227.4	214.6
Exports/GDP	24.5	20.2	25.8	28.1
Current account balance/GDP	?	?	-3.5	-1.2
Interest payments/GDP	1.2	3.0	2.2	2.7
Total debt/GDP	35.6	53.7	56.7	64.3
Total debt service/exports	-	-	35.5	-
Poverty and Social indicators, 1997				
Population, millions	200.1			
GNP per capita, $	$ 1,110			
Population growth, annual %	1.6			
Poverty, % of pop below poverty line	15			
Life expectancy at birth	65			
Infant mortality per 1,000 live births	47			
Child malnutrition, % children under 5	40			
Illiteracy, % of population age 15+	16			

Source: World Bank Development Data 1999

The Indonesian economy with its underdeveloped banking sector and its high degree of speculative foreign investment was highly susceptible to the flight of capital that spread across East Asia in the second half of 1997. Years of development gains were wiped out in a matter of weeks as the local currency, the rupiah, lost 80% of its value against the dollar and inflation soared to over 50%. The Indonesian stock market lost 50% of its value. The economy which had sustained high rates of economic growth for decades contracted by ten to fifteen percent. The crisis hit Indonesia when it was experiencing its worst drought in fifty years, and the international oil price was registering a sharp decline.

Overnight Indonesia became a heavily indebted nation. Estimates put non-performing loans from domestic banks at more than 30 per cent of GDP in Indonesia. To this must be added an overhang of unpayable external debt, estimated at $22bn. The situation in Indonesia is not just a financial and economic crisis but a human one-with the well-being of many millions of people at stake. Rampant unemployment and inflation have pushed literally millions of households back into poverty. In 1996 some 4.5 million people were already unemployed but, due to the effects of the crisis, official estimates suggest that an additional 10 million had lost their jobs by early 1999, although many may have moved into low-paying urban and rural informal sector work rather than open unemployment. School attendance and health are under threat, and the gender gap appears to be widening again. The economic crisis has hit households hard through sharp price shifts and a public spending squeeze. Food security has become a major concern as dramatic price increases for basic foodstuffs affect consumption and nutritional patterns-particularly for women and children.

The IMF bailed out Indonesia to the tune of $43bn to help stabilise its foreign exchange situation and has insisted on a stringent programme of economic reforms. Initially, Fund officials and the US Treasury were confident that macro-economic stability would return as long as the Indonesian government complied with the IMF's reform programme. But it soon became apparent even to the IMF that macro-economic stability depended upon political stability.

Characteristically the IMF displayed complete insensitivity to the socio-economic situation of the Indonesian people by insisting on cuts of government food and fuel subsidies. This had the effect of intensifying the level of riots and demonstrations. In May 1998 the IMF reluctantly adjusted its reform programme to take account of the political and social fragility of Indonesian society. In tandem, the World Bank has implemented a social safety net programme to ameliorate the worst effects of the economic crisis. The economic and political prospects for Indonesia are sobering. Output in 1998 is estimated to have declined by 15%. Given the depth of the crisis, the economy will face ongoing challenges to foster employment and income generating activities for many years to come. While the economy remains in crisis the opportunity for political stabilisation remains remote.

UK Policy Towards Indonesia

Currently the UK government's policy towards Indonesia lacks cohesiveness, reflecting the divided interests of the different departments within Whitehall. Traditionally DfID has refused bilateral support to the Indonesian government because of its poor human rights record. However, the social impact of the financial crisis has caused DfID to reconsider its position towards poverty alleviation in the country. Funding has been allocated to the Community Recovery Programme, a social safety-net programme established by Indonesian civil society. It is also working with the World Bank in the area of health sector finance to help ensure that the IMF structural reform measures do not overlook the needs of the most vulnerable. In addition DfID is providing support to a UNICEF infant feeding programme in West Java. In total, bilateral funding for Indonesian development projects amounted to £7.1m in 1998/99 and is planned to increase to £10m in 2001/02.

In marked contrast to DfID's principled position, the Defence Export Services Organisation of the Ministry of Defence has to all intents and purposes ignored Indonesia's deteriorating economic, social and political circumstances by ruthlessly pursuing arms sales to Indonesia. The decision to sell arms to Indonesia has raised many questions about the strength of the Labour government's commitment to its ethical foreign policy and indeed about its commitment to sustainable development and conflict prevention.

The UK has been selling arms to Indonesia for over two decades. British Aerospace began to sell Hawk jets in 1978. In November 1996, amidst considerably public controversy due to the deteriorating political and human rights situation in East Timor, 16 more Hawk-209 aircraft were licensed for export to Indonesia. The Conservative government at the time argued that they were not 'likely' to be used for internal repression and repeatedly denied that there was substantial evidence that Hawks had ever been used against people in East Timor or Indonesia. The licence was extant but not used when the Labour government came to power.

On 28th July 1997, within three months of announcing 'an ethical foreign policy with human rights at its heart', the Labour government confirmed that it would not revoke the licences for the sale of the Hawks, or for water cannon and Scorpion armoured cars. This decision was made despite calls by international human rights organisations to refrain from supplying arms to the Suharto regime because of its persistent pattern of human rights violations and its occupation of East Timor.

Defending his decision to transfer arms to Indonesia, Cook said that the contracts agreed to under the previous Conservative administration were legally binding and therefore had to be honoured. It is highly doubtful that if the Labour government chose to revoke the licences to Indonesia it would be liable to pay compensation to the UK manufacturers. Article 7(1) of the Export of Goods (Control) Order 1994 states a licence 'may be varied or revoked by the Secretary of State at any time'. Assuming therefore there is no guarantee in the licences about duration or compensation (it would be remarkable if there was), there is no liability incurred by the government if it decided to revoke the Indonesia licences. Moreover, precedents exist for revoking licences as in the cases of Iraq, Somalia, and Yugoslavia. These decisions have not resulted in the UK government facing compensation claims.

One suspects that the real explanation for transferring arms to Indonesia relate to the commercial interests of the UK's most powerful lobbying force, namely the UK's military industrial base. A caveat has been built into the Criteria Used in Considering Conventional Arms Export License Applications, which allows commercial criteria to be placed above ethical considerations in the government's new arms trade policy, captured in the statement; 'full weight should be given to the UK's national interests when considering applications for licenses, including:.....the protection of the UK's essential strategic industrial base.'

In recent years Indonesia purchased 60% of its arms imports from the UK. As a result, Indonesia has been identified as one of the most lucrative East Asian arms export markets for UK companies. The current economic and political crisis in Indonesia has done nothing to dampen the Labour governments resolve to sell arms to the Indonesian regime. The commercial interests of a highly-subsidised industrial sector appear to have overridden the governments ethical and development policies, revealing an enduring contradiction within UK foreign policy, at least as reflected in policies towards Indonesia.

Debt and Arms Sales to Indonesia

In September 1998 the Indonesian government admitted that, because of its financial problems, it could not repay the debt for the Hawks. In February 1998, Margaret Beckett, then President of the Board of Trade, stated that the 1996 Hawk deal had been guaranteed by the Export Credits Guarantee Department to the tune of £280m, which represented 87% of the value of ECGD support for military exports for Indonesia in 1995-6. This sum had risen with interest to £362m in February 1999. Like the Hawk deal, the Alvis vehicles were covered by ECGD to the tune of £65m in 1996 and £2.1m in 1997. Given the instability and continuing economic problems in Indonesia, it is not impossible that the taxpayer might have to cover all of the loan guarantees for arms, an amount of money which could be spent on more socially useful purposes such as humanitarian and development aid for the beleaguered Indonesian population.

South Africa

South Africa is a middle income country with a population of 41 million (1996) and a GNP per capita of $3,160. Twenty five percent of the population lives in extreme poverty. Extreme income inequality and the great differences in human development indicators between different racial groups are a visible legacy of the apartheid regime.

Economic Performance and Development

In April 1994 South Africa held its first democratic election, marking the end of the highly repressive apartheid regime. From the outset, popular expectations of the South African economy were high, but the prognosis is not optimistic. Given a growth rate of 1.7%, a population growth of 1.7% and roughly 50% of the labour unemployed, declining export performance, a devalued currency and a rising debt burden to export ratio, the potential for redistributing wealth to overcome the inequalities of the past are limited.

Since 1994 the government has made considerable headway in refocusing public expenditures and social policies into development priorities. Substantial cuts were made in military expenditures and measures were taken to consolidate a 'peace dividend' from military savings in order to enhance the country's development goals : Between 1994-96 some R1.2bn (£240m) was reallocated from the defence budget to the Reconstruction and Development Programme (RDP). The RDP was a transition strategy designed to remove the structural legacies of apartheid. Its key strategies included meeting basic needs through land reform, housing provision, the supply of clean water, sanitation and electricity to homes, investment in public transport and infrastructure, developing human resources by improving the black education system and diversifying the economy away from the production of primary commodities such as agricultural goods and minerals into higher value added manufacturing.

Table: South Africa Economic and Social Indicators

Key Economic Indicators	*1976*	*1986*	*1996*	*1997*
GDP, $bn	34.5	62.7	126.2	129.0
GDP, % growth	2.3	1.1	3.2	1.7
Exports/GDP	28.3	31.8	27.5	27.8
Current account balance/GDP	-5.5	5.0	-1.6	-1.5
Interest payments/GDP	?	?	0.7	0.6
Total debt/GDP	?	?	20.6	19.5
Total debt service/exports	?	?	11.1	1.5
Poverty and Social indicators, 1997				
Population, millions		38.4		
GNP per capita, $		3,400		
Population growth, annual %		1.7		
Life expectancy at birth		65		
Infant mortality per 1,000 live births		48		
Child malnutrition, % children under 5		9		
Illiteracy, % of population age 15+		18		

Source: World Bank Development Data 1999

The RDP was a carefully articulated social and political programme designed to redress the inequalities of apartheid. It was designed to meet the high expectations of South Africa's impoverished black population and to enhance their economic security. In this respect the South African government had a clear perception of the relationship between security and sustainable development. The 1996 White Paper on Defence argued that 'The RDP is the principal long-term means of promoting the well-being and security of citizens and, thereby, the stability of the country. There is consequently a compelling need to reallocate state resource to the RDP.' Mounting macro-economic pressures, however, forced the government to abandon the RDP in 1996. It was replaced by the Growth Employment And Redistribution (GEAR) strategy which represented a less interventionist and more orthodox approach to macro-economic management. The adoption of GEAR appears to have to put an end to the development and redistribution aspirations of the government.

Economic constraints and pressing development needs combined with the high expectations of the black majority do not augur well for internal stability. Endemic problems such as the Aids pandemic, persistent poverty, unemployment, corruption, criminal violence and the proliferation of small arms make it evident that stability in South Africa is highly fragile. Already the security forces are preoccupied with what some have described as a 'low level civil war situation' in KwaZulu-Natal. Furthermore, internal troop deployments have been made in support of the South African Police's struggle against mounting violent crime. The scale of criminal activity in South Africa has got to a point where it seriously inhibits foreign direct investors. In South Africa, crime is popularly referred to as 'redistribution by other means' and is seen in some quarters as a reflection of the South African government's inability to address the inequities within the South African society.

The UK's role

The UK government provides support to the South African government's development priorities via DfID's bilateral aid programme which promotes:

- pro-poor investment for sustainable job creation and income generation
- improvements in the effectiveness of the Government in delivering essential health, education, water and sanitation services to the poor
- support for sustainable rural livelihoods and initiatives with direct benefit to poor people

In 1998/99 DfID spent £26m on bilateral assistance for development programmes in South Africa. Planned development expenditures for 1999/00-2001/02 are estimated at £30m per annum.

At the same time that DfID has been working with the South African government to promote development programmes, the UK government has relentlessly pursued arms sales to South Africa on behalf of UK companies.

The Rearmament of South Africa

Despite South Africa's urgent development needs and chronic problems of poverty and crime, in January 1999 Deputy Prime Minister Thabo Mbeki announced the cabinet's provisional approval of the decision to re-equip the South African National Defence Force (SANDF). The items to be procured include;

- 28 Gripen fighters from BAe/SAAB for £1.09bn
- 24 Hawks trainer fighters from BAe for £470m
- 4 corvettes-class patrol boats from a German shipbuilding consortium
- 3 diesel submarines from the German submarine consortium
- 4 super Lynx helicopters from GKN-Westland
- 40 light helicopters from the Italian firm Agusta in which GKN-Westland has a stake

The total programme is valued at £3bn or R29bn, to be spread over fifteen years. Because of budgetary constraints the lead in times are very long. The warships and their helicopters delivered by 2002-04, the submarines by 2004-06, the light helicopters by 2003-07, the Hawks by 2007-09, the Gripens not until 2009-14. The costs, spread over fifteen years, will amount to an extra £200m (or R2bn) per annum, representing a 20% increase in the military budget.

The Cabinet has agreed to this increase despite otherwise tight monetary and fiscal policies because of the prospects of easy finance via a soft loan on which no payment is to be made until 2001 and the generous offset deals procured from foreign suppliers. Currently the South African government insists on 80% offsets on all military imports, but has set a target of 100%

for these specific deals, of which 50% will involve investment in the local military industry and 50% will be invested in civil industry. In total the South African government has insisted on a total investment worth £10bn which it hopes will create 65,000 jobs.

While South Africa is in desperate need of employment generation, given an unemployment rate of over 50% within the black townships, the sort of jobs that direct offsets are likely to generate within the military industry will predominantly be for the white skilled workforce that face far less hardships than the black labour force. In justification of the programme, the South African government has claimed that it will enable South Africa to be the policeman of sub-Saharan Africa. Certainly this is a role that foreign powers have been nurturing South Africa for. But within the Southern African region, South Africa's rearmament can only be viewed with consternation. Regional security co-operation via Southern African Development Community (SADC) is at an all time low due to the fundamental differences over policies towards the war in the Democratic Republic of Congo. Moreover, the general remilitarisation of the region, reflected in rising military expenditures, and a general trend towards rearmament suggests that foreign suppliers should err on the side of caution if such early warning signs are to be heeded seriously.

In securing a sizeable proportion of the rearmament programme Tony Blair has promised £4bn worth of investments linked to the UK component of the arms deal. The deal is also likely to increase South Africa's debt burden. Although the UK companies involved are expected to provide the offset investments, export credit guarantees will undoubtedly be supplied to underwrite the risks being taken by UK firms involved in the deal. The weighting of UK resources towards facilitating a controversial arms deal, in contrast with the resources made available for development purposes, raises some uncomfortable ethical questions about UK priorities towards South Africa.

To all intents and purposes it undermines DfID's attempts to restrict arms flows and reduce weapons proliferation in the Southern African region. At the same time it exacerbates the regional 'security dilemma' by enhancing South Africa's military power projection capabilities and effectively increasing the sense of insecurity of neighbouring states. Indirectly this may further undermine regional security co-operation via SADC.

At a time when South Africa is clearly facing economic difficulties which may have serious implications for internal political stability, and when the region is undergoing an alarming process of remilitarisation which is enhancing the role of the military vis a vis civil society within the region, UK priorities towards South Africa appear very short-sighted and highly contradictory.

CONCLUSION

If the UK is to champion development concerns in international forums, it needs to re-examine the current anomalies within its own national practice. Selling weapons to countries facing acute development and debt problems contradicts the government's goal of reducing global poverty, enhancing development and preventing conflict. Scarce national resources used to purchase weapons invariable imply an opportunity cost to development. In highly indebted countries, particularly those that have official HIPC status, arms transfers are unethical, not only because of the missed opportunity for development, which in very poor countries translates into poor quality of life and in some cases loss of life, but also because many of these countries are conflict prone as a result of the systemic problems of poverty and inequality. As witnessed in Indonesia, growing food insecurity has resulted in protest and riots in which the military have indiscriminately turned their weapons on unarmed civilians.

Kofi Annan in his Report on Africa to the United Nations Security Council stated that, 'Arms exporting countries have a responsibility to exercise restraint especially with respect to the export of weapons into zones of conflict or tension'. His appeal was made not only because of humanitarian considerations but also because of the costs of conflict to development. The withholding of weapons sales is a powerful political tool which not only sends signals to the regime concerned, but provides affirmation to the global community of an ongoing commitment to the universal norms and values which uphold the indivisible aims of universal human rights and sustainable development. The UK's persistence in selling arms and extending credit to repressive military or authoritarian regimes in the developing world, represents a missed opportunity to champion international norms and values based on human rights and sustainable development. As a leading developed economy, the UK should foster development for the whole of humanity and eschew the vested interests of its national military industrial base. The government's current arms sales policy undermines this imperative because arms transfers contribute to the impoverishment of developing countries and the burden of unsustainable debt which in turn undermines the security of developing states and its citizens.

Something is fundamentally wrong with the value system of a society that places the subsidisation of the arms market higher on its international agenda than the alleviation of debt and poverty and the promotion of sustainable development. Overseas development aid is much more than a hand out to the worlds poor, it is an essential part of investing in global security.

The current contradictions between the UK's arms trade policies, debt and development are likely to persist until there is greater public accountability in the arms trade decision making process, which allows civil society a chance to challenge the vested interests of the military lobby and the Whitehall mandarins. Until such time, the fundamental dilemma between development and commercial gain in the UK's arms trade policies are likely to remain at odds.

2

Arms Trade and Industry

The arms industry is a global industry and business which manufactures and sells weapons and military technology and equipment. Arms producing companies, also referred to as defence companies or military industry, produce arms mainly for the armed forces of states. Departments of government also operate in the arms industry, buying and selling weapons, munitions and other military items. Products include guns, ammunition, missiles, military aircraft, military vehicles, ships, electronic systems, and more. The arms industry also conducts significant research and development.

It is estimated that yearly, over 1 trillion dollars are spent on military expenditures worldwide (2% of World GDP). Part of this goes to the procurement of military hardware and services from the military industry.

The combined arms sales of the top 100 largest arms producing companies amounted to an estimated $315 billion in 2006. In 2004 over $30 billion were spent in the international arms trade (a figure that excludes domestic sales of arms). The arms trade has also been one of the sectors impacted by the credit crunch, with total deal value in the market halving from US$32.9bn to US$14.3bn in 2008. Many industrialized countries have a domestic arms industry to supply their own military forces.

Some countries also have a substantial legal or illegal domestic trade in weapons for use by its citizens. An illegal trade in small arms is prevalent in many countries and regions affected by political instability.

Contracts to supply a given country's military are awarded by the government, making arms contracts of substantial political importance. The link between politics and the arms trade can result in the development of what US President Dwight D. Eisenhower described as a military-industrial complex, where the armed forces, commerce, and politics become closely linked.

Various corporations, some publicly held, others private, bid for these contracts, which are often worth many billions of dollars. Sometimes, such as the contract for the new Joint Strike Fighter, a competitive tendering process takes place, where the decision is made on the merits of the design submitted by the companies involved.

Other times, no bidding or competition takes place. In the Cold War Era, arms exports were used by both the Soviet Union and the United States to influence their standings in other countries, particularly Third World Countries. Since the fall of the Soviet Union, global arms exports initially fell slightly, but have since 2003 grown again, and now come close to Cold War levels.

Sectors

The AK series of weapons have been produced in greater numbers than any other firearm and have been used in conflicts all over the world.

Land-based weapons

This category includes everything from light arms to heavy artillery, and the majority of producers are small. Many are located in Third World countries. International trade in handguns, machine guns, tanks, armored personnel carriers and other relatively inexpensive weapons is substantial. There is relatively little regulation at the international level, and as a result, many weapons fall into the hands of rebel forces, terrorists, or regimes under sanctions.

Small arms

The Control Arms Campaign, founded by Amnesty International, Oxfam, and the International Action Network on Small Arms, estimated in 2003 that there are over 639 million small arms in circulation, and that over 1,135 companies based in more than 98 different countries manufacture small arms as well as their various components and ammunition.

Aerospace systems

Encompassing military aircraft (both land-based and naval aviation), conventional missiles, and military satellites, this is the most technologically advanced sector of the market. It is also the least competitive from an economic standpoint, with a handful of companies dominating the entire market. The top clients and major producers are virtually all located in the western world, with the United States easily in first place.

Prominent aerospace firms include Dassault Aviation, EADS, Finmeccanica, Thales Group, Lockheed Martin, Boeing, and Britain's BAE Systems. There are also several multinational consortia mostly involved in the manufacturing of fighter jets, such as the Eurofighter. The largest military contract in history, signed in October 2001, involved the development of the Joint Strike Fighter.

Naval systems

All of the world's major powers maintain substantial maritime forces to provide a global presence, with the largest nations possessing aircraft carriers, nuclear submarines and advanced anti-air defence systems. The vast majority of military ships are conventionally powered, but some are nuclear-powered. There is also a large global market in second-hand naval vessels, generally purchased by developing countries from Western governments.

World's largest defence budgets

This is a list of the ten countries with the highest defence budgets for the year 2008. The information is from the Stockholm International Peace Research Institute. Total world spending amounted to $1.464 trillion USD in 2008.

Rank	*Country*	*Spending ($ b.)*	*World Share (%)*
—	World Total	1464.0	100
1	United States	607.0	41.5
2	China	84.9[a]	5.8[a]
3	France	65.7	4.5

4	United Kingdom	65.3	4.5
5	Russian Federation	58.6[a]	4.0[a]
6	Germany	46.8	3.2
7	Japan	46.3	3.2
8	Italy	40.6	2.8
9	Saudi Arabia	38.2	2.6
10	India	32.7	2.1

^a SIPRI estimate

World's largest arms exporters

The unit in this table are so-called trend indicator values expressed in millions of US dollars at 1990s prices. These values do not represent real financial flows but are a crude instrument to estimate volumes of arms transfers, regardless of the contracted prices, which can be as low as zero in the case of military aid. Ordered by descending 2000-2009 values. The information is from the Stockholm International Peace Research Institute.

Rank	*Supplier*	*2000*	*2001*	*2002*	*2003*	*2004*	*2005*	*2006*	*2007*	*2008*	*2009*
1	United States	7220	5694	5091	5596	6750	6600	7394	7658	6090	6795
2	Russia	3985	6011	5773	5202	6260	5321	6156	5243	6026	4469
3	Germany	1603	821	892	1697	1067	1875	2510	3002	2499	2473
4	France	1055	1270	1308	1288	2194	1633	1577	2342	1831	1851
5	United Kingdom	1484	1257	915	617	1180	915	808	987	1027	1024
6	Spain	46	7	120	156	56	108	757	565	603	925
7	China	272	496	515	632	282	306	599	412	544	870
8	Israel	354	360	414	358	612	315	282	379	271	760
9	Netherlands	280	203	243	342	208	583	1221	1322	554	608
10	Italy	189	217	400	312	214	743	525	706	424	588
11	Sweden	306	830	185	515	305	537	417	367	457	353
12	Switzerland	176	193	157	174	250	267	306	324	467	270
13	Ukraine	288	661	244	430	202	281	557	799	269	214
14	Canada	110	129	170	225	268	235	231	343	236	177
15	South Korea	8	165	N/A	104	29	48	94	228	80	163

The information is also from the Stockholm International Peace Research Institute or from the national defence commissions where available and is updated at least once a year.

Next to SIPRI there are several other sources that provide data on international transfers of arms. These include national reports by national governments about arms exports, the UN register on conventional arms and an annual publication by the US Congressional Research Service that includes data on arms exports to developing countries as compiled by US intelligence agencies.

A list of such sources can be found at the SIPRI website. Due to the different methodologies and definitions used different sources often provide significantly different data. For example, according to Statistisk sentralbyrå (Norway state statistics), Norway exports a greater value (in USD) of arms than many of the nations listed above.

Some of the differences are possibly due to deliberate over- or under-reporting by some of the sources. Governments may claim high arms exports as part of their role in marketing efforts of their national arms industry or they may claim low arms exports in order to be perceived as a responsible international actor.

As of 2008 Britain has become the worlds leading developer of arms with British company BAE Systems. Defence group BAE Systems is the first company outside the U.S. to reach the top position, thanks to a deal with the Pentagon for mine-resistant vehicles to be used in Iraq and Afghanistan. According to the Stockholm International Peace Research Institute, a defence think tank, the former British Aerospace group's arms sales are ahead of American market leaders Lockheed Martin and Boeing. The report reveals BAE's U.S. subsidiary was alone responsible for 61.5 per cent of the group's arms sales and around 58.5 per cent of total group sales. This demonstrates BAE's increasing reliance on orders for conventional weapons as the U.S. cuts back on its nuclear arsenal. The British figures were also boosted by orders for Eurofighter Typhoon jets from Saudi Arabia.

World's largest arms importers

The unit in this table are so-called trend indicator values expressed in millions of US dollars. These values do not represent real financial flows but are a crude instrument to estimate volumes of arms transfers, regardless of the contracted prices, which can be as low as zero in the case of military aid.

Rank	Supplier	2000	2001	2002	2003	2004	2005	2006	2007	2008	2009
1	India	911	1242	1872	2802	2227	1036	1257	2179	1810	2116
2	Singapore	622	220	235	88	384	543	52	368	1123	1729
3	Malaysia	30	26	131	135	48	51	410	546	541	1494
4	Greece	710	725	491	2241	1528	389	598	1796	563	1269
5	South Korea	1262	623	461	680	986	686	1650	1758	1821	1172
6	Pakistan	158	397	533	592	385	332	262	613	939	1146
7	Algeria	418	553	237	197	272	156	308	471	1518	942
8	United States	301	449	453	533	512	501	581	731	808	831
9	Australia	364	1191	647	798	505	470	682	629	380	757
10	Turkey	1170	553	1009	438	187	1005	422	585	578	675
11	Saudi Arabia	80	59	555	159	1161	148	185	64	115	626
12	UAE	243	186	213	695	1246	2198	2026	938	748	604
13	China	2015	3366	2819	2207	3080	3511	3831	1474	1481	595
14	Norway	263	148	92	4	6	14	469	494	536	576
15	Indonesia	171	27	63	398	82	31	58	577	241	452

List of major weapon manufacturers

International treaties for arms control

- The Arms Trade Treaty is the name of a potential multilateral treaty that would control the international trade of conventional weapons. The treaty is in the preliminary stages of development and has not yet been officially negotiated.
- The Missile Technology Control Regime (MTCR) is an informal and voluntary partnership between 34 countries to prevent the proliferation of missile and unmanned aerial vehicle technology capable of carrying a 500kg payload at least 300 km.
- The Limitation of Naval Armament included many separate treaties. In general, the treaties involved the United States, United Kingdom, Japan, and France.
- The Convention on Cluster Munitions (CCM) is an international treaty that prohibits the use of cluster bombs, a type of explosive weapon which scatters submunitions ("bomblets") over an area.
- The Outer Space Treaty, formally known as the Treaty on Principles Governing the Activities of States in the Exploration and Use of Outer Space, including the Moon and Other Celestial Bodies, is a treaty that forms the basis of international space law.

- The Ottawa Treaty or the Mine Ban Treaty, formally the Convention on the Prohibition of the Use, Stockpiling, Production and Transfer of Anti-Personnel Mines and on their Destruction, completely bans all anti-personnel landmines (AP-mines).
- The New START Treaty (for Strategic Arms Reduction Treaty) is a bilateral nuclear arms reduction treaty between the United States and the Russian Federation that was signed in Prague on April 8, 2010.
- The Protocol for the Prohibition of the Use in War of Asphyxiating, Poisonous or other Gases, and of Bacteriological Methods of Warfare, usually called the Geneva Protocol, is a treaty prohibiting the first use of chemical and biological weapons. It was signed at Geneva on June 17, 1925 and entered into force on February 8, 1928. It was registered in League of Nations Treaty Series on September 7, 1929.
- The Chemical Weapons Convention (CWC) is an arms control agreement which outlaws the production, stockpiling and use of chemical weapons. Its full name is the Convention on the Prohibition of the Development, Production, Stockpiling and Use of Chemical Weapons and on their Destruction.
- The Convention on the Prohibition of the Development, Production and Stockpiling of Bacteriological (Biological) and Toxin Weapons and on their Destruction (usually referred to as the Biological Weapons Convention, abbreviation: BWC, or Biological and Toxin Weapons Convention, abbreviation: BTWC) was the first multilateral disarmament treaty banning the production of an entire category of weapons. It was the result of prolonged efforts by the international community to establish a new instrument that would supplement the 1925 Geneva Protocol.

The European Council stated to the United Nations General Assembly:

"We are committed to upholding, implementing and further strengthening the multilateral disarmament and non-proliferation framework in the fight against threats which are tending to escape the control of national sovereignty, the challenges deriving from destabilising accumulation and spread of small arms and light weapons, from illicit or irresponsible arms trade, and from the proliferation of weapons of mass destruction, which are creating new and growing hot-spots of international tension. In this regard, the EU welcomes the growing support in all parts of the world for an International Arms Trade Treaty and is firmly committed to this process. "

INSTITUTES PARTICIPATING IN WEAPON RESEARCH AND WARFARE SIMULATION

Ethical issues

For some people, arms exports pose an ethical challenge, as they see supplying the weapons for a conflict as morally akin to becoming involved within the conflict and oppose the support for non-democratic oppressing regimes. Some view the arms industry as a means of profiting from war, repression and death when failure to supply arms could lead to an early disengagement. On the other hand, exporting arms to groups (or states) with "laudable" goals—e.g. a rebel group overthrowing a fascist regime—can be an invaluable equalizer in the conflict. And there is no shortage of parties to a conflict that can wreak incalculable destruction without the assistance of modern armaments—for instance, the Hutus of the Rwandan Genocide conducted most of their carnage using simple machetes and other low-tech implements.

Oscar Arias Sanchez President of Costa Rica (awarded the Nobel Peace Prize in 1987 for his efforts to end civil wars across Central America through the Esquipulas II Accords) has stated: "When a country decides to invest in arms, rather than in education, housing, the environment, and health services for its people, it is depriving a whole generation of its right to prosperity and happiness.

We have produced one firearm for every ten inhabitants of this planet, and yet we have not bothered to end hunger when such a feat is well within our reach. Our international regulations allow almost three-quarters of all global arms sales to pour into the developing world with no binding international guidelines whatsoever. Our regulations do not hold countries accountable for what is done with the weapons they sell, even when the probable use of such weapons is obvious. "

In popular culture

Numerous movies (for example Lord of War), TV shows, comics, video games (for example Far Cry 2), etc. have featured arms dealing. In the Marvel and DC universe, many companies (such as Stark Industries and Wayne Enterprises/Luthor Corp respectively) have an arms manufacturing division. The character Destro in the G.I. Joe comics/toon/toyline has his own private army, The Iron Grenadiers and runs MARS (Military Armament Research Syndicate). MARS is the primary supplier to the Cobra and has sold weapons/vehicles to the US government. The GI Joe team has their weapons/vehicles supplied by the US government, and thus their weapons/vehicles are unknowningly made by MARS. In the comics, the scientist Dr. Mindbender his Battle Android Trooper was made from MARS parts.

THE ARMS TRADE

Unsurprisingly, the West dominates the world arms market in terms of sales. Over the last six or so years, the US has towered over the other countries in weapons sales, clocking up $49,271 million worth of sales (at 1990 prices) between 1996 and 2000. Its nearest competitor, Russia, made $15,690 million worth in the same period, but a large majority of these were of second hand weapons. According to SIPRI, just under half of all transfers (movements) of major conventional weapons between 1996 and 2000 came from the US, Russia and France each accounted for 10 per cent, and Britain and Germany each accounted for between five and 10 per cent. The seven following biggest sellers-the Netherlands, Ukraine, Italy, China, Belarus, Spain and Israel-accounted for around 15 per cent of the world total transfers between them. So it is clear that the global arms market is controlled by just a few players. The six biggest arms selling countries-four of whom, ironically, are permanent members of the UN Security Council-accounted for almost 85 per cent of all arms transfers | over the last six years.

The top 7 largest arms companies, in terms of military sales. The figures in italics represent the percentage of arms in total sales for each company. Figures for arms sales are in US $ billions at constant (1998) prices and exchange rates. Selection of top arms-purchasing countries between 1996 and 2000. Figures are trend-indicator' values expressed in US $ millions, at constant (1990) prices.

The global small arms market

Small arms require a special mention in any assessment of the global trade in armaments, simply because they are so prolific, the trade in them is so difficult to control and the devastation caused by them is so severe. Taking the definition of the UN panel of government experts on small arms, the category includes all of the following military, police and domestic weapons: revolvers and self-loading pistols, rifles and carbines, assault rifles, sub-machine guns and light machine guns, heavy machine guns, hand-held under-barrel and mounted grenade launchers, portable anti-tank and anti-aircraft guns, recoilless rifles, portable launchers of anti-tank and antiaircraft systems, and mortars of less than 100 mm caliber.

So there are plenty of them, and they are everywhere. They are used by police and security patrols, by national armies and by guerrilla and revolutionary groups, they are carried by civilians legally in a number of countries, for sport in many more, and illegally in every country. They feature in practically every armed conflict between nation-states, in internal and civil wars, in gang fighting and as status symbols.

They are so prolific because they are small and relatively cheap, easy to pass on, smuggle, hide, steal, capture from an enemy or buy over the counter. But, they are ubiquitous because of the sheer numbers they are produced in: millions of them, every day, all over the world. It is a myth that the trade in small arms is only one of recycling second-and third-hand weapons. New production merely creates more second-and third-hand guns. In 1999, 45 different countries reported to the UN that firearms, components and ammunition were legally produced in their territories for domestic or export markets. Many more countries didn't respond to the requests for information. The main producers of these little killers are China, Russia and the US. Another 20 or so countries, mainly in Europe and Asia, produce most of the rest of the world's supply. A further 29 countries produce nominal quantities mainly to meet their domestic never be accurate data on which countries have the most of them. Even if there were, accurate figures for exactly which of these were legal, illegal, military or civilian would be impossible to determine.

'The total number and global distribution of small arms remains one of the greatest enigmas in the field of international peace and security', says the Small Arms Survey. The Survey is a project of the Graduate Institute of International Studies in Geneva, which has attempted to profile and estimate the proliferation of firearms (hand-held guns and rifles, rather than hand-held missile launchers and the like), based on rough estimates and incomplete reporting by countries.

Their research estimates that there are at least 550 million legally-held firearms in the world today-at least one gun for every 11 of the world's people. Over half of all of these are privately owned. The group was unable, not surprisingly, to estimate the number of illegally-held arms in the world. The 20th century was the most violent one in human history. Not only did it witness two world wars, and 30 years of major arms-fuelled tension between the world's superpowers, it also featured hundreds of localized conflicts, armed border disputes, civil wars, military coups and counter coups, revolutionary struggles and armed invasions.

According to the Armed Conflicts Report 2000 and the State of the World Report 1999, there were 40 armed conflicts underway in 36 different countries as the 21st century was born. Even in the short time since the millennium, the world has witnessed a new 'war on terror' waged by the US and its allies against Afghanistan, with the threat of extension to Somalia, and the possibility of intensified attacks on Iraq.

Earth is a planet at war, and to a large extent this is a consequence of the legal and illicit sale of arms. In crude but plain terms, without weaponry, combat would be more limited in scale. In most conflict zones in the world, war is a way of life. Waging war is a means of generating money, exerting political power, and providing employment. In some areas of the developing world, children grow up knowing nothing else but bloodshed, dead, injured or maimed relatives, the daily risk of landmines; even bearing arms themselves. If they survive long enough to procreate, their own children will know only the same.

War today

Despite tension between India and Pakistan, the future stability of the world is probably now less at risk from an all-out nuclear catastrophe-as was thought during the Cold War era-than from a slow, insidious, systematic proliferation of small wars and local strife in mainly smaller nations, many of them in Africa. In 1998, Africa suffered 11 major armed conflicts. It is now the most war-torn region in the world. Those small wars are created and sustained in a constant battle to control territory, plunder resources and wield power. William Hartung, of the World Policy Institute, illustrates the problem. When the current Liberian president Charles Taylor invaded Liberia on Christmas Eve in 1989, he did so with just 100 irregular soldiers, armed with AK47 rifles. Within months they had seized mineral and timber resources and used the profits to purchase more light weapons: the first few turns in an ongoing vicious cycle.

According to Hartung: 'This pattern of war as plunder has been repeated with local variations in Sierra Leone, where the Liberian-backed Revolutionary United Front (RUF) has used diamond sales to fuel its campaign of terror; in Colombia, where government forces, right-wing paramilitaries and anti-government rebels have skimmed off profits, fees and bribes from the cocaine trade; in Angola, where UNITA rebel forces have raised billions of dollars through diamond sales and the Angolan Government has countered by stocking its arsenal with revenues drawn from its large offshore oil deposits."

The seizure or trafficking of drugs, diamonds and other valuable commodities produces profits for warring factions. Profits are spent not on peace, reconciliation or education, but on more weapons-bought on the illicit market, and through more 'legitimate' channels. The weapons suppliers to the perpetrators of the 1994 genocide in Rwanda included brokers and shippers in Britain, South Africa and France, working with collaborators in Albania, Belgium, Bulgaria, Egypt, Italy, the Seychelles and the former Zaire (now DR Congo/DRC). Arms and military training are also supplied to warring or revolutionary factions, both openly and secretly, by Western nations to serve their own political ambitions.

Bigger picture

But the arms trade also has a role in sustaining larger, more 'official' tensions and conflicts between states. The deadly dealing increases strains and thereby fuels wars between established nations. Here are some examples. From 1989 to 1998, the US provided over $227 million in weapons and training to African military forces. Of this, over $111 million went to governments that have been directly or indirectly involved in the war in the Democratic Republic of Congo (DRC): Angola, Burundi, Chad Namibia, Rwanda, Sudan, Uganda and Zimbabwe. The big seven arms-selling countries in the world-the US, France, Germany, Britain, Russia, China and Italy have all sold arms to states currently involved in conflict including Sri Lanka, Indonesia, Israel, China, Taiwan, India and Pakistan. And they usually show their deadly wares at arms fairs.

Military training

Military training Military training is an aspect of the industry often overlooked by campaigners and politicians working towards arms control. Yet the provision of training to foreign armies, or warring factions, is commonplace and was clearly illustrated with the allied forces' training and assistance given to the Afghan United Front forces during their reclaiming of Afghanistan at the end of 2001. Just as with the hardware, military training is used by governments to further their strategic and political objectives, as well as being a tool in international relations. But like arms sales, military training of foreign fighters can also bounce back. Since the US armed forces are among the most highly trained and best financially supported in the world, it is no surprise that the US is a major provider of military training. Here's an example. Towards the end of his presidency, Bill Clinton took a special interest in Africa. His proposed 'new partnership' was not to supply aid or help build civil society as was hoped, but apparently to establish a wide program of troop training. In 1998, the US provided $45.8 million in international military education training (IMET) for over 400 African soldiers.

UNDER THE PENTAGON'S JOINT COMBINED EXCHANGE

Training (JCET) program, US Special Forces have trained military personnel from at least 34 of Africa's 53 nations. That includes troops fighting on both sides of the DRC's 'civil' war-from Rwanda and Uganda (supporting the rebels) to Zimbabwe and Namibia (supporting DRC's Kabila regime).

Dirty dozen

The main suppliers of small arms include the same dozen governments that dominate the trade. The main government suppliers include the US, Russia, China, France and Britain, along with Belgium, Bulgaria, Germany, Israel, Italy and South Africa. Innumerable independent arms dealers, criminals, brokers and middlemen control the illicit trade. Some governments and campaigners draw a distinction between legally transferred small arms, and the illegal trade. The vast majority of small arms which infest southern Africa were originally supplied legitimately' by the USSR to 'liberation movements' there. Ukraine, Belarus and Bulgaria remain large suppliers to the region. Worldwide, the 'legal' trade makes up by far the majority of small arms sales. Transfers from established companies, within established nations, make up nearly 90 per cent of the total annual value of the trade. The annual legal global trade in small arms and light weapons is estimated at $4-6 billion.

War in the Congo

The ongoing bloody conflict in the Democratic Republic of Congo (DRC), formerly Zaire, has been called Africa's 'first world war'. In 1965 Mobutu Sese Seko became president of Zaire with the backing of the US Central Intelligence Agency (CIA), who needed a strategic friend in Africa. Mobutu quickly became one of the continent's most brutal dictators, but was nevertheless supported by the US in weapons sales and military training. Even after the Cold War, the United States continued to supply military support to the Mobutu regime. In 1991, more than $4.5 million of military equipment was delivered to Zaire.

In 1996 and 1997, Laurent Kabila and his Alliance of Democratic Forces fought running battles with the Mobutu dictatorship, eventually ousting the despot. The US immediately offered the Kabila regime military training, even as the new president suspended human rights and banned opposition political parties. On 2 August 1998, DR Congo's current brutal conflict began, with nine African nations siding with either the Mobutu faction or Kabila regime in a fight for DR Congo's rich mineral and diamond resources. Foreign troops from Rwanda, Uganda, Burundi, Angola, Namibia, Sudan, Chad and Zimbabwe have all been drawn into the fight, along with irregular and guerrilla movements from surrounding African states. US, Britain, China, Russia, South Africa and other weapons-selling giants have gathered like vultures, gladly supplying the factions with weapons of death. Even after six of the governments involved were drawn together to sign the Lusaka peace accords in July 2000, the battling continues, supported by Western countries and their arms companies.

Despite not sharing a border with the DRC, Robert Mugabe's Zimbabwe has played a major part in the tensions since the mid-1990s in support of the Kabila regime. It is widely known that Zimbabwe sent a steady supply of North Korean weapons to Kabila's rebels before they came to power. In 2000, Zimbabwe had an estimated 13,000 troops fighting in the DR Congo. The Government then estimated its involvement in the DRC cost $3 million a month-though leaked documents have put the figure closer to $27 million, a price the country can ill afford with unemployment at more than 50 per cent, huge debts and massive inflation. Britain has been a good friend to Zimbabwe in terms of arms sales, continuing to supply even after a June 1999 call by the Presidency of the European Union (EU) for states to observe a 'rigorous application' of the EU Code of Conduct on arms sales regarding the region.

In February 2000, the British Guardian newspaper revealed that the Prime Minister, Tony Blair, had pushed through licenses for Hawk fighter jet spare parts to Zimbabwe even though there was evidence that Hawks had been used in the Congo conflict. Only three months later was Robin Cook, the embattled 'ethical foreign policy' British Foreign Secretary, able to announce a full arms embargo on the country-after Zimbabwean white farmers had been attacked by Mugabe supporters. But by that time, many of the Hawk parts had already been exported.

Impact on human rights

'No security assistance may be provided to any country the government of which engages in a consistent pattern of gross violations of internationally recognized human rights. ' Section 502B, US Foreign Assistance Act. 'The President shall consider the following criteria... The government of the country... was chosen by and permits free and fair elections... respects human rights... does not persistently engage in gross violations of internationally recognized human rights, including extra judicial or arbitrary executions, disappearances, torture or severe mistreatment, prolonged arbitrary imprisonment...' US International Arms Sales Code of Conduct Act 1999. 'Member States will not issue an export license if there is a clear risk that the proposed export might be used for internal repression... [including] torture and other cruel, inhuman and degrading treatment or punishment, summary or arbitrary executions, disappearances, arbitrary detentions and other major violations of human rights. '

EU Code of Conduct for Arms Exports 1998... human rights have not been a major barrier to weapons sales at any time in history. The world's worst dictators, despots, human rights abusers and anti-democratic regimes have been the customers of all of the major arms supplying countries in the world-and continue to be so.

According to the Centre for International Policy, during the fiscal year 1998 around 54 per cent of US arms transfers to the developing world went to undemocratic regimes. Between 1991 and 1994, 85 per cent of all US arms transfers were to undemocratic states. According to one calculation by William Hartung of the World Policy Institute, during the 1999 fiscal year, the US delivered roughly $6.8 billion in armaments to nations which violate the basic standards set out in the US's own International Code of Conduct on Arms Sales.

WORST HUMAN RIGHTS ABUSERS:

Turkey

Despite its membership of NATO, and its close relationship with the European Union (EU), to which it aspires for membership, Turkey is the worst human rights abusing state in the European region. There are ongoing tensions between Turkey and Greece, especially over the Turkish occupation of northern Cyprus, but the brutality has been reserved mainly for the ethnic Kurds in the southeast of the country. Since 1984, the Turkish military has been at war against the Kurdish Workers' Party (PKK), a militant Kurdish independent group.

The PKK's tactics have hardly been mild. They include bombings, kidnapping and extortion, but the Turkish response has been the systematic repression of the Kurdish people-some 28 million of whom reside in Turkey. Since the outbreak of the war, more than 37,000 people have been killed, mostly Kurds, and 3 million have been displaced. Turkey is determined not to allow the Kurdish people to live as Kurds in Turkey. Their political parties are suppressed and their leaders summarily arrested or executed. The ban on speaking their own language has only just been revoked. Journalists expressing sympathy for Kurdish rights have been arrested. More than 3,000 Kurdish villages have been destroyed.

The Turkish military has carried out its repression using weapons supplied by the US and Europe. The next biggest supplier is Germany, which has delayed and blocked some arms deals because of Turkey's human rights situation. For their weapons deals, Turkey demands licensed production and joint production deals in order to boost its own weapons manufacturing industry. The weapons are thus produced in Turkey, away from prying eyes, maintaining jobs there rather than for employees of the licensing company.

Despite current financial crisis, the country is embarking on an 8-year military modernization plan, including the purchase of helicopters, battle tanks, small arms and communication systems. The Turkish Ministry of Defence receives 10 per cent of the national budget, a larger proportion than any other government department. The latest EU progress report on Turkey, published in November 2001, states that the country has not improved 'the situation as regards torture and mistreatment'.

Indonesia

Indonesia is the classic example of an anti-democratic, repressive state, sustained in military might by friends in the

West hoping to get their hands on rich oil and logging reserves. Since 1965, the country has been led by an autocratic military regime, the father of which was the infamous General Suharto, who ruled for 32 years and oversaw murder, corruption and repression on an unprecedented scale. Following his resignation after the 1997 Asian economic crisis, a string of short ruling presidents replaced him until the current president, Megawati Sukarnoputri took over on 23 July 2001.

While the Indonesian people themselves suffered horribly under the Suharto regime, it was the people of East Timor who were systematically repressed and murdered after Indonesia invaded in December 1975. More than 200,000 people-a third of the population-died during the occupation, which only came to a fragile close following East Timor's referendum for independence in 1999. Even then, Indonesian-backed and armed militia refused to accept the result, and rampaged through the country murdering civilians. The UN estimates 1,500 to 2,000 people were killed, and 75 per cent of the population were forced into hiding. Today, 60,000 to 80,000 people remain in refugee camps in West Timor.

Saudi Arabia

The Saudi state is illiberal and intolerant, governed by an autocratic and repressive royal family. The practice of any religion except Islam is forbidden and dissent of any kind is heavily punished with the full rigor of shari'a (Islamic law). In 1996, Amnesty International noted a sharp increase in executions, at least 192 having been carried out in the preceding year, as well as many floggings and amputations. In 1998, at least 29 people were executed after grossly unfair and secretive trials. Over 80 executions were carried out in the first 8 months of 1999. In late 2001, three men were executed there for being homosexual.

The Saudi regime is a huge arms customer from western nations, and was on the receiving end of the biggest-ever British arms deals. Britain won the Saudis' favor in arms sales following the reluctance of the US Congress to allow large arms deals to the country. The US had been a major supplier, and the UK exploited Congress' reticence. Saudi has extraordinary levels of. military spending, funded by rich oil reserves, but also beholden to them. Statement by the UN Development Program (UNDP) in 1994, "It is not possible for the community of nations to achieve any of its major goals-not peace, not environmental protection, not human rights or democratization, not fertility reduction nor social integration-except in the context of sustainable development that leads to human security."

Arms sales, conflict and world poverty are so intimately connected as to be almost indistinct. Those same world leaders who shed a tear for the poor and starving in Africa also help sustain the conflict and poverty which infect the continent. The new European Code of Conduct on Arms Sales annual income of $370. In 1997, the average per capita income across Africa was $350 a year, and of course that does not mean that each person actually receives such a sum: the World Bank's figure is an average.

The poorest countries in the world are so poor largely because of huge debts owed to the developed world, much as repayments for past arms sales. Many of the most heavily indebted countries are currently engaged in, or emerging from, conflict of some kind. Arms sales fuel a never-ending vicious cycle of poverty and debt. During the Cold War, developing nations found themselves filing in behind one or the other of the major world powers, buying or receiving free arms to strengthen their position. This in turn fuelled local arms races.

At the same time, dictators and corrupt governments were making large-scale arms purchases, both to bolster their own power and to line their pockets with generous kickbacks and bribes from each sale. High military spending reduced outlay on development and increased the occurrence of cross-border and internal conflicts. This created a need for more arms, which were bought using Western loans, thereby adding to the country's debt. Post Cold War, the cycle continues in many parts of Africa and Asia. In some regions, nations are suffering the economic effects of decades of borrowing, crushed under the weight of debts that do not really belong to them, which they have no hope of ever paying off.

Debt, the Cold War legacy

At the height of the Cold War in the 1970s and 1980s, the world's poorest regions were caught up in an arms race that is, arguably, the foundation for their poverty today. Central America, the Horn of Africa, southern Africa and Indo-China were drawn into the tensions, which exacerbated regional arms races and localized conflicts. In 1985, Nicaragua allocated 26.2 per cent of government spending to the military, Mozambique spent 38 per cent, El Salvador 29.1 per cent, Ethiopia 28.9 per cent and Iran 34.1 per cent. In most cases, arms purchases meant military expenditure had to be increased and budgets for development were tightened. In other cases, the countries borrowed hard currency from international lenders to fund their arms purchases, or simply went into debt with the arms supplying nation.

According to a report by the Campaign Against Arms Trade (CAAT), 'With the end of the Cold War, the Southern African region has witnessed the withdrawal of superpower intervention, the end of apartheid, the termination of conflict in Namibia and Mozambique, a 30 per cent decline in regional military expenditure and the demobilization of tens of thousands of soldiers. However, the debts and costs of destruction that accumulated during the Cold War will remain a burden for generations to come. Children not yet born will have to pay the price of debt for wars they did not fight, for ideas they do not hold, for a regional and global system that no longer exists and for decisions made by regional and world leaders no longer in power.

According to a Jubilee 2000 report, one-fifth of all developing country debt consists of loans given to dictators. The report says the lenders, not the countries currently crushed by former regimes' debts, should be held responsible. CAAT's excellent report on the arms trade and development, cited earlier, reveals that countries which are poverty stricken because of the military spending of their former dictators include Bolivia, Central African Republic, Chad, DRC (Zaire), Kenya, Liberia, Mali, Myanmar (Burma), Uganda and Zambia.

CURRENT MILITARY SPENDING AND ARMS SALES

Despite their being locked into this poverty trap, poorer nations are still regarded as legitimate and profitable arms customers for Western states which helped create their situation. According to a report for the US congress, arms sales to developing countries together far outweigh arms sales to developed countries. According to their definition, countries of the South accounted for 66 per cent of the value of all international arms deliveries in 2000.

Social impacts of conflict

The servicing of debt for arms sales obviously affects health and education, and has other social impacts in the developing world. Money spent on arms, or money spent servicing debts, means less money is spent in social and developmental programs within the country. Countries are prevented by international trade rules from unfairly supporting their own industries above the industries of other nations. Caribbean countries are not allowed to give financial aid to their banana industry on which the region depends, because it is unfair competition for the American-owned banana industry in Central and South America. The Global Agreement on Trade and Services (GATS), which is currently being pushed through the WTO, intends to extend these kinds of rules to other areas such as water, healthcare and education provision.

But at the WTO, and in all other global agreements, the military is specifically excluded from the rules governing global trade. The main WTO governing document, the General Agreement on Tariffs and Trade (GATT), states that a country cannot be prevented from taking any action 'it considers necessary for the protection of its essential security interests... relating to the traffic in arms, ammunition and implements of war and such traffic in other goods and materials as is carried on directly for the purpose of supplying a military establishment.'

In other words, the WTO GATT and other trade agreements do not apply to the arms trade. There are no international restrictions on what munitions a country can buy or sell, how much these should cost, how much a country can spend, who they buy weapons from or to what extent they subsidize their own arms industry. This process has contributed to the pattern of rich countries becoming richer, and poorer nations staying poor, or becoming poorer. Western nations are not prevented by WTO rules from subsidizing their own arms industries, and so are able to acquire military equipment at artificially low knock-down prices, while keeping the finance within the country.

Moreover, the exclusion from WTO regulations means they can buy arms domestically, even when other countries are offering better products more cheaply.

Developing nations rarely have established arms industries and so buy their weaponry from abroad at a cost often way above what the equipment is worth, draining yet more money out of the country. Even when there is a local arms industry, this is usually so small that buying abroad remains cheaper. Developing nations pump cash into their own arms industries too, in attempts to improve their economies, because it is the only industry they can legally support in this way.

When seeing how trade rules benefit the rich countries, especially in the arms arena, it is not surprising that airplane and arms manufacturer Boeing was the prime sponsor of the WTO meeting in Seattle in 1999. Global agreements to break down barriers to trade are having the effect of preventing developing and middle income countries from exploiting the resources they do have to trade on the world market, keeping those countries financially subordinate to the rich West.

The argument that the arms trade creates or sustains jobs, or brings money into the national economy, is one of the most difficult arguments campaigners face. These arguments have strong political currency-people don't vote for governments that threaten their livelihood-but they are based on a fallacy which is only now becoming fully apparent.

The arms trade is an immoral business that cause death, maiming, human rights abuses and suffering around the world. It is also a business that does not bring huge economic or employment benefits to the biggest arms-exporting countries. In many cases, high government subsidies, tax breaks, insurance schemes and promotion for arms manufacturers cost governments more money than weapons producers generate for them. Countries are artificially propping up their arms industries while refusing to explore fully the potential for diversification into areas that are not only more productive and socially positive but also economically viable.

The extent of government subsidies

Governments subsidize their arms sector in a number of ways. The difficult job for campaigners and academics is to show by how much, and why it is a bad thing. Information, such as how much a government spends on its own armed forces, what procurement decisions it makes, how much it spends on military research and development and how much export credit insurance it provides for arms companies, is usually secret or difficult to obtain.

Strong, well-informed estimates based on obtainable information are usually the best that campaigners can muster before issuing the challenge to governments: if we are wrong, it falls to you to prove how wrong. After all, if arms exports are big earners for state economies, wouldn't politicians be shouting it from the roof tops?

With that proviso in mind, valiant attempts to look at this issue have been made. In the US, the defence and foreign aid budgets are the largest single source of federal funding to private corporations. According to the World Policy Institute, more than half of all US weapons sales are financed by taxpayers instead of by foreign arms purchasers. During the fiscal year of 1996 (the last year for which figures were available) the US Government spent more than $7.9 billion to help companies secure just over $12 billion in agreements for new international arms sales.

Direct subsidies

Governments' direct financial support for their arms exports can be roughly placed into a few distinct categories. Each of these subsidies results in taxpayers' money being spent, or risked, helping foreign governments to buy arms.

Export promotion-The major arms-exporting countries each year spend huge amounts of money all over the world promoting and marketing their domestic arms companies' products. Export promotion ranges from diplomatic visits by politicians to the provision of advice and support for companies marketing their systems, to regular attendance and promotion at arms exhibitions and conferences.

At the US Pentagon, nearly 6,000 people were employed in 1996 to promote, broker, administer and finance arms sales abroad, at a cost of $378.2 million. In the State Department a further 75 personnel were employed, part of a defence export promotion budget of $3.7 million. And the US commerce department also plays a role, publishing 'defence market assessments' such as How to do business in Indonesia, and mounting US presence at foreign arms exhibitions. During 1996, the US Government sent equipment and personnel to 19 overseas weapons shows, at a cost of more than $5.1 million.

Export credits-Government insurance schemes to compensate arms companies when their foreign clients default on payment generally make up the bulk of the government direct subsidies. They also provide financing support for deals. Governments then attempt to recoup the cost from the defaulting nations, with usually only limited success. Often the companies insist on some kind of insurance or guarantee from their home government before embarking on large weaponry export deals. Arms sales make up, large proportions of the export credits extended in many major arms exporting countries.

The US Export-Import Credit Bank, which could be seen as the equivalent of an export credit organization, is usually prohibited from guaranteeing arms deals (though not always-Congress occasionally makes exceptions). However the US more than makes up for it in other loans and funding programs which subsidize US arms exporters.

The US Foreign Military Financing Program (FMF) received $3.35 billion in 1999 to support grants and loans for the provision of US military equipment and services to more than 24 countries. Recipients of FMF grants in recent years have included Egypt, Israel, Jordan, Turkey and the Ukraine. More funds were allocated for Africa. Another $16 million of subsidy is granted through the US Defence Export Loan Guarantee fund.

Spending distortions-governments also artificially support their arms industries by distorting their own spending on domestic military purchases. They buy more arms from domestic suppliers than really needed, they pay more than these ought to cost, and they choose domestic arms suppliers even if foreign-made equipment is cheaper and better. In any other industry, World Trade Organization rules and other free-trade legislation would prevent such spending distortions as unfair competition. But as we have seen earlier, the military is exempt from international agreements on trade. In a report by the World Policy Institute, William Hartung decries this kind of spending in the US, which he calls 'defence pork'. He argues that politicians add unnecessary and expensive military equipment purchases to the Pentagon's budget in order to please arms companies, secure or create jobs and so gain campaign donations and votes. In 1998, $3.8 billion was added by senators and officials to the amount that the Pentagon had said it needed to meet its own defence plans. While most 'defence pork' is US-bought-so not an arms export subsidy-the example shows how political pressure distorts procurement decisions.

Other subsidies

The above are just three direct financial subsidies which governments provide for their arms industries. But there are many different ways that governments indirectly financially support their arms industries, and while it is more difficult to quantify this kind of support in concrete terms, the benefits to arms companies can be quite considerable.

Research and development (R&D)-Governments spend large portions of their defence budgets on research and development of new weapons systems, which they contract arms companies to carry out on their behalf. In 1998/99, the three big US weapons manufacturers received over $8 billion in R&D funding. Commissions and bribes-According to one World 1 Bank estimate, the sums distributed worldwide each year as pay-offs and bribes total $80 billion. Campaign group Transparency International (TI) has surveyed attitudes to corruption in business, and found that arms and construction companies were perceived to be the most likely to pay bribes.

Jobs in the arms industry

Off-set deals and joint procurement aside, a further argument-that the weapons business is a thriving employer-is also false.... the global arms industry has been gradually shrinking since the end of the Cold War. Linked to this, the number of people employed in the sector has also fallen.

Moreover, the argument that a government should spend huge amounts of money propping up an industry to safeguard a relatively small number jobs is one that only has so much credibility. Governments should no more subsidize their arms business than any other industry to safeguard jobs. Sir Samuel

Brittan, the British economist and journalist, has written extensively on the weakness of the employment argument.

He says the argument is based on the myth that there is a 'lump of labour' that is engaged in making specific products, that cannot be deployed elsewhere. If defence orders are lost, those people become unemployed and unemployable, runs the line.

Brittan points out that millions of people change jobs, find jobs or leave jobs every year. 'Indeed, it is almost certainly easier for arms workers, many of whom have a wide range of valued skills, to find new jobs... Where will the new jobs come from to replace those lost in exporting weapons? Other jobs, on a much greater scale, arose to take the place of handloom weavers [and] drivers of horse-drawn carts. A report by the British Ministry of Defence and York University, published in 2001, revealed that 40,000 arms export jobs would be replaced by 67,000 civilian posts if arms exports were cut in half, albeit at a lower average salary per job.

Mercenaries: the dogs of war

Selling arms is one side; purchasing people to use them is another. The use of privately hired might is nothing new. The Romans used mercenaries, and the practice probably went back even before them. Italian merchants in the 16th century hired muscle to protect their assets and control trade routes. Colonial explorers were accompanied by hired fighters. From the mid-20th century, Western firms setting up mines and oil exploration in Africa, Asia and Latin America protected their assets by hiring armed heavies.

Mercenaries come under a number of guises, but all include the provision of military might or advice for a profit. Under the guise of 'security' for example, private military companies, consultants, advisors or training outfits, all manner of services to both governments and companies are supplied, including full participation in conflicts, the provision of arms, and armed protection of royal families and industrial plants.

Former members of security services often run modern mercenary companies, exploiting their contacts in the arms and political world. They hire disaffected, unemployed former soldiers wherever they win contracts, and source second-hand weapons and equipment for them to fight with. They will often provide whatever services are required, in exchange for hard currency or interests in mining and oil exploration. UN Special Rapporteur Bernales Ballesteros was appointed by the UN General Assembly in 1996 to report on 'the use of mercenaries as a means of violating human rights and impeding the exercise of the rights of peoples to self-determination'.

Child soldiers

At least mercenaries can usually make their own l choices; it is different for children. There are more than half a million children (under 18s) serving in armed forces, in more than 87 countries. At least 300,000 children are actively fighting in 41 countries, including Colombia, Sri Lanka, Sierra Leone, Uganda and Chechnya.; In some countries, very young children are used as messengers, spies and equipment carriers, but by the age of 10 they are given rifles, or rapid repeating machine-guns and set to fight in conflicts they cannot possibly understand.

As members of armed forces, children become lawful targets for attack, but the use of child soldiers also increases the danger faced by civilian children who come under suspicion from warring parties. Within armed forces, children are often treated brutally, suffering physical, emotional and even sexual abuse. But it is not only faraway nations mired in internal conflicts that use child soldiers. The US is the country most opposed to setting 18 as the minimum age limit for recruiting and participation in armed forces. One in every 200 of its armed personnel is 17, while many more become temporary members as part of youth military training programs.

The UK continues to recruit 16-year-olds leaving school, and the recruitment process begins even while they are still at school. British soldiers under the age of 18 fought-and died-in both the Falklands/Malvinas conflict and the Gulf War. Other countries that recruit under-18s to the armed forces, via conscription or voluntary enlistment include: Australia, Bangladesh, Belgium, Brazil, Burundi, Canada, Chile, Croatia, Cuba, Denmark, El Salvador, Estonia, Finland, France, Germany, Honduras, India, Indonesia, Iran, Iraq, Ireland, Israel, Italy, Japan, Jordan, Libya, Luxembourg, Mexico, Namibia, Netherlands, Aotearoa/New Zealand, Norway, Pakistan, Peru,

Portugal, Republic of Korea, Sudan, Switzerland, Uganda and Yugoslavia.

A number of factors lead to the use of children as soldiers. Technological advances have made semi-automatic rifles light enough to be used and simple enough to be operated by a child, while rabid proliferation has made them cheap and easily obtainable. The longer a conflict goes on, the more likely children are to be 'recruited' as manpower becomes short-both young girls and boys are recruited-and new soldiers are needed to replaced the killed and injured.

Children are perceived to make obedient soldiers, they are cheap and are easy to manipulate. Children 'volunteer' or are coerced to join-up in order to survive, to prove their 'adulthood' or because it is a natural step in a culture of violence. In the Revolutionary United Front in Sierra Leone, children are held and trained for two or three months, threatened with death if they disobey orders or attempt to escape. In the Kamajors militias, they are initiated into secret societies and told they will gain magical powers and be immune to bullets if they join military forces.

Prevailing international law at the United Nations sets 15 as the minimum age for military recruitment and participation in armed conflict, though there is widespread agreement that this age is too low. The Coalition to Stop the Use of Child Soldiers is an international movement of organizations seeking the adoption and implementation of an Optional Protocol to the Convention on the Rights of the Child (CRC) setting the minimum age for all forms of military recruitment and use in hostilities at 18 years of age.

By the end of 2001, a total of 92 countries had signed or ratified the Optional Protocol, but implementation will take many years and a great deal of effort. Programs to prevent child recruitment, including monitoring, providing alternatives, and establishing proper procedures, as well as programs to ensure safe demobilization and integration of former child soldiers are particularly needed.

Landmines: the legacy

Children, whether child soldiers or not, are often the main victims of landmines, perhaps the most vicious weapons brokered by the arms dealers. In the words of the International Campaign to Ban landmines, Put simply, anything that landmines can do to an enemy's army, they can do to a civilian population. What they cannot do is discriminate between the soldier and the civilian. Their impact cannot be confined to the duration of the battle. Thus, under the laws of war, they are an illegal weapon.'

More than any other weapon of war, landmines have received much public and legislative attention over recent decades. They are horrific because their effects on civilian communities, after battles have ended, are so long-term and devastating. Under internationally recognized definitions, landmines fall into two broad categories:

* Anti-personnel (AP) landmine-'A mine designed to be exploded by the presence, proximity or contact of a person and that will incapacitate, injure or kill one or more persons'.
* Anti-tank (AT) landmine-A device designed to detonate by more than 100 kilograms of pressure.

Whether anti-tank or anti-personnel, the effect of landmines on civilian communities is the same. They kill and maim indiscriminately, taking children just as easily as heads of households. Families are devastated not only because of the loss of a loved one, but also because their means of income or a future generation is destroyed. In the same way, those who are not killed when a landmine explodes are maimed or permanently disabled, becoming a long-term financial and emotional burden on families. Some landmines are designed to scatter thousands of shards of metal up to 50 meters, specifically to injure rather than kill.

Landmines also have devastating effects when they don't kill or maim, rendering thousands of acres of land unusable for farming or livestock. Families are forced to make a terrible choice between starvation or risking their lives on mined fields. In Cambodia alone there are over 35,000 amputees as a result of landmines, and they are just the survivors. Mine deaths and injuries in the past few decades amount to hundreds of thousands. They are a daily threat in Afghanistan, Angola, Bosnia, Cambodia, Chechnya, Croatia, Iraq, Mozambique,

Nicaragua, Somalia and dozens of other countries. In December 1997, following decades of pressure from campaigners, a total of 122 governments signed the Ottawa convention, officially titled 'The Convention on the Prohibition of the Use, Stockpiling, Production and Transfer of AntiPersonnel Mines and on their Destruction'. Less than one year later the treaty became international law when Burkina Faso became the 40th country to ratify.

It is the most comprehensive international treaty of its kind, and became law quicker than any other treaty of its kind in history. But despite worldwide support, and condemnation of the use, sale and stockpiling of anti-personnel landmines, a total of 53 countries still refuse to sign including China, Egypt, Finland, India, Israel, Pakistan, Russia and the US. The US's refusal has a devastating political influence, giving credence to other countries' refusal. The campaign continues to demand that these countries drop their opposition to the treaty, and to expand it to cover anti-tank mines and other 'area denial weapons'-a euphemism meaning they blow you up if you stray where you 'should not'-like cluster munitions and unexploded ordnance.

The 'trade' in landmines, as traditionally defined at least, is all but non-existent. Cuba, the United States, Russia, Egypt, Iran, Iraq, Burma, China, India, North Korea, South Korea, Pakistan, Singapore and Vietnam are still classified as producers of the weapons by the International Campaign to Ban Landmines, though some of them have only failed to prove written attestation to the contrary. Military monitor Jane's Mines and Mine Clearance 2000-2001 revealed there has been a 'virtual absence of mines-legitimate or otherwise-at arms shows and military equipment exhibitions this year'. Thirty-four countries are known to have exported anti-personnel landmines in the past. All but Iraq have attested that they no longer do so. The trade in anti-personnel landmines has been confirmed to exist only in a relatively small amount of illicit trafficking.

For a book on the arms trade, it could be argued the issue should stop there-the trade in anti-personnel landmines no longer exists, and the manufacture is nominal. Unfortunately, the step is not so easily taken. The Ottawa treaty covers only certain types of antipersonnel landmines, leaving vast loopholes where area denial weapons, including anti-tank weapons, remain available and traded.

The campaign against landmines concentrates now on encouraging the states who have so far failed to sign and ratify the Ottawa treaty to do so, but it has also broadened its outlook to the new and next generations of landmines and weapons that are landmines by any other name. The weapon causing most concern for campaigners is the cluster bomb. Usually dropped from a plane, it explodes just above the ground, scattering hundreds of miniature 'bomblets' over a wide area. Many of these bomblets fail to explode, remaining in the ground, just like anti-personnel landmines, until disturbed.

Like landmines, unexploded ordnance (UXO) poses a serious threat to lives and livelihoods. Between 1964 and 1973 the US dropped a huge number of cluster bombs over Laos. It is estimated that millions of unexploded bomblets remain. Cluster munitions were used in Kosovo and Vietnam, during the Gulf War, in the Falklands/Malvinas conflict, and during the recent attacks on Afghanistan. NATO admits to a failure rate of between 8 and 12 per cent in Kosovo, leaving as many as 35,000 live bomblets on the ground. The campaign against landmines is far from won. Many countries, having signed Ottawa, pour money and research into mine clearance programs-an expensive and time-consuming business. But while taking mines away with one hand, the landmines of the future are being created and delivered across war zones all over the world. The arms companies which are earning millions from developing mine clearance equipment are also at the forefront of developing new generations of weapons, laying the foundation of devastation in the future. The International Campaign to Ban Landmines is calling for a moratorium, banning the use of cluster weapons because of their devastating and long-lasting effects.... government ministers, advisers and senior members of the armed forces frequently move into the employment of arms companies and vice versa. The supposed wall between government and the industry has a huge gaping hole in it, in which a constantly revolving door has been established.

In Frank Vogl's Earth Times article on bribery and corruption in the arms trade, he outlines how the George W

Bush regime in the US takes 'this game of political pressure to an unprecedented new level'. 'Rarely before has US business taken such total charge of the Pentagon. Not only does the Secretary of Defence [Donald Rumsfeld] come from big business, but so too do the new heads of the Army, Navy and Air Force... President Bush has nominated James Roche a vice president at military aircraft seller Northrop Grumman, to become Secretary of the Air Force; Gordon England from arms and naval vessel manufacturer General Dynamics to become Secretary of the Navy.

For good measure, US Vice President Dick Cheney's wife, Lynne, serves on Lockheed Martin's board, a company which is a major contractor to the US Government and its allies.

Purchasing power

Donations from private companies to political parties and candidates are nothing new, and have been the foundation of many scandals for governments across the Western world. Not surprisingly, because there are lucrative domestic contracts to be won, and restrictive legislation to be challenged, the arms business is a major player in the cash-for-influence money-go-round. As Lumpe and Donarski note in The Arms Trade Revealed, 'Whenever and wherever arms export policy is being made, financially self-interested representatives of the arms corporations are present. Generous campaign contributions from the weaponeer's political action committees (PACs) open doors, providing access and influence on the policy making process. According to the World Policy Institute, the 25 leading weapons-exporting companies contributed a record $10.8 million during the 1995-96 general election cycle in the US. Of this, $6.6 million came in regulated PAC donations and $4.2 million in unregulated 'soft' money-donations theoretically targeted for party-building activities, but often used to benefit specific candidates. Lockheed Martin was the leading arms corporate donor during this time. The Republican Party, more military-minded than the Democrats, received the bulk of donations.

A US Code of Conduct?

Although the US has relatively strict legislation governing the involvement of its citizens in arms brokering the world's largest arms-exporting country has comprehensively stalled on drawing up its own code of conduct on arms exports. Progressive Congress representatives have been attempting for nearly a decade to introduce a Code of Conduct on arms exports into US legislation. In 1995 International Relations Committee member Cynthia McKinney (Democrat) introduced the 'Code of Conduct on Arms Transfers Act' into the 104th Congress.

Campaign for an International Code | Finally, the US President has now been instructed by Congress to pursue multilateral steps for controlling and monitoring the arms trade. There is a real possibility that within a generation, perhaps even before, an International Code of Conduct on Arms Transfers could be introduced, building on the EU Code. In 2000 the US and the EU signed a declaration to work towards a common vision on the question of arms export controls. In May 1997, 14 Nobel Laureates met in New York to launch their own International Code as a first step to persuade arms exporting countries to adopt standards: 'Today, we speak as one to voice our common concern regarding the destructive effects of the unregulated arms trade. Together, we have written an International Code of Conduct on Arms Transfers, which, once adopted by all arms-selling nations, will benefit all humanity, nationalities, ethnicity, and religions.

Their proposed Code requires that arms transfers are only granted if transfer would complement and comply with international human rights standards, international humanitarian law, respect for international arms embargoes and military sanctions, promotes peace, security and stability, promotes human development and opposes terrorism. It calls too for public accounting of the Code's implementation, and transparent international co-operation through the UN and other bodies to improve and adjust the code as appropriate. While the proposal needs updating to account for recent changes in the international arms trade, it is a bold attempt to set in motion some international moves to curb the arms export business. It is perhaps the best tool arms trade campaigners currently have to effect change on a global scale.

A broader view of campaigning

From Seattle onwards, politicians and executives of the biggest and richest transnational corporations realized that wherever they went, and whatever they did, an inspired, passionate group of united people was watching, criticizing and acting for social justice and equality. Also for the first time, campaigners on widely diverse issues, from gay rights to third-world poverty, from peace and nuclear disarmament to environmental activists, joined together. They realized their concerns overlapped in many different and complex ways. They discovered that united campaigning, using the concerns they shared as a foundation, was more effective than disparate, isolationist campaigns along strictly issue-based lines.

The campaign against arms trading cannot, and should not, be considered in isolation from other concerns of social justice, except perhaps for convenience' sake. In almost every area of global injustice, the arms trade plays its deadly role. It was revealed how the trade exacerbates conflict, promotes human rights abuses and worsens poverty in developing countries. The trade is also intimately connected to environmental destruction, inequality, immigration and asylum, gender and cultural rights, privatization and worker exploitation-in fact, most of the world's evils have their roots in the fighters, tanks, mines, guns and bullets that corrupt individuals and destroy lives.

3

Socio-Economic Impact of Arms Transfers in Developing Countries

INTRODUCTION

This part of the book will provide a general background about the problem of arms imports to developing nations. This part will elaborate upon the origins of arms transfers, define socio-economic indicators, and reconcile the two by providing a methodology for further discussion.

Origins

The supply side of the global arms trade is no secret. The largest producers and exporters are developed countries, the top six in 2005 being: United States, Russia, France, United Kingdom, China, Germany and Italy. The largest recipients tend to be in the developing world, with Taiwan, Saudi Arabia, Turkey, South Korea, China, India being the top six importers in 2005.

This poses a very important question: why is it that the developed nations, with more development and economies, are exporting arms to developing nations, countries which lack infrastructure and development? The most fundamental problem in this dynamic is that developing nations, with low human development index ratings, are prioritizing arms over development. This book will address the impact of arms imports upon socio-economic factors in developing countries.

Socio-Economic Dimensions

The term socio-economic is a bit problematic as it could mean several different things. For the purpose of this book, the term will be used synonymously with human development index (HDI). The HDI will provide a measure of the well being of the general population of a nation. The HDI will also be used comparatively to measure the relationship between socio-economic strength and arms imports.

Methodology

In order to further analyse the relationship between arms transfers and socio-economic factors, three types of charts were created. The first chart illustrates the level of arms imports, and monetary expenses spent on arms transfers. The second chart helps to evaluate socio-economic standards based upon the HDI, life expectancy, adult literacy, and GDP. A final grouping of charts was created to aid in the comparative analysis of the impact of arms imports on socio-economic factors based upon the conflict situation of the country (inter-state conflict, intra-state conflict, or no-conflict).

CASE STUDIES

This part of the book will provide comparative case studies of Colombia, Egypt, Eritrea, India, Iran, Namibia, Pakistan, Sudan, Venezuela, and Vietnam. The countries which were selected for the case studies were based upon achieving as wide a sample group as possible in order to understand the impact of arms transfers upon socio-economic factors. In selecting the countries for case studies the following was taken into consideration: (1) region, (2) conflict status, (3) level of arms transfers, (4) and available data. Finally, each nation was further analyzed in order to provide a qualitative analysis to complement the quantitative data.

Colombia

Although Colombia is in the midst of a civil war, it maintains a middle level HDI, the highest out of the sample group, a close second in life expectancy and adult literacy, and the highest GDP per capita. Baring these figures in mind, out of the sample group, Colombia also spent the second least on arms imports, and the lowest per capita and percent of its GDP. The connection between low arms imports and a high HDI in relation to the sample group is visible through Colombia's statistics. Colombia had a low arms import number, the second lowest out of the entire sample grouping, and the highest HDI. However, Colombia ranked the highest in the world in kidnapping, crime per capita, and second for firearms murders. Colombia also ranked 70th in the world for health expenditures. Colombia held the 14th highest amount of the world's poor with 0.76%. Based upon these statistics, though some socio-economic factors are very weak, it appears that Colombia has balanced its military and socio-economic interests, at least more so than other nations in this study.

Egypt

Egypt is a nation which is highly militarized, ranking 11th in arms imports yet 111th in its HDI. This is quite an astounding contrast between its prioritization of arms imports over social programmes. The numbers show that Egypt invests heavily into its arms imports, but its adult literacy remains relatively low, though its life expectancy is at a moderate level for the sample group (5th). Egypt had a high level of arms imports, with a very low level of HDI. This relationship demonstrates an explicit link between high expenses on arms results in a lower standard of living. Egypt appears to have the second highest conviction rate in the world, and the fifth highest percentage income inequality for the poorest 10%. Egypt also ranked 111th in world on health expenditures. Egypt held the 33rd greatest number of poor people in the world with 0.18%. It is obvious from these statistics that Egypt's socio-economic problems are being placed behind its military interests, due to the fact that their arms imports numbers were far higher.

Eritrea

One of the strongest demonstrations of the link between arms imports and socio-economic factors comes from Eritrea. Eritrea was found to be spending the highest amount of its GDP per capita on arms imports, than any other nation. Continuous tension with Ethiopia may play a large role in this militarization. The two nations fought a war between 1998 to 2001 leading to an unstable conclusion with the 2000 Algiers Agreement. The 2000 Algiers Agreement led to a Boundary

Commission ruling in favour of Eritrea, which Ethiopia rejected. This conflict has resulted in aggravation of already large socio-economic problems in both nations. Eritrea comparatively ranked in the bottom tier of the HDI rankings, with an extremely low life expectancy rate, and its adult literacy rate not being reported. Furthermore Eritrea is considered a high risk area for bacterial diarrhea, hepatitis A, malaria, and typhoid fever. It can easily be inferred from the data that socio-economic conditions are being sacrificed for the sake of Eritrea's arms imports. The conflict with Ethiopia has resulted in the heavy militarization of Eritrea. It should be noted that Eritrea spends 17.70% of it's GDP on military expenses, the highest in the world. It also had the 33rd highest HIV/AIDS rate in the world. Furthermore the BBC reports that the Eritrean government has been unable to provide food as two thirds of the population receives foreign food aid. Also, a large part of the labour force in Eritrea is composed of the army. Eritrea also remains 157th place for health expenditures.

India

India is another nation that is highly militarized, in a perpetual state of armed conflict with its neighbor Pakistan. India's HDI is extremely low, yet it is ranked first in the world in terms of arms imports. The visible prioritization of arms over social programmes is evident since its HDI rank is a dismal 126 in contrast to its first place finish in arms transfers. Both India's adult literacy and life expectancy were starkly lower than other nations.

A direct correlation can be drawn from India's socio-economic conditions and its arms imports. Perhaps a reason for this discrepancy is its state of insecurity due to long standing armed inter-state conflict and arms race with neighbouring Pakistan. India ranked 75 out of 101 countries with its average adult having 5.1 years of education. India also ranks 126 in health expenditures in the world. India appears to be another high risk nation for bacterial diarrhea, hepatitis A and E, typhoid fever, dengue fever, malaria, Japanese encephalitis, and rabies. India also holds the title of having 41.01% of the world's poor, the highest in the world. India's prioritization of arms over socio-economics is very visible.

Iran

Iran has been in a process of nuclearization, declaredly for civilian use, though contested by other nations. Notwithstanding the heavy toll the population has paid for sanctions placed upon Iran for its pursuit of nuclear technology outside the IAEA framework, Iran ranks seventh in the world for arms imports with an astounding $1.5 billion, though that number was third last in the sample group in terms of its percentage of GDP. Though Iran held the highest GDP per capita, it ranked below Colombia and Venezuela on socio-economic factors, and a moderately low adult literacy. This analysis demonstrates that it is due to its allocation of funds that it is not achieving as high socio-economic conditions as other nations who have a lower GDP per capita (Colombia, Venezuela). Iran is the seventh leading arms importer in the world, though maintains a fairly moderate HDI rank. This discrepancy could be explained by Iran's large oil exports, the country ranks third in oil production and reserves. The large oil industry in Iran allows the government to allocate large funds towards arms imports, but also provide a significant amount towards social programming. An example of this is that it ranks third in the world for the immunization of newborns for hepatitis B. Iran ranked 96th in the world for health expenditures.

Namibia

Namibia provided for a very interesting case. Though its arms imports were not relatively high compared to other nations, 45th overall, a more nuanced analysis demonstrated a very interesting discovery. Namibia placed ninth overall for the percentage of its GDP spent upon arms imports, as well as for its per capita expenditures on arms imports. Furthermore Namibia placed 125 in its HDI ranking, the lowest out of the sample group for life expectancy. An interesting note about Namibia was that, though its overall arms import dollars were relatively low, it ranked ninth in terms of percentage of GDP spent on arms imports. This development comes from a nation which is under no immediate threat of war, and with an extremely low life expectancy. Even with this lack of emphasis on socio-economic programming, funds allocated towards arms imports were extremely high. Namibia also ranked 125th in the world in health expenditures. Namibia also has the sixth highest HIV/AIDS rate in the world at 21.30%, in addition to the 50th most poor people in the world with 0.06%, even with its small country size of just over two million.

Pakistan

In a constant arms race with India, Pakistan holds sixth place in terms of arms imports, yet a ranking of 134 for HDI. In terms of per capita and GDP percentage spent on arms imports, the number is moderately high. Pakistan's average adult had 3.9 years of schooling, 75th out of 101 countries. Pakistan also ranks 134th in the world for health expenditures. Pakistan is considered a high risk for several diseases including bacterial diarrhea, hepatitis A and E, typhoid fever, dengue fever, malaria, and cutaneous leishmaniasis. Pakistan is the country with the fourth largest percentage of the world's poor with 3.86%. The high level of arms imports, coupled with low HDI and high disease risk demonstrates that Pakistan's investment into arms imports comes at high socio-economic costs.

Sudan

Sudan is another nation which has invested heavily into arms imports. It should be noted that the arms import numbers are quite high considering an illicit flow of arms continues into Sudan, even despite a UN arms embargo. Even with this embargo, Sudan sits as the 10th leading arms importer, and 10th for expenditures on arms imports as percentage of its GDP. Sudan's socio-economic factors are also low, ranking second last out of the sample group for HDI, and very low in adult literacy and life expectancy. It truly appears that arms expenditures are being prioritized over social programmes, leading to a negative impact upon socio-economic factors. Sudan is very visible in the media due to its intra-state conflicts, most notably the crisis in Darfur. The situation in Darfur has been called a "humanitarian crisis". Even with an arms embargo in place, Sudan has managed to get a large amount of arms through its borders, as it is the 10th largest arms importer in the world. Sudan also has the 44th highest unemployment rate out of 198 countries. More striking was the fact that the average adult in Sudan had just two years of school, 96th out of 101 countries. And Sudan is ranked 141st in ranking for health expenditures. The lack of focus on socio-economic issues in favour of arms imports has had a huge negative impact upon the socio-economic factors in the nation.

Vietnam

Vietnam appeared to be at the high middle range of sample group for arms imports (27) HDI rank (109), and life expectancy. Surprisingly its adult literacy rate was very high given that the other nations with higher HDI's had lower adult literacy rates. Vietnam surprisingly invested a significant amount into arms import. Interestingly it had a high adult literacy rate. Vietnam ranked a surprisingly high 20th in per capita GDP expenditures on arms imports, and 27th overall. This is coupled with the fact that Vietnam ranks 109th in the world in health expenditures. This coming with the fact that it is a high risk for bacterial diarrhea, hepatitis A, typhoid fever, dengue fever, malaria, Japanese encephalitis, plague, rabies, and leptospirosis. It appears that avian influenza is also becoming a risk in Vietnam. Once again the focus of Vietnam on arms import appears to have de-prioritized socio-economic issues, especially health.

Venezuela

Hugo Chavez's Venezuela is in a rapid process of militarization as well. Though it ranks the lowest out of the sample group in terms of arms imports, another study says that it secured $1.9 billion in arms transfer agreements in 2005 alone (fifth in the world). Venezuela had the second lowest arms imports, along with the second highest HDI rank out of the sample group. Out of the non-conflict ridden nations, Venezuela fared the best, with the highest life expectancy and adult literacy. This should demonstrate a correlation between arms import numbers and socio-economic factors. Venezuela ranked 72nd in the world in health expenditures, and 69th in arms imports. This, similar to Colombia, is a demonstration of the capability to balance arms interests with socio-economic concerns, at least within the sample group. Venezuela came in 22nd largest amount of the world's poor with 0.51%. Though Venezuela fared better than all but Colombia on HDI factors, it was nevertheless below medians for the world.

ANALYSIS

Based upon the statistics found above, a closer analysis will be given of the sâmple countries. The analysis will encompass three parts: inter-state conflict countries (Eritrea, India, and Pakistan), intra-state conflict countries (Colombia and Sudan), and nations in non-conflict zones (Venezuela, Iran, Vietnam, and Namibia). The basis of the analysis should provide a comparative insight into the socio-economic impact of arms imports on countries based on region, size, conflict conditions, and more.

Inter-state conflict countries

The first broad groups of countries to be analyzed are those in the midst of inter-state conflicts: Eritrea (with Ethiopia), India, and Pakistan. These nations state that their pressure to import arms is due to their state of insecurity. This argument comes at the expense of social programming as this grouping of nations had the worst HDI ranks, especially vis-a-vis the amount the spent on arms imports. The obvious deduction from these statistics is that nations in the midst of conflicts have their socio-economic factors suffer the most from arms imports.

Intra-state Conflicts

Among the countries analyzed who were in the midst of inter-state conflicts are Colombia and Sudan. These countries justification for importing arms is in order to overcome internal rebellions. There appeared to be a significant discrepancy between the two nations studied, which may be accounted for different regions, intensity of conflict, or other factors. An interesting observation is that Colombia invested significantly less than Sudan on arms imports, and ranked significantly higher on HDI. Sudan conversely, as the 10th highest arms importer, had an extremely low HDI rank, as well as life expectancy and adult literacy. The contrast between these two nations should demonstrate the negative relationship which arms transfers have upon socio-economic factors.

Non-Conflict

The final grouping of nations is those who are not involved in a significant inter-state or intra-state conflict. In general, these nations have very little justification to arm themselves other than national security concerns. Interestingly, once again, the country that invested the least in arms imports, Venezuela, ranked the highest in HDI. However an exception occurred when Iran ranked the highest in arms imports but ranked the second highest in HDI, though its life expectancy and adult literacy were very low. It shows that non-conflict nations demonstrate a high disparity between prioritizing arms imports with other socio-economic interests.

Summary

Based upon the statistics it appears that, as can be presumed, nations involved in inter-state armed conflicts must prioritize arms over socio-economic concerns, which in turn led to a severely negative impact upon the latter. The results of states within inter-state conflicts appeared to be fairly consistent.

In intra-state conflicts, there appeared to be a variance between the emphasis they place upon arms imports and socio-economic concerns. The difference may possibly be accounted for due to regional security, as for example Colombia, with a high HDI yet lower arms imports come from a region of relative security. Conversely, Sudan, with higher arms imports and lower HDI, comes from a very volatile region which includes neighbouring conflicts in Ethiopia, Uganda, Central African Republic, and Chad.

Similar to the findings in intra-state conflicts, nations in non-conflict zones appear to vary in the importance they place upon arms imports, though regional insecurity may account for this disparity. Non-conflict zones appear to have the greatest variance in terms of arms imports and HDI rank. However, an interesting observation provided by the statistics showed that the higher the percentage of GDP spent on arms imports, the lower the HDI rank. Given these results, it appears that the greatest indicator of the negative impact of arms imports and socio-economic factors depends upon *the percentage of GDP spent on arms imports*. The greater the percentage of GDP nations spend upon their arms imports, the greater the negative impact upon socio-economic conditions. For instance, Eritrea ranked first in percentage of GDP spent on arms imports but also ranked near the bottom for HDI ranking. As mentioned above Namibia is another example of this relationship between percentage of GDP and socio-economic conditions.

THE ETHICS AND ECONOMICS OF THE ARMS TRADE

Every sensible market economist should accept that a market must operate within a framework of law and moral convention.Investment Bankers are not permitted to finance firms that sell poison and there are strong constraints on the emission of lead into rivers or on pollutants into the chain of foodstuffs.My contention is that exports of arms to dubious regimes should come within the sphere of what is out of bounds – and more decisively so than at present. Would we have to pay a heavy economic price for such restraint? There is indeed sometimes a conflict between national self-interest and ethical actions, just as there can be a conflict between personal self-interest and moral behaviour. But in both cases this is often exaggerated. In the national case it is exaggerated by an inflated view of the role of arms and export promotion in the British economy.

The promotion and *de facto* subsidisation of arms sales is – like most other industrial subsidies – wealth destroying; there would be very little, if any, sacrifice involved in doing away with the whole effort. Behind the arms promotion lobby is the primitive belief that if one source of overseas sales dries up, the workers and other resources involved would waste away. This is rubbish in view of the millions of people who change jobs every year. If other countries want to compete with us in foolish subsidies, let them.

The ethical case

It might be best to examine the ethical case before the economic arguments. It is not my intention to argue against all arms sales. It would be absurd for each member of an alliance to try to make a full range of weapons, simply out of *amour propre*, when specialisation would pay far better. In 1998-99 the Ministry of Defence spent 13% of its equipment budget on 64 co-operative equipment programmes involving 19 partner nations. The most important of these, by far, were France, Germany, the USA, Italy and the Netherlands.

Subsidised credit for exports of arms or major capital goods have far worse effects than just the economic ones. Western nations are undoubtedly rich enough to waste some resources. As Adam Smith said: 'There is an awful lot of ruin in a nation.'

The worst effects are political and moral. They are both illustrated by the instance of the Pergau Dam in Malaysia in the mid 1990s when the Conservative government overturned a publicly minuted reservation by the Permanent Secretary of the Department of Overseas Development and insisted on supporting credits for this dam. One of the unstated arguments for going ahead was that this would act as a sweetener to persuade the Malaysian government to buy other goods, including arms, from Britain. On the other hand arms sales are justified because they are supposed to persuade governments that buy them to use British equipment in their capital projects. Thus one bad consequence is called in aid to support another; and Third World despots are encouraged to devote still more resources to military spending on prestige projects of dubious value.

More recently, the Labour Prime Minister was said to have overruled the Foreign Secretary when he authorised a statement by Stephen Byers on 21 December 1999 that he was 'minded', subject to certain conditions, to grant export credit for the Ilisu dam project in Turkey, which will flood several valleys with sites of unique cultural and religious value to the Kurds. You can imagine what this will do to promote ethnic harmony inside Turkey. In the spring of 2001 we were still waiting for a decision.

We cannot leave out of account the enormous part that bribery plays in this trade. A forthcoming study by Joe Roeber concludes that: 'Because of the structure, complexity and capacity of the market, and above all, because of the secrecy that surrounds every aspect of its activities, the international arms trade is the most corrupt of all legal trades.' He finally asks: 'Can we justify bribing people to buy arms they may not need with money their taxpayers cannot afford, simply to inflate the number of jobs in a declining industry?'

All these follies are supported by the myth that exports are valuable for their own sake, however small the return the

British nation gets from them. Business lobbyists are able to persuade a succession of prime ministers, ranging from ultra-dry Conservatives to New Labour that, if the government does not support them, their overseas rivals will win the contracts instead.

Orders of magnitude

The official estimate for British arms sales is that they amounted in 1999 to about £4bn or appreciably less 0.5% of GDP. A great part consisted of aircraft and aerospace parts. A good academic estimate of the direct cost of government support is about £400m per annum. This does not cover the arms promotion aspects of many royal, political and military visits and activities, which are ostensibly for other purposes. Indirect support for what is known as the Defence Industrial Base is a good deal larger. The number of workers employed is put at 90,000 or just over 0.33% of UK employment. There are two practical inhibitions that limit official export promotion. The first and obvious one is the Exchequer cost. Secondly there is the fear that official promotional activities will be self-defeating, and still more expensive, if all governments follow them in a competitive race. Accordingly, international organisations such as the European Union, the World Trade Organisation, the OECD and the Berne Credit Union have set rules to limit – but not stop – government support.

Unfortunately these agreements do not prevent the never-ending procession of royalty, ministers and ambassadors who promote arms sales abroad, to say nothing of the military and trade attachés. Then there is the Defence Export Services Organisation, which provides marketing and military assistance. Above all, arms sales are often backed by the Export Credits Guarantee Department (ECGD), which provides 'insurance and finance packages for exporters of capital goods and services and political risk insurance' – in other words, taxpayer support for sales that would not pass muster on purely commercial terms. While public enterprises are set a target real rate of return of six per cent, the ECGD has to do no more than break even on average. The ECGD covers medium to long-term capital goods exports from three years up to 16 years duration. In a typical year it underwrites about £7bn of cover. The business is concentrated almost entirely on civil engineering projects and military and civil aerospace. The largest recipient is China. The military share of ECGD business has averaged over 25% in the most recent five years.

The much-maligned Treasury tends to fight many ECGD deals, but is often defeated. Huw Evans, a former Treasury deputy secretary, has said that the ECGD is too vulnerable to intensive lobbying of ministers by large corporations and that it should become an independent agency. As Andrew Tyrie MP, a former adviser to Conservative chancellors has written, 'It is illogical to indulge in a competition to give away our own exports through an auction of subsidies.'

SMALL ARMS

The problem, however, is not confined to officially supported exports of high technology equipment such as aircraft and missiles. It is most often small arms that have been used for domestic repression in armed conflict in the last decade – the vast majority of them civilians and most of them killed by small arms. Clare Short's 2000 White Paper on International Development stated: 'Of the 40 poorest countries in the world, 24 are either in the midst of armed conflict or have only recently emerged from it. This problem is particularly acute in Africa... An estimated five million people have died.' Sophisticated defenders of arms sales agree that there is a case for banning exports of small arms altogether except for the armed forces of western democratic states. For instance Philip Towle argues that the profits Britain makes from this trade are very small despite the benefits to some specialised manufacturers.

The Scott Report of 1996 advocated legislation to put control on arms exports and arms brokering on a permanent non-emergency basis. In the spring of 2001 the Labour government undertook to introduce such legislation in the next parliament and published a draft bill with explanatory memoranda. This will introduce a licensing requirement for trafficking and brokering in arms between overseas countries. It will also introduce licensing requirements for export of military technology by electronic means. Nevertheless the government is still likely to be inhibited by two factors: its reluctance to move too far ahead of competitor countries and its belief that small arms can legitimately be sent to official governments as distinct from so called rebels.

Al Yammamah

There is a further category which is not overtly a subsidy, but is certainly a special arrangement. This is the obscure Al Yammamah deal with Saudi Arabia under which weapons were exchanged for oil. Full details have never been published, but a great deal of information has been collected in *The Arabian Connection*, published by the Campaign against the Arms Trade, which is a useful source even for those who might not agree with all the objectives of the Campaign.

The first Yammamah deal was negotiated in the middle to late 1980s and has its origin in the reluctance of the US Congress to sanction weapons exports to Saudi Arabia. American policies have fluctuated since then; but a second Yammamah agreement was negotiated in the late 1980s; and despite may difficulties it became operational in the early 1990s. Its biggest 'achievement' was to produce a market for the Tornado aircraft, which was said at one time to have saved 19,000 jobs.

The Blair government shows no sign of wanting to banish this kind of agreement, despite the distortions that the heavy investment in arms is producing in Saudi Arabia, the horrific human rights record of the regime there, and the basic instability of that regime. As for the argument about oil supplies, the US, Britain and France cannot – like other western countries – buy their oil on the international market, remembering that Middle Eastern countries often need to sell the oil even more urgently than we need to buy it. It is interesting that this so-called argument of economic strategy usually comes from foreign ministries rather than ministries of finance or economics.

The UK record

The recent UK record is not all bad. In July 1997 the then new British Foreign Secretary Robin Cook stated that the new Labour government would not permit the sale of arms to regimes that might use them for internal repression. It is the least he could have said after the *Arms for Iraq* scandal. The government has fulfilled an election pledge to publish annual reports on UK's strategic export controls. These have gradually improved in quality; and the third one, issued in July 2000, has been described by Saferworld as 'the most transparent report published by any European country and one which offers a potential template for best practice through the EU.' But even this latest report is criticised for failure to provide information on ultimate end users, the absence of summary information on licences refused and lack of detailed information on actual deliveries, as distinct from licences.

The Blair government inherited various international obligations such as membership of the Australia Group of 30 countries aiming to discourage the proliferation of chemical and biological weapons. An international convention was reached in December 1997 banning the production and transfer of anti-personnel mines. This came too early to be attributed to the Labour government elected in the same year. But the new government indeed took a lead in pressing for a European Union Code of Conduct on Arms Exports which was agreed in June 1998. The Chancellor of the Exchequer, Gordon Brown, began the millennium by adding 22 new poor countries over and above the previous 41 covered by the ban on export credits 'for unproductive expenditure'.

Indonesia, however, remains off the banned list. And because the Chancellor's action was in the context of debt relief for poor countries, it did not affect Saudi Arabia, which has accounted for about one third of British arms sales. It is thus fair to say that there is still a long way to go. Amnesty International's view has been that the Department of Trade and Industry 'is not meeting its responsibility to promote trade in a manner which is not harmful to human rights.' It was also worried that this same department is responsible both for the licensing of arms sales and for their promotion. A joint report of four House of Commons committees reiterated that a serious error of judgement was made in late 1998 and early 1999 in granting several open export licences for military equipment to the government of Zimbabwe, despite that government's heavy involvement in the fighting in the Congo and its domestic infringements of human rights. The same report urged considering a stricter interpretation of the arms embargo on China and also raised issues about licences for arms to other countries.

At the height of the East Timor crisis in early 1999 there appeared a telling *Times* cartoon. On one side of the cartoon a buoyant Tony Blair was shown exclaiming: 'We need a hawk' – meaning a more determined military effort to put pressure on the government of Indonesia. On the other side he was shown piloting one of the Hawk aircraft that the UK had been delivering to Indonesia for many years for the use of the country's former military dictator, General Suharto.

Export Promotion

A popular view is that some arms sales may be undesirable, but that they help promote jobs, growth and employment. Therefore a balance has to be drawn between these two considerations – a compromise always appeals to the so-called practical man. We will thus never really stop dubious arms sales until the myth of the export drive is nailed once and for all. The root of the matter is the belief throughout the political and business establishment that exports are worthwhile for their own sake, irrespective of the terms on which they are sold and how much they have to be subsidised. It is for this reason that prime ministers, whether Thatcher, Major or Blair, time and again come down against the Treasury in favour of controversial arms deals or dubious overseas capital projects. These attitudes are a hangover from the siege economy days of Stafford Cripps (Labour Chancellor in the late 1940s) and have no place in a global market economy.

The balance of payments preoccupation goes back many centuries. Mercantilist writers in the 16th, 17th and 18th century, campaigned for a favourable balance of trade and for an inflow of gold and silver. These writers were refuted as conclusively as anything can be in political economy by 18th century members of the Scottish Enlightenment such as David Hume and Adam Smith. During the subsequent period of rapid world economic growth towards the end of the 19th century huge current account surpluses and deficits built up, far greater than any of the imbalances which commentators have bemoaned in recent decades. The origin of both the export drive and the reinvention of so-called balance of payments problem was in the immediate post-war years when sterling was on a fixed exchange rate and was also inconvertible. The financial policy regime was then one of suppressed inflation, which tended to spill over into the balance of payments, and which was held down by a mixture of controls and exchange rate overvaluation. It was, moreover, a world with strict controls over capital flows. These controls could not be severe enough to protect determined speculators from launching an attack on a suspect currency, but they were enough of a deterrent to the regular flows of capital across borders which normally finance imbalances on current account. The post-World War Two generation of political and economic leaders was brought up on slogans and posters such as 'export or die', the 'dollar drive' and even on one occasion 'exporting is fun'. By contrast we are now back in a world of relatively free capital flows. There are bound to be large imbalances between countries with high savings ratios and relatively few investment outlets and other countries, such as the United States, which have had low savings but many investment opportunities. Moreover we now have floating exchange rates.

Advanced industrial countries with floating exchange rates need never have balance of payments problems. They may suffer from unwelcome downward pressure on their exchange rate due to financial market's distrust of their policies or of fears about domestic inflation. If so, such fears should be tackled directly. In today's circumstances export drives really amount to the diversion of public resources towards special interest groups under the guise of patriotic slogans. The basic political and business fallacy is not to realise that exports, like investment, are a cost and not a benefit. If we could finance the imports that British citizens want to buy without any exports – say by interest-free loans from overseas on indefinite repayment terms – we would be better off. Of course this would require a period of adjustment. But such adjustments are necessary after any kind of economic or industrial change. In the world as it is, exports are a waste of resources and serve no purpose if they are not paid for, or are paid for very late and on a heavily subsidised credit basis and with a strong political risk factor.

The jobs argument

The most popular argument for subsidising exports is the effect on jobs. We should be on our guard when politicians defend dubious policies by declaring 'jobs are at stake'. This is so whether it is an 'Old Labour' supporter wanting to protect manufacturing, a Tory spokesman talking about the employment provided by hunting, or a business lobbyist pushing for arms sales to dubious regimes. The argument that jobs derived from exporting weapons cannot be replaced is akin to the argument for keeping open uneconomic coalmines for the sake of employment. Yet it is often just those people who lecture us on the need for workers to change jobs, and who say that full employment cannot the same employment, who are most keen to promote the sale of arms.

Such arguments are based on the myth that there is a lump of labour that is engaged in making specific products. Then, it is supposed, if orders or output are lost in one area they cannot be regained anywhere else. But people change jobs constantly. Well over three million people leave the unemployment register each year even in recession periods, over half of them for new jobs or training. Indeed, it is almost certainly easier for arms workers, many of whom have a wide range of valued skills, to find new jobs than it was for miners, whose training was more specific There are those who ask, 'Where will the new jobs come from to replace those lost in exporting weapons?' The onus is on them to explain how it is that other jobs, on a much greater scale, arose to take the place of handloom weavers or the drivers of horse-drawn carts – or for that matter the owners of pack-asses replaced by wheeled traffic at the dawn of history. The multiplication of population and the multiple rise of productivity in the last two centuries, so far from these having caused mass unemployment, have been accompanied by a multiple increase in the number of jobs.

One of the key ideas of economics is that of the circular flow of income. The point is that there is a continuing flow between purchasers who desire to buy products, the incomes received from supplying their needs, and still further purchases. The idea is so basic that economists regard it as too obvious to mention and take it for granted rather than discuss it explicitly. The smoothness of this flow can be helped by sensible policies, such as efforts by the Bank of England Monetary Policy Committee to maintain an adequate, but not excessive, flow of total spending, and by sensible exchange rate policies. The interested citizen needs to know mainly that there is or can be such a circular flow, and that there therefore need be no fear of one country being undercut in everything by another.

Terms of trade

A slightly more respectable argument is that relating to the terms of trade. A royal visit or a small amount of official publicity, or arm-twisting by the Foreign Office, might enable a company to sell more overseas at a given price or to sell a given amount of goods at a higher price. This enables the home country to exchange exports for imports on slightly more profitable terms. The argument has very little application in a highly competitive world where a country of the size of Britain has little monopoly power. If e-commerce means anything at all this should vanish completely as buyers are able to find the most competitive offer unaided by royal visits.

A further argument relates to small exporters, who might not have the resources to engage in the required market research and export promotion. But surely this kind of thing is the job of market research and advertising agencies, chambers of commerce and industry associations. If it does not pay them to engage in such promotion, it is because government support agencies are providing these services on a free or subsidised basis.

Spillover benefits

The last resort of any sector or industry whose subsidies are challenged is to say that it brings spillover benefits to the rest of the economy. Concorde was virtually launched on such arguments. Weapons producers argue that the government should continue to support exports because the proceeds contribute to the overhead costs of firms supplying the British military. These considerations cut both ways. The drive for arms sales itself distorts the design and production plans of British manufacturers and, in the view of some defence economists, offsets the savings in overheads. In any case, only some arms exports would be affected by a ban in the spirit of our supposedly ethical foreign policy. The posited economies of scale could readily be achieved by greater specialisation among Nato counties – a process inhibited by the desire of so many governments to protect domestic firms.

The NERA report

A report on export credit by the National Economic Research Associates (NERA). There has been some misguided celebration of the fact that NERA did not recommend that ECGD should be privatised. But the more important question is whether the provision of insurance cover should be subsidised. Until 1991, the Department showed heavy cash flow losses. It was then instructed to break even in cash flow terms in line with Berne procedures. But the ECGD is still, not required to show the positive return of 6% in real terms normally required on public sector investment projects. NERA could not find any justification for the subsidy – a most important finding which the vested interests involved have contrived to bury.

NERA's first preference is for an internationally negotiated phasing out. We must also face the question of whether there is a case for the UK moving further ahead on its own. But much more important than any of these details is the fact that reports such as NERA's are based on a mutually convenient misunderstanding. Economic research organisations, trying to unearth a case for intervention and subsidy, tend to focus on lapses from perfection inherent in almost all markets: matters such as informational barriers facing potential new exporters, and which governments might be able to help overcome by activities such as trade fairs or start-up credits. NERA indeed found such imperfections.

Politicians and opinion leaders take such reports, however, as confirmation that, without export promotion, the balance of payments would go haywire, the country become bankrupt and thousands of jobs would be lost. They conveniently overlook the fact that these bankruptcy and job fears are dismissed in polite terms as fallacies not worth serious consideration. NERA for instance remarked that the last thing the overheated British economy needed was extra demand for labour. Even in the year 2001 when there was a risk of recession, selective aid to a few heavy goods or arms manufacturers would have been an extremely inefficient way of stimulating demand.

INDUSTRIAL CASE STUDIES

Few critics would suggest a complete ban on arms sales; but a cut of one-third would effectively eliminate the most dubious items. Let us suppose, then, that British arms exports were cut by £1 billion or £2 billion a year. Let us grant that these exports would have to be replaced or imports reduced in their stead. But there is no more a fixed lump of exports than there is a fixed lump of jobs. In fact, this arithmetic is far too generous to the arms lobbies. It would apply if we were talking about an industry that does not receive special government help; in that case, the resources involved would have to move to their next best use. But arms sales do not represent, even in the narrowest economic terms, the best use of national resources. They are so heavily supported by the taxpayer that there might actually be a gain in moving the workers, plant and technical skills to other activities that could pay for themselves.

Let me cite two related bottom-up industrial studies. These have examined the impact of a one-third reduction in arms exports based on the average of the decade 1985-95 when the size of the arms sector was somewhat larger than it became at the of the century. The output of weapons and ammunition would have been cut by about 12% and of aero products by nine per cent.

The maximum number of jobs lost would have been 40,000. On the basis of labour turnover estimates, the authors estimated that 40% would have found new work within a year and another 13% the year after that. About 27% would have taken more than two years to find a new job. Some 20% would have left the labour force. The impact would have been greatest where defence employment is concentrated in one or two plants in individual towns such as Bristol, Plymouth, Yeovil and Preston.

The hypothetical one-third cut in arms exports would have initially reduced total exports of all goods and services by some 0.5%. Nearly half of this half would have been replaced by alternative exports produced by redundant workers finding new work within a year. The remainder could be found partly from those finding work later and partly through other shifts within and between industries. We are talking about the loss of 0.25% of UK exports of goods and services. This might, at worst, involve a miniscule devaluation and some slight adjustment in monetary and fiscal policy. If we cut through the technicalities, the cost could be a tiny deterioration in the terms of exchange between British exports and imports from overseas.

The academic authors search for some positive overspill benefits from promoting military exports. The largest they can find is the contribution of exports to the overhead cost of firms which serve the home market as well. The second largest comes from the contribution of exports to development costs. Against these modest industrial costs have to be set government budgetary savings. A more subtle saving is that the government now has to take into account not only value for money but supposed industrial and employment benefits in placing military orders. In 1995 a recommendation by the Equipment Approvals Committee in favour of the American designed Chinook helicopter was overridden by the Secretary of State for Defence in favour of a mixed order involving Westland. Netting all their estimates out, the defence economists arrive at an annual budgetary gain of £76m from the postulated cut in arms sales. One does not have to pretend that these estimates are precise or that the cost saving is enormous. The thrust of the argument is that the net effects on the British economy of reducing arms sales are negligible or even favourable.

Similar results have been emerging in France. A Committee of the French National Assembly was given an analysis of 21 of 42 programmes of French arms exports which were said to have reduced purchasing prices for the French armed forces. The conclusion was that for half of these the gains of scale were countered by various factors, such as changes in specifications and delays. For the other half the scale effect did not lead to any reductions in the prices paid by the French government because the profit from the extended production lines went to the companies. The Committee also quotes Denis Ranque, chairman of the Thomson-CSF group who told the Defence Committee of the Assembly on 28 March 2000 that "although many of the group's non military activities sprang from earlier defence programmes, the reverse was becoming more and more frequent, as the new civilian technologies were now being incorporated in weapons systems. This development.. encouraged the group to seek a presence in the new civilian technology sector in order to maintain competitiveness in defence production.'

Why size matters

That is the relationship of the *a priori* argument about the circular flow of income and the automatic adjustment of the balance of payments, to numerical estimates of the size of the sector and the modest nature of the adjustments involved in eliminating dubious exports. Suppose we were talking about 50% of total exports or four or five million workers? Would this affect the argument? The answer is mainly in the time dimension. Any change in the pattern of demand leads to some adjustment problem. If the adjustment is large, care has to be taken by monetary and fiscal policy to maintain total demand; special efforts have to go into retraining; and there is a case for phasing out the change, if at all possible, to give those concerned time to adjust. But when we are talking about a modest fraction of a small and declining industry these adjustment problems are second order. Obviously a few constituencies are involved; but the change is much less than the normal adjustments which take place in a typical year through economic circumstances without any change of policy.

Others will take the trade

The favourite business argument, which one hears particularly, but not only, in relation to arms sales, is that if the British government does not promote them, the American, French or Chinese or other governments will, leaving Britain as usual as the mug. But supposing that other countries do not go all the way? It is like saying that you should not stop knocking your head against a brick wall until your friends have also stopped knocking theirs. Or to drop the metaphor: national resources should be left to go to where they enjoy the highest rate of return even if this causes a loud protest from companies that have been used to being artificially supported. The argument that others will export weapons if Britain desists is a dangerous defence for any aspect of the arms trade. 'The very same argument was used to defend the slave trade in the 18th century and the opium trade to China in the 19th century.'

4

International Cooperation to Control the Intergovernmental Small Arms Trade

INTRODUCTION

Legal small arms imports and illicit supplies "fuel grave human rights abuses" among FARC and ELN rebels, paramilitaries and state security forces in Colombia; Rearmament on all sides of conflict stymies possible benefits of a UN arms embargo in Cote d'Ivoire; A long history of armed conflict and rising violent crime in Guatemala linked to the arms trade; Overt and clandestine arms provisions to Somalia "worsen a human rights catastrophe"; protestors massacred with arms supplied to Guinea in years prior to their use; US, UK and NATO military sales "worsening the carnage and despair" in an increasingly armed Iraq; arms transfers abused and misused in repressive Myanmar; the intensification of a borderline genocide fiasco resulting from the continuous inflow of small arms directly—and indirectly by way of neighbouring Chad—into Sudan by both transparent and illegal means. International news sources need only look to the world's most violent conflict zones to be constantly equipped with an array of disturbing headlines directly related to flagrant international human rights' violations exacerbated by the flourishing global arms trade.

As the international community struggles to respond to the human rights crises associated with the globalized trade in small arms and light weapons (SALW), cooperation efforts have done little to curb the harmful implications of the legal and illegal transfer of arms to conflict-ridden areas of the world, where profit-seeking business endeavors seem to trump ethical social responsibility. "According to the Congressional Research Service, the value of all arms transfer agreements worldwide in 2005 was approaching $45 billion, with the sales to the developing world accounting for two thirds of that total." Among government militaries, armed militias and rebel guerrillas in countries wrought with civil war, destroyed by humanitarian disasters and plagued by factionalist infighting, the demand for weapon provisions is constantly on the rise, with a high price to be paid to those willing to provide the supply. Academicians, ambassadors, human rights' activists and politicians from all corners of the world condemn the "irresponsible" arms trade that continues to provide governments and non-state armed groups with a plethora of SALWs at the snap of a finger, many times in outright disregard for UN and regional sanctions prohibiting their dissemination.

How has the international community attempted to respond to such a widespread threat to international peace and human rights? What are the fundamental obstacles to restricting the arms trade to prevent the proliferation of SALWs in conflicts under scrutiny for human rights violations? How can governments and international organizations cooperate to promote a regulated, responsible and legal global arms trade? This paper touches on these questions as it analyses the main challenges associated with the small arms trade, particularly as it relates to the legal intergovernmental transfer of arms, highlighting the case study of China's continued supply of arms to human rights' hotbed, Sudan, despite international pressure urging the contrary. References include United Nations documents, task force and international NGO campaign reports, contemporary media coverage and University for Peace lecture discussions. As human rights crises rage on from Colombia and Guatemala to Sudan, DR Congo, Somalia, Myanmar and dozens of conflict zones in between, regulating the legal arms trade has become a hot policy topic in national governments, among peace advocating international NGOs and within the UN system. Despite their efforts and minimal progress, a key challenge remains: Is the international community ready and willing to commit to such an ethical task when there are billions to be made in defecting? At the start of the twenty-first century, the answer remains dubious at best.

CONTROLLING THE INTERGOVERNMENTAL SALW TRADE

For our purposes of analyzing international cooperation on controlling interstate arms transfers and given the limited scope of this topic, the illicit non-governmental trade in SALW, arguably one of the most dangerous threats facing our global humanity today, will not be treated here. However, it is significant to mention that the illicit trade by private individuals and groups acting outside state control is a worrisome outcome of the versatility of today's globalized economy such that these non-state actors may provide arms to belligerents despite international sanctions or other mechanisms to control the arms trade. In this way, we must recognize the illicit arms trade as a force to be reckoned with alongside efforts to control the legal intergovernmental trade in SALW, as it exacerbates the already challenging aim of regulating the interstate transfer of arms to conflict zones ripe with human rights violations.

With the end of the Cold War, new global challenges emerged with the rise of grave human rights' concerns in Somalia, Rwanda and Kosovo, to mention a few. As the superpower nuclear threat gave way to intra-state conflict in cases of genocide and human rights violations, the need to regulate the small arms trade resurfaced as a key priority on the international policy agenda.

The mid-1990s saw the resurgence of the same preliminary attempts of the old League of Nations days to regulate international arms transfers through a process of registering who is trading with whom on the intergovernmental level. From its inception this idea lacked overarching support and was buried by the outbreak of World War II and the ensuing global Cold War environment primarily concerned with the threat of nuclear weapons as opposed to regulating the trade in small arms. Although the advancement of economic globalization and its dizzying implications for the SALW trade have created a much different world than that of the inter-World War period, international cooperation on this issue continues to target the same general aim of creating an environment of governmental responsibility, accountability and transparency through regulation, registration and monitoring of the international SALW trade. Within the past decade, cooperative efforts on the national, intergovernmental, international NGO and United Nations levels have established overarching campaigns in attempts to prevent the transfer of arms to governments implicated in grave human rights' violations.

A principal outcome of 1990s international cooperation on arms control was the development in 2005 of a draft Arms Trade Treaty (ATT), "drawing on the principles of the 1997 Nobel Peace Laureates' International Code of Conduct on Arms Transfers proposed by Dr. Oscar Arias and a group of seven other laureates... an effort to codify states' existing responsibilities under international law and [provide] an operative mechanism for their application to the arms trade." The Code of Conduct and the ATT relate specifically to the legal intergovernmental arms trade, calling on governments to exercise ethical responsibility and recognize their role in condemning human rights' abuses by restricting arms transfers to governments in violation of international law, particularly human rights abuses. In 1997, the Code of Conduct called for "a ban on transfers of weapons or military technology to governments that violently repress fundamental democratic rights, are guilty of gross violations of human rights, or commit acts of armed international aggression." In 2005, with the hopes of becoming a binding, universal and comprehensive treaty, the draft ATT adopted and expanded this ban to encompass the single principle of "No more weapons for violations of international law." At the time of its creation, the ATT Steering Committee members included: the African Peace Forum, Amnesty International, the Arias Foundation for Peace and Human Progress, Caritas International, Friends Committee on National Legislation (USA), International Action Network on Small Arms, Non Violence International, Oxfam, Project Ploughshares (Canada), Saferworld (UK), Albert Schweitzer Institute (USA), Sou de Paz (Brazil), Viva Rio (Brazil), and the Women's Institute for Alternative Development (Trinidad and Tobago).

As international NGOs lead the cooperative campaign urging the implementation of the Arms Trade Treaty to regulate and restrict the legal intergovernmental transfer of SALW, the United Nations system has responded quite favorably with a landmark First Committee of the UN General Assembly vote in 2006 to move forward on the process of creating a comprehensive ATT within the UN body. Passing with a margin of 139 to 1 (24 abstentions and the United States the only vote in opposition), this vote "paved the way for a feasibility report by the Secretary General and the establishment of a Group of Governmental Experts to consider the scope and content of the Treaty." In this case, we may consider the proactive response of the UN to move forward on creating a comprehensive ATT a major success of the international NGO cooperation between those organizations mentioned above in influencing the international UN policy agenda.

As the ATT process trudges along in the General Assembly as an overarching attempt to regulate the global intergovernmental arms trade, the role of the UN Security Council in this matter has taken on a much more specific, ad hoc character in its efforts to prevent the governmental dissemination of arms to states implicated in human rights violations. In the majority of cases, sanctions and embargoes have become the standard practice in Security Council responses to governments under scrutiny for human rights' abuses. This has been the case most recently in Sudan, DR Congo, Myanmar and Somalia, where the Security Council has voted to condemn through sanctions the sale or transfer of arms to the governments of these countries. Although a majority of UN member nations have heeded UN sanctions prohibiting arms provision to these states' governments, defection on the part of a limited number of governments within the international community has weakened their capacity to put real pressure on the governments in question to change their inhumane policies and put an end to human rights' violations. A devastating result of this practice of arms sanction defection is the perpetuation of violent intrastate conflict characterized by gross human rights violations at the hands of the official state military apparatus, rebel groups and hired militias. The following section examines this phenomenon in the case study of China's ongoing provision of arms to the Sudanese government in disregard of UN sanctions against it.

CHINA-SUDAN ARMS TRADE

Darfur, Sudan, one of the world's most talked-about intrastate conflicts in the international media, among members of the UN system and within the scope of international human rights' NGOs, is an illustrative example of the ways in which sovereign states may thwart international cooperation on efforts aiming to end human rights' violations through restricting the arms trade. In the case of the Sudan, where 300,000 people, the vast majority civilians, have been killed and 2.5 million displaced, the Chinese government is under international scrutiny for continuing to provide the Sudanese government with SALW and military transport vehicles despite a UN Security Council embargo forbidding the transfer of arms to the Darfur region since 2004.

Security Council Resolution 1591 (2005) bans the transfer of arms to all parties to the Darfur conflict: "All States shall take the necessary measures to prevent the supply of arms and related materiel of all types and also of technical training and assistance to the following actors operating in the states of North Darfur, South Darfur, and West Darfur: all non-governmental entities and individuals, including the Janjaweed; all parties to the N'djamena Ceasefire Agreement; any other belligerents." Within the international community, there is very little doubt that the Sudanese government continues to play an active, if not entirely protagonist role in the Darfur conflict and its heavy list of human rights violations. In this light, governments and international NGOs have cast blame on the Chinese government for its ongoing arms provisions to the Sudanese government in disregard for the Security Council arms embargo.

The Chinese government, on the other hand, claims that it has not acted in breach of the embargo on the grounds that arms sales to Sudan support the self-defence of the Sudanese government, who it denies as a perpetrator of human rights violations in Darfur. China's "arms sales exploit a gray area in the resolution, which may technically allow the government to buy weapons as long as they are not used in Darfur." However, international rights groups in particular have reported on the link between Chinese arms provisions to the Sudanese government and their subsequent use in Darfur. According to a 2007 report by Amnesty International, "Sudan had transferred six K-8 attack aircraft recently acquired from China to Darfur in breach of the ban...[noting that] Khartoum was expecting six more....In 2005, the year a United Nations resolution banned the transfer of weapons to all parties in Darfur, China supplied $24 million in arms and $57 million in aircraft equipment." Through this type of 'gray-area' arms provisions that may or may not be in breach of the Security Council embargo depending on differing interpretations of its terms, China has successfully undermined international arms control efforts attempting to put an end to one of the most troublesome human rights crises in contemporary history.

Cooperative international efforts within the INGO, intergovernmental and UN spheres have responded to the China-Sudan arms trade in two significant ways: a) recommendations by the US, European Union and Security Council Committee on Sudan to strengthen and expand the current arms embargo; and b) international media and public opinion pressure through a successful awareness movement led by the Control Arms Campaign. On the international elite level, the US, EU and Security Council Subcommittee for Sudan are in the process of coordinating efforts to strengthen and expand the jurisdiction of the UN Security Council arms embargo.

The US and EU are leading the campaign to induce other Security Council members to threaten or invoke sanctions on governments who do not comply with the Sudan arms trade embargo. In a recent report, the Security Council Subcommittee has recommended the expansion of the current embargo to include arms transfers to Chad and possibly, Libya. These measures respond both to China's arms sale to Sudan and the reality that despite the embargo, SALW are leaking into Sudan by way of the Chad and Libyan borders. Although progressive by Security Council standards, these collaborative efforts remain in the planning stages, lacking overarching support from the Security Council with the impending threat of a veto exercised by China and/or Russia.

Through the publication and dissemination of official reports, observer testimonies and press releases, the Control Arms Campaign has made significant headway in its efforts to stimulate international awareness of the link between China's arms trade with Sudan and the human rights crisis in Darfur. Comprised of three leading international human rights NGO's, Amnesty International, Oxfam and International Action Network on Small Arms, the Control Arms Campaign has been highly successful in influencing public opinion as well as national and international policy agendas to regulate the intergovernmental arms trade in general, and the China-Sudan trade in particular.

As media outlets and grassroots campaigns vociferously respond to reports such as Amnesty's "Blood at the Crossroads," a detailed compilation of the connections between the SALW trade and the world's most perilous human rights' crises, it is becoming increasingly impossible for governments to ignore their role in the perpetuation of human rights' violations through questionably legal intergovernmental arms transfers. As awareness increases on the popular and elite levels, some journalists point to its effect on the arms providers themselves, in this case China. An Economist special report notes, "China has [...] changed its stance on Sudan as international outrage about events in Darfur has grown and activists have branded the Beijing games as 'the genocide Olympics'. Last year China helped to persuade Sudan to admit UN peacekeepers—a move it had long resisted, with China's blessing. China has even sent troops of its own to join the UN force." As UN sanctions and embargoes may prove weak in their capacity to influence states' behaviour in regard to the sale of arms irrespective of human rights, international pressure through cooperative awareness campaigns may be a way forward in prompting governments like China's to reevaluate their role as arms providers in conflicts wrought with human rights violations.

SMALL ARMS TRADE

In the age of nuclear and other weapons of mass destruction, the vast majority of all warfare continues to be conducted using conventional weapons: machine rifles, grenades, landmines, explosives, and light rockets. These small arms, and the ability to obtain them, are the operational means of warfare. The much-touted efficiency of "high-tech" warfare based on computer-guided rockets and remote-controlled war machinery has been generally successful only as bombardment in advance of ground-based attack which ultimately depends on soldiers wielding hand-held weapons. Thus, even when blessed with unlimited war capability and unlimited weaponry options, militaries such as those of the United States and Russia depend on small arms to subdue populations and control territory. So do guerilla revolutionaries and those defending themselves against their own violently abusive governments. This essay will consider the issue of the global trade in small arms, examining its scope, its global economic underpinnings, its relationships to the economies of conflict-plagued countries, its particular connections to the current war in Sudan, and finally possible initiatives for reform of the global small arms trade.

The Scope of the Problem

As recently as World War II, the ability to prosecute war depended on developing the industrial capacity to produce these "small arms." During the Cold War, the United States and the Soviet Union provided conventional weapons for their respective client states fighting "proxy" wars. The high-geared military-industrial economies of the two leviathans have stimulated France, China, Germany, the UK, Italy, Ukraine, and Israel to compete in the lucrative worldwide business of weapons export. In 2002 these nine weapons-selling countries exported $14.8 billion in conventional weapons to the rest of the world. Forty percent of this staggering volume of weapons flows from Russia; 27% is shipped from the USA. The USA, UK, and France earned more in small arms sales to developing countries in 1998-2001 than they gave in aid.

The gigantism of this industry renders it a force in national economic policies. It is in the national interest of these nations, to some degree, to promote violent conflict and war around the world. As is apparent in the case of Sudan, the economic leverage of the weapons industry, including the small arms industry, may determine whether major first-world nations support or impede peace processes in war-torn countries. This positive self-interest that weapons-supplying first-world nations have in the negative interest — the active destruction and resulting impoverishment — of third-world nations is a very dark side of the economic colonialism that typifies neo-liberal economic globalization.

Classic game-theory analyses of arms race determinants assume arms development and production to come at the expense of a nation's economic well-being. While that may actually be true in terms of benefit to an entire nation's economy, it is *always* true that war yields positive economic benefit to national military industries, and that military industries hold disproportionate power over their governments' decision-making processes. In result, the world is flooded with weapons, and the potential to pursue violence is immediately and endlessly available to all. As Mary Kaldor notes, "violence is increasingly privatized both as a result of growing organized crime and the emergence of paramilitary groups." There are reported to be more than 639 million small arms in the world today; in the case of South Asia, 80% are in civilian (non-governmental) hands.

The availability of small arms is further assured through the worldwide financial deregulation that is a cornerstone of neo-liberal economic globalization. The deregulation of financial transactions has effectively rendered the financing of war exempt from national or international governance. Arms merchants and, significantly, diaspora supporters of civil conflicts are easily able to move funds instantly and covertly behind the screens of small states specializing in such banking services, thanks to the blessings of deregulated economic globalization. Weapons procurers are similarly enabled to operate with impunity, even when supplying arms illegally to the perpetrators of humanitarian crimes and genocides. Even when legal "controls" are in effect, sales and movement of small weapons to parties in conflict can proceed unabated. The illegal arms trade is estimated at more than (perhaps much more than) $1 billion per year. Conflict entrepreneurs — weapons manufacturers, gun-runners, merchant middle-men, and the weapons users themselves, profit both from the supply of weapons and from their use in protracted conflict.

During the Cold War massive supplies of conventional and more sophisticated weapons systems were pumped into client states by the Cold War powers, providing vast stores of machinery for ensuing post-Cold War wars. Weapons fed into the Afghanistan and Cambodian conflicts have been the foundation of supply for current South Asian violence. Massive supplies of weapons supplied to the Congo and Angola wars provided the stockpile for succeeding West African wars. The killing lives of such weapons may last many years. During the Cold War, the Coordinating Committee for Multilateral Export Controls (CoCom) operated as the Western self-regulation of which weapons and technologies were to be restricted. By 1989, however, the appeal of economic gains effectively overwhelmed security concerns. CoCom was disbanded in 1994, and first-world weapons producers have since fed arms to parties in conflict with unrestricted, free-market eagerness.

THE SOCIAL AND ECONOMIC IMPACT OF SMALL ARMS IN WARRING NATIONS

Small arms trade plays a prominent role in the economies of nations at war, and particularly in intrastate conflicts. The availability of small arms makes war possible, and their continuing availability fuels the protraction of war. War economies require continuing violence for sustenance. In many protracted civil wars, the availability of weapons exceeds that of soldiers, leading to the mushrooming prevalence of child-soldier "recruitment" by kidnapping (Sudan, Uganda, Sierra Leone, Sri Lanka, and elsewhere).

Thus, the small arms market helps to drive the diverse disabling economic and social effects of war. Wars fed by small arms supply divert economic investment and energy from normal productivity, and suck up resources otherwise available for domestic services and infrastructure (education, health care, social welfare, and productivity-related infrastructure like roads, energy provision, and water supply). "War interrupts, and indeed reverses, economic development." War destroys physical and social capital, and erodes what Sen calls the "capacities" and "entitlements" of people's lives.

Small arms warfare is intimately connected to poverty and arrested economic development in conflict-affected areas. Agriculture suffers both from the loss of opportunity to work in fields and from the weapons themselves, especially land mines. Looting and the ruination of croplands are common tactics. Commerce suffers as well; necessary safety, reliable transportation, and open communication become extremely difficult in areas infused with small arms. Industry and international trade suffer for all these reasons, plus the increased risks of loss to combatants. The stability of government and policy, required for the smooth function of economies, suffers in the presence of active violence. When war concludes, conflict-damaged societies must then face the economic burdens of both weapons disarmament and disposal and the education and employment of habituated combatants.

The ready availability of small arms enables conflict economies of robbery and looting, extortion systems, and kidnapping. Lives lost to small arms violence are a major economic loss to societies torn by conflict, with long-reaching adverse effects on the economic function of families and communities. Small arms violence results in major dislocations of refugees and internally-displaced persons, who are rendered both severely needy and unable to be productive. And the supply of small arms stimulates drug-running and other smuggling economies. Finally, when active warfare abates, the presence of abundant small arms and abundant ex-soldiers fosters the escalation of crime rates and the development of organized crime that has been a virtually constant sequel to recent wars.

Even the ability of outside humanitarian donors to ease the suffering of people in conflict-infected regions risks being hijacked for economic gain by warring groups empowered by small arms. In many situations, armed independent gangs or unofficial militias derive significant funding from regular looting or "taxation" of humanitarian aid providers.

The Case of Sudan

The individual case of the complex, protracted intrastate war in Sudan clearly exemplifies the terrible hazards of the global small arms market. In Sudan, the genocidal campaign of the Sudanese (Muslim) government against native Muslims living in the newly-discovered oil field lands of Darfur has been actively pursued through government-assisted militias, primarily the Janjawid. The Janjawid are able to carry out their program of mass terror, murder and intentional starvation by virtue of their wealth of small arms provisions — Kalashnikov AK47 assault rifles, rocket-propelled grenades, and jeep-mounted machine guns — despite the UN adoption in 2001 of Article 16 of the UN International Law Commission's Articles on Responsibility of States for Internationally Wrongful Acts. The agreement is binding on *all* states, and forbids any assistance of another state in the commission of "any internationally wrongful act." The Janjawid's atrocities clearly surpass international definition as "Internationally Wrongful Acts," and the Sudan government's claims to be uninvolved and opposed to the arbitrary and indiscriminate killing, "disappearances," systemic rapes, and torture fly in the face of heavily documented evidence of the government's supply of and government troop participation in the atrocities. In 1994, the European Union joined in an arms embargo against all non-governmental entities in Sudan in order to "promote lasting peace and reconciliation within Sudan," but the world weapons industry has continued to sell arms to the Sudanese government without restriction. Given the clear evidence of the Sudan government's programmatic support of and participation in the Darfur genocide and crimes against humanity, any sale of arms to Sudan violates Article 16 of the UN International Law Commission. Every nation fully understands this, yet the world community of weapons exporters have continued to feed small arms into Sudan, fueling the Darfur genocide. In March, 2004, The UN Security Council voted 13-0-2 to demand that Sudan disarm its paramilitary militias, but issued its demand without teeth. Further, small arms shipments to other East African countries from the USA and Germany, among others, is certain to bolster Sudan's stockpile of weapons. It is estimated that 85% of the personal assault weapons in Africa originate in the five countries of the UN Security Council: the USA, the UK, Russia, China, and France.

Finally, only two weeks ago, the UN Security Council approved a total weapons embargo, targeted economic sanctions against atrocity perpetrators, a 10,000-person peacekeeping force, and an International Criminal Court investigation and prosecution of criminals against humanity in Sudan. Principal exporters of small arms to Sudan appear to be Iran, China,

France, Saudi Arabia, Switzerland, and the UK (this tally excludes further volumes of arms sales in terms of fighter jets, helicopters, etc.). The fact that UN Security Council nations have stakes in the illegal arms supply of the Janjawid/Sudanese government genocide in Darfur (and China's strong oil-supply relationship with the Sudanese government) helps explain the Security Council's failure to act to stop the war. In November 2004, Amnesty International revealed densely documented details of the uncontrolled arms exports that have fueled massive human rights abuses in Sudan, including the killing, rape, torture and displacement of more than a million civilians since the Darfur conflict escalated in February 2003 after the discovery of Darfur oil deposits.

The inability (or unwillingness) of the Swiss, paragons of organization, to regulate their own export of weapons demonstrates the degree to which the weapons market is out of control. After being told by the Geneva-based Graduate Institute of International Studies that Swiss small arms exports to Sudan totaled more than $4 million in 2002, the Swiss Finance Ministry promised that Switzerland would review its weapons exports. The Swiss government records reveal less than *$4,000* worth of handgun exports to Sudan, to be used "for use as personal protection or sporting purposes." "Such trade would not have been approved by us," stated Ottmar Wyss, responsible for export control. "Either there is illegal export trade going on, or the numbers are wrong." Reason and experience suggest that the wrong numbers are those of Mr. Wyss.

The Sudanese government estimates that "two to three million" landmines cover 32 % of the country; the original exporters of the landmines were Russia, China, the UK, Iraq, Iran, the USA, and a list of others.

While Sudan's population is impoverished and has been victimized by its two decades of civil war, and although Sudan is one of the 38 "Heavily Indebted Poor Countries" eligible for favourable borrowing terms, Sudan is also sitting on major oil reserves — a resource pool that could possibly deliver economic stability and domestic freedoms to the people of Sudan. Instead, oil production is bankrolling the government's pursuit of genocide against its own people, through the purchase of small arms and other weapons, a political economic decision founded on abuse of one part of its population for the benefit of a relative few. The main foreign direct investors in Sudan are companies from China, Malaysia, and India.

HALTING THE GLOBAL SMALL ARMS MARKET

What measures might effectively govern the worldwide small arms market and reduce the likelihood of violence? Given the present prevalent system of deregulated trade and finance, and the monstrous productive capacity of a profusion of nations to produce the weapons that fuel conflict, it is hard to be sanguine about the prospects for real change. Rhetorical advocacy for peace and human rights is often a smokescreen to cover the transnational corporate "national" interests of weapons producers. The following measures must be pursued as part of an aggressive world response to the calamity of the global small arms market system and its contributions to the Sudan civil war:

1. The UN Security Council must aggressively pursue all of its new measures against Sudan's criminal war against its own people, and apply this same standard to all conflicts.
2. The United Nations, regional interstate security unions, and individual weapon-producing nations must be aggressively and resolutely pushed to reform policy in order to reduce and govern weapons manufacture and export. The economic benefits of the global small arms market enrich a few while impoverishing the interrelated economies and lives of most of the world. Targeted financial sanctions against non-compliant producers might enable this reform, if the Security Council permanent members can find the political and moral will to curtail their own weapons industries. Real change will take determination, and will not be a short-term project.
3. All weapons should be given international registry marks, so that manufacturers and countries of origin can be determined.
4. A fund should be created to pay for the purchase and destruction of small arms, initially in areas of conflict

and then globally, in order to reduce the massive world stockpile of such weapons.

5. The neo-liberal system of economic globalization itself must be progressively reformed. It is time for the world to again implement regulatory governance of trade, finance, labour, environment, and community, on state and transnational bases.

This essay allows space only for an introductory analysis of the global small arms system of manufacture, export, trafficking, and use in violent conflict; and economic bases and effects of this system. Small arms, and the broader concern of all weapons production for sale, are a major piece of the conflict and peace puzzle. Weapons manufacture and traffic, and particularly that of small arms, is a beast that will require taming if the world's wildfires of violence are to be contained.

THE INTERNATIONAL ARMS TRADE: DIFFICULT TO DEFINE, MEASURE, AND CONTROL

The international arms trade apparently has weathered the financial crisis quite well. Available data indicate that the impact to date on the volume of orders and deliveries has been limited.

As has been shown in the past, financial resources—from domestic budgets or foreign military assistance—are not the only factor that influences arms acquisitions. Perceived internal or external threats to national security, the need to replace or upgrade military inventories, demonstrations of international status, development of domestic arms industries via licensed production and offsets, the desire to strengthen ties with suppliers, and the influence of the military play important roles in the arms acquisition process. Before permitting exports of arms and military equipment, suppliers will assess the potential economic gains and the potential impact of the transfer on their strategic interests and foreign policy. Will the transfer harm or help friendly states or the supplier's international commitments, reputation, or standing?

For several reasons, there is no straightforward answer to the question, "How big is the international arms trade?" First, there is no globally agreed definition of "arms." States and international organizations that seek to measure or control the arms trade use lists of items that vary in their complexity and coverage, most notably with regard to their inclusion of "dual-use goods," items with both military and civilian applications. Second, there is no common agreement on what types of activities constitute the arms trade. Examples of areas where differences exist include arms leased to other states; gifts and donations; the transfer of technology to produce arms and military equipment; and upgrades, parts, and services related to the transfer of arms and military equipment. Third, the lack of openness and transparency by many arms suppliers and recipients regarding the value and volume of their arms exports and imports makes it difficult to collect accurate data. As a result, a variety of different definitions of the international arms trade and estimates of its scale exists. This has implications for efforts to establish controls on arms transfers via a future international arms trade treaty (ATT). This article will outline some of the challenges in defining, measuring, and controlling the international arms trade.

Definitions and Estimates

The national lists of arms and military equipment to be subject to export controls (control lists) maintained by most states and all major arms exporters provide a useful starting point for defining "arms" and the international arms trade. The Munitions List and Lists of Dual-Use Goods and Technologies of the Wassenaar Arrangement on Export Controls for Conventional Arms and Dual-Use Goods and Technologies provide the basis for the control lists of the 40 states that are members of the group. The Munitions List covers a wide range of arms and military equipment, from small arms to ships, as well as ammunition, information and communication technologies, training equipment, and equipment for producing arms. Several significant arms-exporting nonmembers, including China, have fully or partially aligned their national control lists with the Munitions List. As a result, all of the top 10 arms suppliers during 2005-2009 have control lists derived from the Wassenaar Arrangement.

National control lists serve as the basis for national reports on arms exports. As of January 2010, 32 states had published at least one national report on arms exports since 1990, and a further nine states provided information on the value of their export licenses and exports to the 2009 European Union (EU) Annual Report on Arms Exports. These reports vary in detail but, at a minimum, tend to provide data on the financial value of arms export licenses or arms exports. Several major exporters (e.g., Russia) do not produce such reports, but do release official data on the financial value of their arms exports. Using national reports and official statements, the Stockholm International Peace Research Institute (SIPRI) has attempted to provide estimates of the financial value of the international arms trade.

The now-defunct U.S. Arms Control and Disarmament Agency (ACDA) created the following comprehensive definition of the arms trade, which has been widely used by researchers: weapons of war, parts thereof, ammunition, support equipment, and other commodities designed for military use.... Dual-use equipment...when its primary mission is identified as military. The building of defence production facilities and licensing fees paid as royalties for the production of military equipment.... Military services such as training, supply operations, equipment repair, technical assistance and construction are included where data are available.

A similar definition of the arms trade is used to compile the U.S. Congressional Research Service's (CRS) annual report, "Conventional Arms Transfers to Developing Nations." In spite of the name, the report contains estimates for the value of the global arms trade, not just trade with developing countries. The CRS estimated the financial value of deliveries of arms to be $34.5 billion for 2007. Despite using a narrower definition of arms transfers than the CRS, SIPRI's accounting of official financial data contained in national reports and official statements for 2007 generated a figure of $51.1 billion for arms exports, representing 0.3 percent of world trade. This figure is likely to be lower than the true figure because a number of significant exporters, including China, do not release data on the financial value of their arms exports. The difference between the SIPRI and CRS estimates is a further demonstration of the difficulty of estimating the financial value of the international arms trade.

The SIPRI arms transfers database provides information on international arms transfers from 1950 to the most recent calendar year. Its coverage is narrower than that of the ACDA, CRS, and national control lists; for example, it does not include transfers of most small arms and light weapons (SALW). However, it provides information on the number of units transferred and employs a unique pricing system to measure the volume of arms transfers. The SIPRI trend indicator value allows researchers to track developments in transfers to and from different suppliers, recipients, and regions. SIPRI data form the basis for the discussion below.

Arms Trade Trends

The volume of international arms transfers in the post-World War II period peaked in 1982. Following the end of the Cold War, there was a steady decline in global arms transfers. They reached their lowest point in 2002, when transfers amounted to only 38 percent of their Cold War high. This decline has reversed, and the volume of international transfers of major conventional weapons during 2005-2009 was 22 percent higher than during 2000-2004.

One of the most marked aspects of the international arms trade has been its dominance by five suppliers. During 1980-1984, when global arms transfers were at the highest level, the Soviet Union (37 percent), the United States (29 percent), France (8 percent), the United Kingdom (5 percent), and the Federal Republic of Germany (5 percent) accounted for 84 percent of all exports. The five largest suppliers of major conventional weapons during 2005-2009 were the United States (30 percent), Russia (23 percent), Germany (11 percent), France (8 percent), and the United Kingdom (4 percent), collectively accounting for 76 percent of exports.

The governments of these major suppliers are actively engaged in assisting the export efforts of their domestic arms industries in the competitive international arms market. Some governments also provide military equipment to allies at beneficial rates as a key plank of their foreign and defence policies, something that often has clear benefits for commercial arms manufacturers based in these states.

Since 2001, the United States has increased foreign military aid for allies in regions of tension or conflict. President Barack Obama has maintained the Bush administration's pledge to increase foreign military financing aid for Israel, which is set to reach $3 billion in 2012. Egypt and the members of the Gulf Cooperation Council have been the recipients of increased assistance as well.

Russia has announced its willingness to develop and produce arms jointly with other countries to help strengthen ties, accept payments through barter, participate in joint economic projects, and offer credit and exchanges of debt for arms. In 2009, Russia extended a $2 billion line of credit to Venezuela for arms purchases. In addition, it agreed to cancel Vietnam's debt to Russia and help modernize its shipbuilding industry in exchange for Vietnam's commitment to purchase 20 Su-30MK combat aircraft and six Type-636 Kilo-class submarines and further expand the involvement of Russian companies in the exploration and extraction of Vietnamese oil.

In 2007 the French government simplified and modernized France's arms export licensing system and began taking a more active role in promoting exports abroad. It has demonstrated a willingness to engage in far-reaching technology transfer agreements in order to win contracts. In September 2009 French President Nicolas Sarkozy visited Brazil to conclude an almost $10 billion deal to supply four conventionally powered submarines and technology to assist in the development of Brazil's first nuclear-powered submarine.

Attempts by countries beyond the traditional major producers to develop their own arms industries and increase their share of global arms exports have typically had limited success, largely because of high technological barriers or an inadequate civilian industrial base. Yet, many countries still seek to increase their levels of autonomous capability in arms production, with some developing state-of-the-art products for particular niche items. For example, Israel is widely recognized as a leading producer and supplier of unmanned aerial vehicles (UAVs), supplying systems and licenses for production for more than 100 UAVs to 18 states, including all of the top five suppliers, during 2005-2009.

In addition, licensed production agreements have led to an increase in the number of states that are capable of manufacturing less-advanced weapons systems, particularly small arms and light weapons. Although licensed production agreements often include controls on who can receive the weapons produced, this is not always the case, or the agreements are not enforced. Soviet Avtomat Kalashnikov (AK) and German Heckler and Koch G3 assault rifles serve as classic examples of cases in which licensed production has led to exports being made without the express permission of those issuing the original license. Russia perceives the production of Kalashnikov rifles in a number of former Warsaw Pact countries to be unlicensed and illegal, claiming that arrangements concluded during the Soviet era have expired. The decision to give designs and information on product technology to Warsaw Pact states and clients during the Soviet era therefore remains a source of concern. Nonetheless, Russia continues to issue licensed production agreements for Kalashnikov rifles, revealing recently that 10 states had applied to build factories. The possibility remains that today's license holders could produce or export Kalashnikovs without the express permission of Russia in the future.

In contrast to the largest suppliers, the largest recipients of major conventional weapons have varied considerably over the years. During 1980-1984, the five largest recipients of military equipment—Iraq (7 percent), India (6 percent), Libya (5 percent), Syria (5 percent), and Egypt (4 percent)—accounted for 27 percent of total imports. The five largest recipients of major conventional weapons during 2005-2009 were China (9 percent), India (7 percent), South Korea (6 percent), the United Arab Emirates (6 percent), and Greece (4 percent), accounting for 32 percent of total imports. After the end of the Cold War, China imported a large volume of aircraft, ships, submarines, air defence systems, and missiles from Russia, but Chinese arms imports from Russia have declined dramatically in recent years. One explanation for this drop is that China appears to have overcome many of the problems that have dogged its arms industry and is now able to manufacture advanced weapons systems domestically. There are persistent allegations that many of China's "indigenous" weapons systems are actually copies of other countries' designs. It continues to rely on imports of components and subsystems for a number of its weapons systems, but is regarded as an example of a country in which arrangements for licensed production and technology transfers as part of arms import deals have helped with the development of an indigenous arms industry. India has sought to develop its own arms industry and decrease its reliance on arms imports but with limited success to date. It is expected to replace China as the largest arms importer in the coming years.

Recent acquisitions by states in Latin America, the Middle East, North Africa, and Southeast Asia indicate the possible emergence of reactive arms acquisition patterns that could develop into regional arms races. The volume of deliveries to Southeast Asia nearly doubled during 2005-2009 compared to 2000-2004. Deliveries were 722 percent higher to Malaysia, 146 percent higher to Singapore, and 84 percent higher to Indonesia. In 2009, Malaysia received six Su-30MKM combat aircraft with advanced missiles from Russia, two Scorpène submarines from France and Spain, two MEKO-100 frigates from Germany, and 21 PT-91 tanks from Poland. Singapore received eight F-15E combat aircraft with advanced air-to-air and air-to-ground missiles from the United States, two La Fayette frigates from France, and 40 Leopard-2A4 tanks from Germany.

There is limited empirical evidence to suggest a direct causal link between an increase in the volume of arms imported and the outbreak of conflict or an increase in the intensity of conflict. It has been suggested, however, that states that acquire significant quantities of military equipment may be more prone to use armed force to resolve disputes. For example, the recent conflicts in Sri Lanka and Georgia, both of which are relatively minor arms importers, were preceded by significant increases in transfers. In both cases, governments sought to restore what they perceived to be their state's territorial integrity against forces that were seeking independence and had established high levels of autonomy to some degree within clearly defined regions.

As the graph on this page demonstrates, the volume of Georgian imports of major conventional weapons in the years preceding the August 2008 conflict in South Ossetia increased significantly, with the largest volume of arms imports for Georgia, excluding acquisitions by forces in Abkhazia and South Ossetia, taking place in 2007. Significant increases in arms imports and military spending were perceived by some as indicating that the Georgian government was preparing to use force to restore Georgia's territorial integrity.

TRADE CONTROL EFFORTS

At present, UN Security Council arms embargoes are the only global, legally binding prohibitions on arms transfers. Since 1990, the United Nations has imposed 28 arms embargoes against targets in 17 countries and one nonstate entity (Osama bin Laden and al Qaeda). The most recent new arms embargo was introduced against Eritrea on December 23, 2009. Recent UN arms embargo resolutions recognize that nonstate actors play an important role in the contemporary arms trade and in the facilitation of arms transfers to "undesirable" end-users. States retain primary responsibility for enforcing arms embargoes and controlling the activities of arms brokers and dealers operating from their national territory or registered with their national authorities.

Sanctions committees and panels of experts charged with monitoring arms embargoes have documented the role different states have played in violating arms embargoes, such as in the case of Eritrea's involvement in transfers to Somalia. Also, states have been accused of giving shelter to individuals and entities accused of violating embargoes and of failing to investigate alleged violations but in such instances have not been sanctioned themselves. Stronger transfer control policies and increased political will are of central importance for preventing violations of UN arms embargoes.

States have long been reluctant to give up any element of national control in the field of arms transfer controls. Yet, the Iraqi invasion of Kuwait in 1990 and the scandals involving Western states and companies in the arming of Iraq prompted the development of the guidelines for conventional arms transfers, under which the permanent members of the UN Security Council agreed to exercise restraint in exports of conventional arms transfers. Suppliers were required to ensure that exports met only the "legitimate self-defence" needs of the recipient and did not contribute to conflict or regional instability or introduce "destabilizing military capabilities in a region." There is no international agreement on what constitutes legitimate self-defence or "destabilizing military capabilities."

Efforts to improve controls on international arms transfers have primarily been driven and directed by suppliers in North America and Europe. Motivations have included protecting national industries by preventing the spread of technologies and limiting potential adversaries' access to key technologies. The prevention of conflict and human rights abuses also has long been at the heart of efforts to control the arms trade. States, export control regimes such as the Wassenaar Arrangement, and regional organizations (e.g., the Economic Community of West African States, the EU, the Organization for Security and Cooperation in Europe, and the Organization of American States) have developed various sets of best-practice guidelines and model legislation to help ensure that arms exports do not provoke or exacerbate conflict and are not used to commit violations of human rights and humanitarian law. In addition, efforts have been undertaken to prevent the diversion of arms to terrorists, criminals, and armed groups.

Experience with existing regional mechanisms and export control regimes demonstrates some of the problems that an ATT is likely to face when it comes to ensuring harmonized interpretations of the criteria it puts in place. Despite developing agreed export criteria and mechanisms of consultation and information exchange, members of the Wassenaar Arrangement have demonstrated contrasting attitudes toward exports of arms and military equipment to a range of destinations. Although the EU and the United States have arms embargoes against Iran, Myanmar (Burma), Sudan, and Zimbabwe, Russia continues to supply weapons systems to these states. Meanwhile, Russia has repeatedly called for restraint on arms transfers to Georgia, but Wassenaar Arrangement members the Czech Republic, Turkey, and Ukraine have continued to supply arms to Georgia. It appears that bilateral pressure on nonmembers Bosnia and Herzegovina, Israel, and Serbia led to some deals to Georgia being canceled.

Even within the EU, where states have agreed that their export license decision-making should be guided by eight criteria relating to issues such as conflict prevention, human rights, and economic development, there appear to have been differences of opinion among members regarding exports to Georgia. EU member states reported issuing licenses worth more than $180 million between 2004 and 2007 for exports of arms and military equipment to Georgia and making exports worth almost $96 million during that period. Also during this period, EU member states denied 41 export licenses for arms and military equipment for Georgia because of concerns about the potential impact of the transfer on the possibility of conflict within Georgia. In several cases, EU member states denied an export license for the export of a particular type of military equipment that other EU member states had exported.

Researchers have found evidence of a correlation between the introduction of the politically binding EU Code of Conduct on Arms Exports in 1998 and a decline in arms exports from EU member states to countries in conflict or considered violators of international human rights and humanitarian law, but differences in decision-making on "responsible" recipients continue within the EU. In this regard, the impact of the EU arms exports code and the legally binding Council Common Position 2008/944/CFSP, defining common rules governing the control of exports of military technology and equipment, which replaced the EU arms exports code, continues to illustrate the challenges of reaching agreement on how to interpret and implement a set of agreed common standards among (supposedly) like-minded states. Disagreements in the Wassenaar Arrangement show the difficulties in achieving similar objectives when the group is composed of states that hold very different opinions on what constitutes a responsible end-user.

RELEVANT PROVISIONS APPLICABLE TO NON-INTERNATIONAL ARMED CONFLICTS

Due to the frequency of these internal armed conflicts, the international community was forced to realise that some form of regulation of non-international conflicts was needed. The effort to extend IHL to non-international armed conflicts ultimately resulted in the bold and ambiguous Common Article 3. IHL applicable in non-international armed conflict is the result of a compromise between the concept of sovereignty and humanitarian concerns. Internal conflicts involve a high intensity of violence and cannot remain beyond the reach of international law providing protection to both civilians and combatants. Non-international armed conflicts are covered by Common Article 3, Protocol II (156 State Parties to date), several other treaties, as well as by customary law. Customary law acts both as a complement and a confirmation of the basic standards set by both Protocol II and Common Article 3. As already noted, many provisions applicable in international armed conflicts have also become applicable in non-international armed conflicts as customary international law. Under the following analysis you should have in mind that the part of IHL governing non-international armed conflict is the result of a compromise between the concept of sovereignty and humanitarian concerns.

COMMON ARTICLE 3

When Common article 3 was first adopted, it was considered a major step in the right direction in the development of the IHL. Indeed, it is the result of the first attempt ever to impose some basic humanitarian legal restraints upon both parties to an internal conflict carried out within the territory of a State Party to the Conventions. As is well known, States do not welcome any interference in their domestic security matters. So to agree upon imposing limitations in dealing with internal violence directed against? is still considered a great achievement. This "mini convention" is viewed as a part of *jus cogens*.

The article states that: In the case of armed conflict not of an international character occurring in the territory of one of the High Contracting Parties, each party to the conflict shall be bound to apply, as a minimum, the following provisions:

1. Persons taking no active part in the hostilities, including members of armed forces who have laid down their arms and those placed *hors de combat* by sickness, wounds, detention, or any other cause, shall in all circumstances be treated humanely, without any adverse distinction founded on race, colour, religion or faith, sex, birth or wealth, or any other similar criteria.

   To this end the following acts are and shall remain prohibited at any time and in any place whatsoever with respect to the above-mentioned persons:

   a) violence to life and person, in particular murder of all kinds, mutilation, cruel treatment and torture;

b) taking of hostages;
c) outrages upon personal dignity, in particular, humiliating and degrading treatment;
d) the passing of sentences and the carrying out of executions without previous judgment pronounced by a regularly constituted court affording all the judicial guarantees which are recognized as indispensable by civilized peoples.

2. The wounded and sick shall be collected and cared for. An impartial humanitarian body, such as the International Committee of the Red Cross, may offer its services to the Parties to the conflict. The Parties to the conflict should further endeavour to bring into force, by means of special agreements, all or part of the other provisions of the present Convention.

The application of the preceding provisions shall not affect the legal status of the Parties to the conflict. Despite the undisputed significance of Common Article 3, as an improvement of the traditional international law approach to internal conflicts, it barely employs the most basic principles preserved in the Conventions onto non-international conflicts. It is true that the parties to the armed conflict are encouraged to apply all the provisions of the Conventions, but it fails to provide the full application of the entire body of IHL on its own. When governments have been reluctant to recognize the lower threshold in Common Article 3, namely that there is an internal conflict taking place within their territory, it seems rather unlikely that they would consider applying any additional provisions from the Conventions. To be clear, the application of Common Article 3 starts automatically when the objective criteria listed in this article are met.

Nevertheless, the governments refusal to acknowledge this rule may contaminate the attitude of the armed group involved in the conflict, especially that they neither participated in the process that produced this rule, nor were allowed to become a party to the treaty. The reciprocity between the government and the ANSA remains important, though it is not a direct requirement for its application. Of course they may be other reasons why an armed group might refuse to comply with the law. Armed groups that do not have an aspiration to achieve international recognition and legitimacy, lack the intention to comply with international norms. They are merely interested in controlling economical/natural resources or running criminal activities. On the other hand, a governments reluctance to admit that an internal conflict existed within its territory had totally different reasons. It was grounded in its concern that such recognition would give legitimacy to the armed groups cause and at the same time reveal the weak points of the State. It should be pointed out in this context that Common article 3 does not confer by any means recognition to the ANSA involved in the conflict, nor does it change their status in international law. It certainly does not provide any legitimization to their cause.

By this provision, it is no longer required that the members of ANSA exercise control over any amount of territory or that they have the characteristic of a government. The threshold for the application of Common Article 3 is lower than that for recognised belligerency; such recognition would bring the whole corpus of IHL, not just the minimum rules of common Article 3, into application. As already mentioned, there are a lot of violent activities left outside the scope of this provision. Under this provisions rather low threshold lies a range of conflicts, from passing sporadic challenges to State authority to insurgency, which could, conceivably, come within the scope of Common Article 3.

The greatest weakness in Common Article 3 is the absence of a clear definition of what is to be considered a non-international conflict. This ambiguity of its threshold makes it uncertain if and when violent actions in a State can be regarded as a non-international armed conflict and thereby trigger its application. Common Article 3 also lacks of the expression of the necessity or even better the formation of a competent authority who can decide if a certain conflict constitutes an ' Article 3 conflict'. As if all these deficiencies are not enough, Common Article 3 fails to take into account the special type of warfare involved in most internal conflicts, i.e. guerrilla warfare. Yet the article fails to take it into account. The Diplomatic Conference of 1949 failed to define the scope of the conflict which is covered by Common Article 3. A lot of difficulties and disputes had to be resolved by the committee of the non-international conflict at the Diplomatic Conference when the drafting of the provision of non-international conflicts came up for discussion. Judging from the conclusion of the article, they obviously had a hard time reaching a consensus. So the limitations and defects of this articles final composition must be regarded with this in mind. Indeed, Common article 3 has been the object of more attention and dispute than any other provision in the Conventions. In the end its conclusion can be regarded as an achievement despite the defects it holds.

ADDITIONAL PROTOCOL II

Protocol II, like Common Article 3, was considered innovative as it was the first separate treaty to establish standards for the protection of persons involved in internal armed conflicts. It provided basic rules on methods of warfare applicable by both States and ANSAs involved in non-international armed conflicts. Protocol II was meant to define and supplement Common Article 3. But the strong resistance it received from developing States that, although they supported a distinctive treatment for ANSAs fighting against colonial and racist regimes, strived to secure their fragile existence by decreasing the regulations in non-international armed conflicts that occurs within their territory and threaten their authority, led to the failure of this intention. The States severely limited Protocol II and introduced a high threshold for its applicability, since the status of ANSAs combating colonial and racist regimes was established, and they had no interest in adopting a comprehensive framework in Protocol II. It should be stressed at this point that a compliance with the provisions of Protocol II does not imply recognition of any particular status for armed opposition groups.

Protocol II turned out to be limited to ensuring the application of the basic rules of IHL to internal conflicts. Thereby, it does not limit the rights of the States or the means available to them to maintain or restore law and order. It cannot even be used to justify humanitarian intervention. A government faced with an insurrection can in no circumstances use the argument that the insurgents have illegally taken up arms to justify refusing to apply Protocol II, since the instrument was adopted precisely to govern situations of that nature. With respect to the obligations it creates, Protocol II therefore rules out any subordination of *jus in bello* to jus ad bellum. Nevertheless, Protocol II has had a significant influence on State Practice and the following formation of customary law applicable in non-international armed conflicts. As a result, many of its provisions are now considered to be part of customary international law. States practice has also created a significant number of customary rules that are more detailed than the elementary provisions in Protocol II. Customary law has a very important complementary role as it fixes the deficiencies and fills the gaps in both Protocol II and Common Article 3.

Both Article 3 and Protocol II can apply simultaneously to a conflict, providing for the minimum amount of protection. However, protocol II provides a much greater substantive protection, introducing new fundamental rules concerning the protection of civilians against the effects of hostilities, as well as the protection of medical personnel and transports.

Article 1

Article 1 of Protocol II comprises the foundation of the protocol as it lays down the scope of its application. In order to remedy the shortage of Common Article 3, mentioned earlier, and to improve the protection of victims of non-international conflicts it was necessary to develop rules and define objective criteria to determine the applicability of Protocol II. The uncertainty regarding definitions often led to the rejection of the applicability of Common Article 3. At the same time a strict and rigid definition would have also led to the same result. Article 1 is the result of many extensive and protracted negotiations. The outcome of the entire protocol hinged on this single provision.

The article states:

1) This Protocol, which develops and supplements Article 3 common to the Geneva Conventions of 12 August 1949 without modifying its existing conditions of application, shall apply to all armed conflicts which are not covered by Article 1 of the Protocol Additional to the Geneva Conventions of 12 August 1949, and relating to the Protection of Victims of International Armed Conflicts

(Protocol I) and which take place in the territory of a High Contracting Party between its armed forces and dissident armed forces or other organized armed groups which, under responsible command, exercise such control over a part of its territory as to enable them to carry out sustained and concerted military operations and to implement this Protocol.

2) This Protocol shall not apply to situations of internal disturbances and tensions, such as riots, isolated and sporadic acts of violence and other acts of a similar nature, as not being armed conflicts.

While Common Article 3 does not provide a definition of "non-international armed conflict", Article 1 of Protocol II, clarifies that the Protocol applies to armed conflicts which take place (1) in the territory of a State Party to the protocol, (2) between its armed forces and ANSAs which (a) are organized under a responsible command, (b) exercise control over part of its territory, (c) are able to carry out continuous and intensive military operations and to implement the Protocol.

The condition of having a responsible authority and an organization does not imply that a hierarchical system of guerilla organization similar to that of regular armed forces is required. It simply points out the obligation of having an organization that exercise control over a certain amount of territory and capable of planning and carrying out continuous and concerted military operations. In addition to that, it should have a *de facto* authority imposing discipline on its members and capable of implementing this protocol. The amount of territory which should be occupied is not stated and in fact is not relevant: the occupation of the territory only has to be such as to allow sustained and concerted military operations and to apply the protocol. Therefore, internal conflicts resulting in a temporary occupation of a small territory without total control over another national territory do not fall under Protocol II. On the other hand being under command and in control of a large amount of the territory is a crucial requirement to be able to implement the protocol, for instance to set up of hospitals and prison camps. So this rather high threshold is fairly realistic since the conditions provided in this article correspond with actual circumstances in which the parties may reasonably be expected to apply the rules developed in Protocol II. In practical terms, if the ANSA is organized in accordance with the requirements of the Protocol, the extent of territory it can claim to control will be that which escapes the control of the governments armed forces. However, there must be some degree of stability in the control of even a modest area of land for it to be capable of effectively applying the rules of the Protocol. This condition of territory control in the mother State is rarely achieved as most ANSAs have their base outside of the mother State. Obviously, these criteria restrict the scope of application of the Protocol to conflicts of a high intensity only. Therefore, only very few non-international conflicts are covered by Protocol II, unlike Common Article 3.

Once this threshold is passed, the Protocol applies to the conflict in question. The application of Protocol II is automatic, i.e. no declaration has to be made by the parties to the conflict as long as the requirements of Article 1 are met. Therefore, the question of the applicability of Protocol II can be answered differently in each case, according to the prevailing circumstances. Despite the efforts made to clarify the problem of the threshold of Protocol II, much ambiguity still surrounds its application. Protocol II does not clearly state how much territory must be under the control of the non-government party to the conflict. Even the implementation of this Protocol by the ANSA remains unclear. A lot is left up to the discretion of the State, which is not a very satisfactory position. If States are allowed to characterise a situation and in accordance with that dictates of their individual disposition, then the broader base of humanitarian concerns may be sacrificed in the process.

The second paragraph of Article 1 reveals the exclusion of situations of internal disturbances and tensions, such as riots, isolated and sporadic acts of violence and other acts of a similar nature, from the scope of Protocol II. As already mentioned, these forms of hostilities are not considered as armed conflicts, not even in the framework of Common Article 3. A State may use armed force to maintain order caused by or even causing internal tensions or when force is used as a preventative measure to maintain respect for law and order without getting to be considered internal disturbances. However, situations of this kind are covered by regional and universal human rights according to the Article. Nevertheless, practice has laid down certain criteria to draw up the boundaries of non-international armed conflicts from internal disturbances. Firstly, the hostilities have to be carried out by force of arms and reveal such intensity that the government is compelled to utilize its armed forces against ANSA. Secondly, the hostilities are meant to be carried out by the entire ANSA, and not by a single group within. Additionally, the ANSA has to exhibit a minimum amount of organization. Its armed forces should be under a responsible command and thereby be capable of meeting humanitarian requirements. The conflict must demonstrate certain similarities to an armed conflict without fulfilling all conditions necessary for the recognition of belligerency.

While in conflicts that come within the scope of Common Article 3, the ANSA and the State party involved are also encouraged to apply all the other provisions of the Conventions relating to international armed conflicts, thus offering a much broader base of protection to those involved in wars of national liberation, including a limit on the means and methods of warfare and on the conduct of hostilities. Protocol II only applies to situations of conflicts between ANSA and the established government and not between two or more ANSAs, resulting in a scope of application that is much narrower than that of Common Article 3.

COMBATANT AND POW STATUS

The status of combatants in internal conflicts differs dramatically from the status of combatants in international conflicts. However, the restrictive combatant status offered in Common Article 3 can be accorded to both recognized and unrecognized ANSAs. But Article 4 of the POW Convention, which automatically applies in international conflicts, does not apply to a non-international conflict unless the parties to such conflict choose to apply it, either by an expressed agreement or by concession. For instance, US Military command applied this article to the captured enemy in Vietnam.

The combatant status offered in Common Article 3 and Protocol II fail in providing any protection from prosecution to captured combatants. This is rather peculiar considering that both instruments establish a separation, if only to a limited extent, between *jus ad bellum* and *jus in bello*. The constraints on States provided by Common article 3 or Protocol II, such as the obligation to treat members of ANSAs in a humane manner, have been proven difficult to achieve. Indeed these instruments fail to achieve any constraints on the penalties these combatants are forced to endure for participating in the hostilities. This failure is extremely alarming bearing in mind the absence of specific rules and definitions with respect to the principles of distinction and proportionality that makes the distinction between combatants and civilians very minimal in Protocol II.

Article 44 (3, 4, and 5) of Protocol II states:

3. In order to protect the civilian population from hostilities, civilians are not to be harmed if they are not taking part in attacks or war activities or preparing attacks. Because in certain armed situations it is not possible to differentiate between the combatants and the civilians, people are to be granted combatants status if they: a) are openly carrying a weapon during a military manoeuvre; b) are openly carrying a weapon in view of the enemy while on a military march prior to an attack which they are supposed to take part in.
4. A combatant who falls into enemy hands and who is not covered by the provisions of Section 3/2 is to be considered a Prisoner of War; he is entitled to all rights guaranteed by the Third Convention and this Protocol.
5. A combatant who falls into enemy hands, not while taking part in an attack or preparing for an attack, is not considered a combatant or a Prisoner of War because of his prior activity.

To be regarded as combatants, members of ANSAs have to fulfil certain conditions. They have to be carrying arms openly either during the attack or in the preparation preceding the attack that they are participating in. If the combatants are caught participating in a military operation or preparing such but not abiding by the distinction rules they are still granted a POW status. Even civilians participating in these conflicts are granted both combatant and POW status under the same conditions. However unlike Protocol I, Protocol II does not grant either combatant or POW status on members of any armed group, for their mere membership. In addition to that domestic law still remains in force in situations where Protocol II is applicable. Obviously the protection offered by Protocol I regarding combatants and POW, is to be much preferred. However, Article 6, concerning penal prosecutions, lays down the judicial guarantees provided for in Common Article 3; independence of the courts, rights of defence, individual responsibility, non-retroactivity of penalties, presumption of innocence, information on judicial remedies. The fifth paragraph of this article contains a provision that even urge the established government to grant amnesty to the participants. There are also various resolutions granting POW status to members of ANSAs when captured, especially those fighting for a certain political objective, such as freedom. Most recently the US Supreme Court has declared the applicability of Common Article 3 with regard to trying individuals captured in Afghanistan during the conflict there between US and Al Qaeda. The Supreme Court declared that Common Article 3 applies even to that conflict. In the meanwhile, since neither common Article 3 nor Protocol II contains any provision on criminal responsibility for any violations of IHL in an internal armed conflict, the International Criminal Tribunal for the former Yugoslavia (ICTY) concluded in an important decision that horrific crimes committed in a non-international armed conflict are to be considered as international crimes. As a result, rules concerning international armed conflicts apply when trying a person prosecuted for a crime committed in a non-international armed conflict.

Both Common Article 3 and Protocol II apply simultaneously and automatically to internal conflicts when certain threshold criteria are reached. However, the ambiguity surrounding the application and scope of Common Article 3, caused by its lack of definition of what constitutes an internal conflict, made it difficult to distinguish between a non-international armed conflict and internal disturbances or other sporadic acts of violence. This has expectedly helped States escape their international obligation in applying these instruments by denying that such a conflict is taking place in their territory. Protocol II, however, describes its scope in considerable detail, excluding low-intensity conflicts. Article 1 makes the application of Protocol II dependent on the exercise of *de facto* control of part of the national territory and on the ability of on material circumstances linked to the nature of the hostilities, i.e. the ability to carry out organized and sustained acts of violence and to implement the Protocol. It applies to all armed conflicts in which these conditions are met, regardless of who triggered the conflict and why. Protocol II rules out any subordination of *jus in bello* to *jus ad bellum*. Protocol II, reaffirms the separation between *jus ad bellum* and *jus in bello* established by Common Article only as far as the obligations it creates are concerned and only to a limited extent as it fails to provide any protection from arbitrary persecution to the participants in these conflicts. It is fair to say that the protection offered by both Protocol II and Common Article 3, to captured members of unrecognized NSAs is very modest and in many cases non-existence.

5

Recent Trends in International Arms Transfers

ARMS EXPORTERS

One of the most marked aspects of major arms transfers over time is the stable composition of the list of the five biggest suppliers, with only slight changes in the ordering. For the period 1980–1984, when global arms transfers were at the highest, the Soviet Union, the United States, France, the United Kingdom and Germany accounted for 84 per cent of all exports. The five largest suppliers of major conventional weapons for the period 2004– 2008 were the USA, Russia, Germany, France and the UK. These suppliers accounted for 78 per cent of world exports for this period, compared with 81 per cent for the period 1999–2003. The USA and Russia remain by far the largest exporters. More than a third (37 per cent) of US deliveries of major convention weapons for the period 2004–2008 went to the Middle East, including around 207 combat aircraft and over 5000 guided bombs. Several major new deals were under discussion in 2008, including the sale of Patriot Advanced Capability-3 (PAC-3) and Terminal High Altitude Area Defence (THAAD) antiballistic missile (ABM) surface-to-air missile systems to the United Arab Emirates (UAE).

Russia's arms exports were 14 per cent higher in 2004–2008 than in 1999– 2003, although its overall share of the global market remained roughly the same. Around 71 per cent of Russian arms were exported to the Asia–Pacific region for 2004–2008, with deliveries of advanced combat aircraft and naval vessels to China and India accounting for a considerable share. At the same time, deliveries to Africa and Latin America have increased by around 200 per cent and 900 per cent, respectively. The majority of these transfers went to Algeria and Venezuela.

The volume of Germany's arms exports increased by 70 per cent between 1999–2003 and 2004–2008, and its share of the global market rose from 7 per cent to 10 per cent. Much of this increase was due to exports to European destinations, which grew by 123 per cent. Greece and Turkey accounted for nearly a third of German exports. In recent years, both countries have received Leopard-2A4 tanks and licensed produced Type-214 submarines. For the period 2004–2008, 40 per cent of France's arms exports went to states in the Middle East. For the second year in a row, there were no outstanding orders for newly built French combat aircraft. However, France was reported to be in advance negotiations for deals with Libya and the UAE. The UK's largest customers in recent years have been the USA and India, which accounted for 21 per cent and 14 per cent, respectively, of British transfers for the period 2004–2008. India is in the process of receiving 66 Hawk-100 trainer aircraft and 20 Jaguar-S combat aircraft from the UK. In 2009 the UK began the delivery of 72 Typhoon combat aircraft to Saudi Arabia, which will help to cement its position among the top five suppliers.

While countries in other parts of the world may lack modern defence industries, they can still provide surplus or second-hand equipment, or newly produced but less technologically advanced weapon systems such as SALW and their related ammunition.

Arms importers

In contrast to the largest suppliers, the group of the largest recipients of major conventional weapons has varied more over the years. In addition, relative to the largest suppliers, the largest recipients account for a smaller share of the total market due to the large number of minor recipients. For the period 1980–1984 the five largest recipients of military equipment—Iraq, India, Libya, Syria and Egypt—accounted for 26 per cent of total imports. For the period 2004–2008 the top 5—China,

India, the UAE, South Korea and Greece—accounted for 35 per cent of all imports. This change illustrates a shift in the major arms import markets over the past 30 years from the Middle East to Asia. However, recent data indicates that this process may be reversing, with the Middle East again emerging as a major destination for military equipment. Nonetheless, in recent years the composition of the list of largest recipients has remained relatively stable. China and India were the world's two largest arms importers for both 1999–2003 and 2004–2008. The most significant change in the composition of the five largest arms importers in recent years has been the entry of the UAE, which rose from being the 16th largest importer in the period 1999–2003 to being the third largest for the period 2004–2008.

Africa

African states accounted for 7 per cent of international imports of major conventional weapons over the period 2004–2008, compared with 6 per cent for 1999–2003. During the period 2004–2008, Algeria and South Africa were the two largest arms importers in Africa, accounting for 35 per cent and 27 per cent, respectively, of the continent's imports. The third largest recipient of major conventional weapons was Sudan, which accounted for 8 per cent of Africa's imports. Excluding South Africa, arms transfers to countries in sub-Saharan Africa accounted for only 2 per cent of the world total for the period 2004–2008. However, even small volumes of transfers of major conventional weapons can have a significant impact on conflict dynamics in the region. Deliveries to Algeria in 2008 included the last of 180 T-90 tanks and an estimated 18 of a total of 28 Su-30MK combat aircraft, both purchased from Russia. Two Project 636 Kilo Class submarines and a significant number of air defence systems are also on order from Russia. Morocco, Algeria's neighbour and long-term rival, embarked on a significant military modernization programme in 2008, ordering 24 F-16C combat aircraft from the USA, large FREMM frigate from France and 3 smaller SIGMA-90 frigates from the Netherlands.

Chad's arms imports were five times higher over the period 2004–2008 than in 1999–2003, although globally it remains a minor recipient. Weapons delivered to Chad in 2008 included the first of 6 Su-25 ground-attack aircraft from Ukraine and the last of approximately 82 armoured vehicles from Belgium. Sudan, which has tense relations with Chad, took delivery of an estimated 10 Su-25 aircraft from Belarus.

During 2007 and 2008 Ukraine delivered an estimated 110 T-72 tanks and 11 BM-21 multiple rocket launchers to Kenya. In September 2008 a consignment of 33 T-72 tanks and 6 BM-21 launchers en route from Ukraine to Kenya was hijacked by Somali pirates. The cargo was held for four months, during which time there was much speculation that its final destination was intended to be the government of Southern Sudan, rather than Kenya, despite Kenyan and Ukrainian protestations.

The Americas

States in the Americas accounted for 11 per cent of imports of major conventional weapons over the period 2004–2008, compared with 8 per cent for 1999–2003. Transfers to South America were 94 per cent higher in 2004– 2008 than in 1999–2003. The USA was the largest importer of conventional weapons in the Americas for the period 2004–2008, and the seventh largest in the world, up from 14th place for 1999–2003. Chile was the largest importer of conventional weapons in South America for the period 2004–2008 and the 11th largest in the world, up from 36th for 1999–2003. Several states in South America are undergoing force modernization programmes, indicating that the volume of transfers to the region will remain high. Most significantly, in December 2008 Brazil signed an €8.6 billion ($11.3 billion) agreement with France for the licensed production of 50 EC-725 helicopters, 4 conventional submarines and 1 nuclear-powered submarine.

For the period 2004–2008 Venezuela was the world's 18th largest recipient of military equipment, up from 55th place for 1999–2003. In 2008 the final delivery took place of many weapons that had been ordered from Russia in 2006 and 2007, including the last of 24 Su-30MK combat aircraft. During 2008 there was considerable speculation regarding follow-on deals with Russia, but no new contract was signed.

Almost half of US imports for the period 2004–2008 came from EU member states. Nominally, European products have been favoured over rival US products in several recent high-profile competitions, including for EC-145 helicopters and C-27J transport aircraft. However, most of the actual production under these contracts will take place in the USA.

Asia

Asian states received 37 per cent of all transfers of major conventional weapons in the period 2004–2008, compared with 40 per cent for 1999–2003. Transfers to East Asia (including South East Asia) accounted for 67 per cent of transfers to Asia in 2004–2008, those to South Asia for 25 per cent, to Oceania for 7 per cent and to Central Asia for only 1 per cent. Three of the four largest importers for 2004–2008 globally are Asian states: China, India and South Korea. Transfers of major conventional weapon systems to China in 2007 and 2008 were less than half their average annual volume in 2002–2006. The volume of deliveries to Taiwan has also fallen, dropping by 44 per cent between 1999–2003 and 2004–2008. However, in late 2008 the USA agreed to a long-discussed weapon package for Taiwan.

The volume of deliveries to Pakistan has increased significantly in recent years. Forty-one per cent of all transfers to Pakistan over the past 5 years took place in 2008. Over the period 2004–2008, 40 per cent of Pakistan's imports of major conventional weapons came from the USA. Significant deliveries in 2008 included M-109A5 155-mm artillery systems, P-3CUP Orion maritime patrol aircraft and F-16A combat aircraft. South Korean imports of major conventional weapons were 61 per cent higher in 2004–2008 than in 1999–2003. In 2007 and 2008 South Korea was the world's largest importer of major conventional weapons. The USA accounted for 73 per cent of arms transfers to South Korea for the period 2004–2008, including long-range F-15K combat aircraft along with engines and other components for South Korean-designed aircraft and ships.

Europe

European states received 24 per cent of all transfers of major conventional weapons for the period 2004–2008, compared with 26 per cent for 1999– 2003. EU member states accounted for 19 per cent of global arms imports over the period 2004–

2008 and 17 per cent over the period 1999–2003. The largest importer of major conventional weapons in Europe in recent years has been Greece. However, it has fallen from being the third largest recipient of major conventional weapons for the period 1999–2003 to fifth place for 2004–2008. Turkey has fallen from being the fourth largest recipient of major conventional weapons for the period 1999–2003 to eighth place for 2004–2008. Turkey signed a number of significant deals in 2008, including those for 6 Type-214 submarines from Germany and 51 A-129 combat helicopters from Italy, which will be produced under licence in Turkey.

Arms transfers to Georgia received a significant amount of media attention in the run-up to the conflict over South Ossetia in August 2008. Georgian arms imports were nearly four times higher over the period 2004–2008 than for 1999–2003. The largest supplier of arms to Georgia was Ukraine, which accounted for 65 per cent of transfers over the period 2004–2008. During 2004–2008 states in Europe imported an estimated 211 combat and ground-attack aircraft, compared with total world imports of over 1300. During 2008 there were at least 10 European states with ongoing competitions for combat aircraft acquisitions. However, a number of these deals may be delayed, downsized or cancelled as a result of the global financial crisis.

The Middle East

Middle Eastern states received 18 per cent of international transfers of major conventional weapons for the period 2004--2008. Transfers to the region were 38 per cent higher in 2004–2008 than in 1999–2003. During 2004– 2008, 34 per cent of all transfers to the Middle East went to the UAE, while Israel received 22 per cent and Egypt 14 per cent. Despite significant speculation about Iran's arms import plans, it accounted for only 5 per cent of transfers to the Middle East for the period 2004–2008 and was the 27th largest recipient of major conventional weapons worldwide

During the period 2004–2008 the UAE was the largest recipient of major conventional weapons in the region and the third largest in the world. Imports in this period included around 80 F-16E combat aircraft from the USA and around 50

Mirage-2000-9 combat aircraft from France. The UAE placed a number of significant orders in 2008 and looks set to remain a significant importer in the coming years.

During the period 2004–2008 Iraq was the world's 28th largest recipient of major conventional weapons, with 40 per cent of its imports coming from the USA. In 2008 Iraq ordered 140 M1A1 tanks from the USA and announced plans to obtain advanced combat aircraft and additional armoured vehicles. Israel's arms imports in 2004–2008 consisted primarily of 102 F-16I combat aircraft and related air-to-air and air-to-surface weapons. The vast majority of weapon systems ordered by or transferred to Israel during this period came from the USA, mostly in the form of military aid. Israel also imported components for its weapon systems from a variety of countries, including EU member states.

THE FINANCIAL VALUE OF THE ARMS TRADE

It is not possible to ascribe a precise financial value to the international arms trade. However, by aggregating financial data on the value of their arms exports as released by the main suppliers, it is possible to make an indicative estimate. According to official government data, the estimated financial value of the international arms trade in 2007, the last year for which data is available, was $51.1 billion, which represents 0.3 per cent of world trade. This figure is likely to be lower than the true figure since a number of significant exporters, including China, do not release data on the financial value of their arms exports. Although the SIPRI data on international arms transfers and official government data on the financial value of the arms trade are based on different methodologies, both have tended to increase since 2001.

According to official government data, the USA was the largest arms exporter in 2007, with exports worth $12.8 billion; Russia was in second place, with $7.4 billion; France was in third place, with $6.2 billion; Israel was in fourth place, with $4.4 billion; and the UK was in fifth place, with $4.1 billion.

Comparing SIPRI's data on international arms transfers with national data on the financial value of arms exports reveals some of the differences in the methodologies used to create these data sets. For example, a significant proportion of Israel's arms exports consists of electronics and other components, which are not included in the SIPRI Arms Transfers Database. This partly explains why Israel is among the five largest arms exporters according to reported financial values but not according to SIPRI data on international arms transfers. Meanwhile, a significant proportion of German arms exports consists of military aid and the sale of second-hand equipment. Since the SIPRI data is based on the notional equivalent values of the weapon systems (the TIV), and not their cost at the point of sale, these transfers may be valued more highly in the SIPRI data on international arms transfers than in Germany's national data on the financial value of its arms exports. This may partly explain why Germany appears among the five largest arms exporters according to the SIPRI TIV, but not among the five largest according to reported financial values.

INTERNATIONAL TRANSFERS OF SMALL ARMS AND LIGHT WEAPONS

Since the mid-1990s global attention has become increasingly focused on transfers of SALW, which have come to be regarded as the type of conventional weapon that can cause the most instability in a country or region. Governmental transparency in international transfers of SALW continues to lag behind transparency levels for other types of conventional weapon transfers, although advances have been made in recent years. For example, in December 2003 the UN General Assembly invited member states to provide information on SALW transfers to the UN Register of Conventional Arms (UNROCA), which had previously covered only major conventional weapons, and in 2006 states were invited to do so using a standardized reporting form.

As of 31 December 2008, 56 states had submitted data to UNROCA on their SALW transfers on at least one occasion since 2003. The major suppliers and recipients according to UNROCA data. However, the information submitted to UNROCA covers only a fraction of international transfers of SALW because many significant exporters (e.g. China, Russia and the USA) have not submitted data. In addition, since a high proportion of European states have submitted SALW data to the UNROCA, they are over-represented among exporters.

The only other regularly updated source of information on the global trade in SALW is the customs data that states submit to the UN Commodity Trade Statistics Database (Comtrade). The Norwegian Initiative on Small Arms Transfers (NISAT) collects and collates customs data from Comtrade and compiles an annual register of international SALW transfers.

However, this source is also far from complete. For example, many countries omit data related to arms exports in their reports to Comtrade or omit information about the destination of arms exports.

RECENT TRENDS IN WORLD MILITARY EXPENDITURE

There is no necessary, direct relationship between global military spending and the volume or value of the global arms trade. Movements in one do not necessarily correlate to movements in the other. For example, the majority of most states' military budget is spent on personnel costs, rather than equipment acquisitions. Among member states of the North Atlantic Treaty Organization (NATO), the median share of military spending allocated to equipment purchases was 17.6 per cent in 2008. Also, many of the world's biggest spenders, including Russia and the USA, acquire the majority of their equipment domestically, and so increases in their procurement costs will not lead to a rise in international arms transfers. In addition, many states, particularly in the developing world, often exclude money spent on arms acquisitions from published military budgets. Such purchases may be funded through non-military budget lines or simply may not accounted for in the budget. Finally, many states receive considerable amounts of military equipment in the form of military aid, which would not necessarily be reflected in the recipient states' military budget.

Nonetheless, a general increase in military expenditure in a particular region or worldwide is likely to be a strong indication that arms procurement expenditure has also increased, whether on-or off-budget. In addition, many states, particularly in the developing world, rely on arms imports, rather than domestic production, as their main source of military procurement, and increases in their military spending may well translate into increases in the global arms transfers. While patterns over previous time periods vary, since 2001 there have been consistent year-on-year increases in the SIPRI data on both international arms transfers and global military expenditure.

Over the first decade following the end of the cold war (1989–98), world military spending fell in real terms by more than one-third. Many states downsized or restructured their armed forces while making deep cuts in procurement. The deepest cuts took place in Russia and the other former members of the Warsaw Treaty Organization; there were smaller reductions in Africa, the Americas and Western Europe. However, military spending continued to rise in Asia (by 27 per cent) and the Middle East (by 17 per cent). Since 1998 the downward trend in military spending has reversed. Global military spending increased by 45 per cent in real terms over the 10-year period 1998–2007, reaching $1339 billion in 2007. This corresponded to 2.5 per cent of world gross domestic product (GDP) or $202 for each person in the world. The increase in spending has accelerated since 2001, with an annual average increase of 5.3 per cent, compared with 2.2 per cent during the period 1998–2001.

The factors driving increases in military spending since 2001 constitute a mixture of foreign policy objectives, real or perceived threats, armed conflict and policies to contribute to international peacekeeping operations. However, the primary driver of the high rate of growth has been the USA, which accounted for 63 per cent of the post-2001 increase in global spending and 45 per cent of total global military spending in 2007. While much of this increase is attributable to spending on military operations in Afghanistan and Iraq, the core military budget has also risen significantly. Many other states have also increased their military spending since 2001. Around two-thirds of countries that make data available increased their military spending annually between 2001 and 2006. Of the 121 countries for which such data was available, 88 had higher military spending in real terms in 2007 compared to 2001. The following regional trends can also be observed.

In Eastern Europe military expenditure rose by 162 per cent over the period 1998–2007, the highest increase in any subregion. It was also the region with the highest increase in

2007, at 15 per cent. Russia, with a 13 per cent increase in 2007, accounted for 86 per cent of this regional increase. In North America military expenditure rose by 59 per cent over the period 1998–2007. This rise was driven almost exclusively by the recent increases in US military spending. By 2007, US spending was higher than at any time since World War II.

In the Middle East military expenditure rose by 62 per cent over the period 1998–2007. There have been strong increases in all Gulf Cooperation Council member states apart from the UAE. There have also been significant increases in military spending in Iran, Jordan and Lebanon.

In South Asia military expenditure rose by 57 per cent over the period 1998–2007. The upward trend was largely due to a real-terms increase of 64 per cent in Indian military spending. In Africa military expenditure rose by 51 per cent over the period 1998– 2007. This increase was largely driven by a 97 per cent increase in Algeria's military spending. While military budgets in much of Africa remain low by global standards, the economic burden that they represent can be considerable. For example, in 2005 military spending in Angola and Burundi represented 5.7 and 6.2 per cent of GDP, respectively, among the highest proportions in the world. Angola and Burundi also have some of the lowest human development indices.

In East Asia military expenditure rose by 51 per cent over the period 1998–2007. Three countries increased their military spending by more than 50 per cent during this period: China, by 202 per cent, Indonesia, by 100 per cent, and Malaysia, by 153 per cent. While China increased its military spending threefold over the decade, its rapid economic growth, means that the economic burden of military spending is still moderate, at 2.1 per cent of GDP in 2006. The subregions with the lowest growth in military spending over the period 1998–2007 were Western Europe (6 per cent) and Central America (14 per cent).

RECENT TRENDS IN WORLD ARMS PRODUCTION

The global arms industry, especially the production of modern major weapon systems and technologies, is dominated by North America and Western Europe, although significant capabilities also exist in Australia, China, Israel, Japan, South Korea and Russia. There are no available reliable estimates for the overall size of the global arms industry. However, SIPRI produces an annual list of the top 100 arms-producing companies (the SIPRI Top 100), which captures the majority of the financial value of the global arms industry. The total value of arms sales (military-specific goods and services) by the Top 100 companies was $315 billion in 2006, a 60 per cent increase on the 2002 value. This rapid rise is mostly linked to increases in US military expenditure. US-owned companies accounted for 63.5 per cent of the 2006 total and West European-owned companies accounted for 29.2 per cent. These shares have not changed greatly over the past few years. 19 Following the end of the cold war the global arms industry contracted significantly due to the substantial decreases in military expenditure by both NATO members and former members of the Warsaw Treaty Organization.

In the USA and Western Europe, while this decline led to substantial job losses, it took place at a fairly managed pace and was accompanied by largescale consolidation of the industry. In the USA a few giant companies were formed through mergers such as those of Northrop and Grumman in 1994 and of Boeing and McDonnell-Douglas in 1997. In Europe consolidation led to the creation or rapid growth of BAE Systems in the UK, Thales in France, Finmeccanica in Italy, and the trans-European company EADS. These four companies are the only non-US companies among the world's 10 largest arms producers. In some countries, particularly the UK and the USA, the reductions in spending on military equipment were to some extent mitigated by the growth of outsourcing of services formerly performed by the military. The period of post-cold war consolidation in the Western arms industry had largely ended by the early 2000s, which was also when US military expenditure began to increase significantly, especially following the terrorist attacks on the USA of 11 September 2001. The rapid growth of US military expenditure has led to increasing efforts by overseas companies to access the US markets through acquisitions of US companies. British companies, due to the UK's close political relationship with the USA, have been most successful in acquiring US companies. Led by BAE Systems, which is now one of the top 10 sup pliers to the US Department of Defence, many British companies now carry out as much or more of their operations in the USA as in the UK. Continental European companies have been far less able to make acquisitions in the USA, but in 2008 an Italian company broke this pattern with the acquisition for $5.2 billion of DRS Technologies, a US military electronics company. In Russia, the former Soviet arms industry virtually collapsed as Russian military spending fell to just 6 per cent of the former Soviet level. While in recent years the Russian industry has revived somewhat, helped by strong export performance, and is beginning to receive new injections of state capital and domestic orders, it still suffers from severe problems of aged equipment and obsolescent technologies. The Russian arms industry is currently undergoing a major reorganization, with the creation of a few large stateowned holding companies to consolidate different sectors of the arms industry. These include the United Aircraft Corporation, the United Shipbuilding Corporation and Rostekhnologii.

Attempts by countries outside the traditional major producers to develop their own modern arms industries have typically had limited success. This is in large part due to the high technological barriers to producing modern major weapons systems and, in many cases, an inadequate civilian industrial base. However, many countries are continuing efforts to increase their levels of autonomous capability in arms production, sometimes with increasing success.

China is increasingly able to produce a wide range of modern weapon systems, including fourth generation-plus combat aircraft, although in most areas it is still one to two generations behind the most advanced technology. Israel has for some time now maintained an advanced arms industry. In some areas, such as unmanned aerial vehicles (UAVs), it technology is among the best in the world and is sold to major Western powers. South Korea has had considerable success in a number of areas in recent years. In 2007 Turkey signed a $459 million deal to buy 40 KT-1 Woong-Bee trainer aircraft from South Korea, reflecting the country's emergence as a significant arms exporter. India is pursuing a strategy of off sets to obtain technology transfers when importing arms, as a way of developing its indigenous capabilities. It is too early to judge how successful this strategy will be. Brazil had the most successful arms industry in Latin America during the 1980s and was the 11th biggest supplier in the world for the period 1984–88. Its industry contracted rapidly in the early 1990s, but the Brazilian Government is placing a strong emphasis on revitalizing the sector. South Africa developed a significant military industry during the apartheid era and has sought to keep the sector going in the years since. As of 2008, Denel Group, South Africa's largest arms-producing company, had about 7300 employees.

While countries in other parts of the world may lack modern defence industries, they can still act as sources of surplus or second-hand equipment or of newly produced but less technologically advanced weapon systems, such as SALW and their ammunition. According to one estimate, at least 1249 companies in more than 90 countries are involved in some aspect of SALW production. The means of producing weapons and military systems, particularly SALW, has spread through the licensed and unlicensed transfer of production facilities around the world. The level of technological know-how attained by the host country through licensed production is highly variable. In some cases the host country is responsible for no more than the final assembly of components made by the licensing country, while in other cases it may be used as a step towards mastering the full production process. According to one estimate, 60–80 per cent of all military rifles, assault rifles and carbines are manufactured by producers that acquired the necessary technology from elsewhere. Examples of countries that lack a significant defence industry, but which nonetheless maintain some level of SALW production capacity, include Colombia, Indonesia, Jordan, Nigeria and Sudan.

RECENT TRENDS IN EXPORT CONTROL MECHANISMS

Arms export policies are policies that govern 'The dispatch of conventional weapons, weapon platforms and related equipment (that would normally be found on a military list of controlled goods) from one country to another'. 32 Along with other defence-and security-related issues, the development and implementation of such policies is almost universally considered to be the exclusive prerogative of states. States have traditionally pursued widely divergent arms export policies and, with the exception of multilateral arms embargoes, have been reluctant to give up any element of national control in this area.

Nonetheless, numerous states have also sought to increase the level of coordination and harmonization in this area—as a means of both increasing international standards and off setting the commercial costs of maintaining a more restrictive system than other states. Such efforts have intensified in recent years. While they have largely focused on regional organizations such as the Organization for Security and Co-operation in Europe (OSCE) and the EU, the UN has also made extensive and long-standing efforts. Numerous UN Security Council and General Assembly resolutions have reiterated the importance of states maintaining functioning controls on the export of military goods. For example, under the 2001 Programme of Action to Prevent, Combat and Eradicate the Illicit Trade in Small Arms and Light Weapons in All Its Aspects (POA), states have agreed to ensure that they have adequate laws, regulations and administrative procedures to control transfers of SALW.

Transfer prohibitions and guidelines

At present, arms embargoes imposed by the UN Security Council are the only global, legally binding prohibitions on arms transfers. UN arms embargoes are imposed by resolutions adopted under the authority of Chapter VII, Article 41, of the UN Charter. Like all Security Council resolutions, embargoes require the affirmative votes of at least nine of the 15 members of the Security Council, and each of the five permanent members (China, France, Russia, the UK and the USA; the P5) has a veto. As of 1 January 2009 there were 11 mandatory UN arms embargoes in force. However, according to the sanctions committees and panels of experts monitoring these embargoes, many UN arms embargoes have been repeatedly violated, by both states and private individuals.

The development of regional and global guidelines for conventional arms transfers has been on the international agenda since the 1920s. In 1925 the League of Nations produced a draft convention on the arms trade, but it was never adopted. While global conventions govern the transfer of nuclear, biological and chemical weapons, there is currently no equivalent, global mechanism covering the transfer of conventional weapons. During the cold war the two competing blocs and individual countries used conventional weapon transfers in order to establish or maintain spheres of influence. At the regional level, the coordination of export control policies was mainly focused on preventing transfers to members of the opposing bloc. For example, in 1949 the Western bloc formed the Coordinating Committee for Multilateral Export Controls (COCOM) to manage an embargo on transfers of arms and related technologies to the Eastern bloc. COCOM was disbanded in 1994.

In the early 1990s states concluded that the accumulation of major conventional weapons in Iraq in the period preceding the 1990 invasion of Kuwait had contributed to Iraq's decision to invade. Partly as a result, during the early and mid-1990s different state groupings developed several sets of guidelines or principles on arms transfers. Rather than targeting specific groups of states, they sought to lay down rules that would apply to all conventional arms transfers, regardless of their destination.

In October 1991 the P5 adopted a set of guidelines for conventional arms transfers which called on the P5 and other arms exporters to export conventional arms only in line with the legitimate self-defence needs of recipients and appropriate and proportionate responses to security threats. It was also agreed that transfers that were likely to prolong existing conflicts and tensions, introduce 'destabilizing accumulations' or contravene international commitments, such as arms embargoes, would be avoided. In November 1993 the OSCE reaffirmed its commitment to a similar set of principles governing conventional arms transfers.

Other principles emphasized in these guidelines include the need to prevent transfers that might contribute to destabilizing military build-ups, prolong or aggravate an armed conflict, or fall into the hands of terrorists. However, the guidelines lack enforcement mechanisms, and their interpretation has been left entirely at the discretion of individual states. Concerns such as these have played a significant role in the recent push for the development of an international arms trade treaty. A 2006 draft UN General Assembly resolution states that the 'absence of common international standards on the import, export and transfer of conventional arms is a contributory factor to conflict, the displacement of people, crime and terrorism'.

Export control regimes and other regional mechanisms

The post cold-war period has also seen the development of more formal mechanisms aimed at coordinating the policies of supplier and recipient states. These mechanisms involve the application of guidelines and principles, but they also include some level of coordination between the states involved to try to ensure some level of harmonization in how they are implemented. Other mechanisms cover exports of missiles (e.g. the Missile Technology Control Regime), nuclear technologies (e.g. the Nuclear Suppliers Group) and chemical and biological agents (e.g. the Australia Group). The Wassenaar Arrangement on Export Controls for Conventional Arms and Dual-Use Goods and Technologies was established in 1996 in an attempt to replicate some of the benefits of COCOM but on a broader and non-adversarial basis. It currently has 40 participating states, including Russia, the USA, most members of NATO and most former members of the Warsaw Treaty Organization. The Wassenaar Arrangement was designed to promote transparency and responsibility in transfers of arms and dual-use items in order to prevent 'destabilizing accumulations'. Participating states exchange information on their exports and discuss policies on particular regions or destinations.

The EU's Common Rules Governing Control of Exports of Military Technology and Equipment (known as the Code of Conduct on Arms Exports until 2008) was first formally adopted in June 1998.41 It consists of eight criteria on which EU member states should base their export licensing decisions, relating to issues such as conflict prevention, human rights and economic development. Under the EU Common Rules, governments agree to exchange, in confidence, information on any application for an export licence that is denied, including the reasons for the refusal. If a member state is considering granting an export licence for a transaction that it believes might be 'essentially identical' to one that has previously been denied, then it is obliged to consult the state that previously issued the denial in order to clarify the situation. In 1998 members of the Economic Community of West African States (ECOWAS) adopted a moratorium on the manufacture, importation and exportation of SALW. A 2002 evaluation report highlighted a number of weaknesses in the moratorium and cases where certain states had failed to uphold its principles. In response, the ECOWAS Convention on Small Arms and Light Weapons, Their Ammunition and Other Related Materials was adopted in June 2006. The convention retains the moratorium's prohibition on SALW imports, but states can apply to the ECOWAS Commission for exemptions 'in order to meet legitimate national defence and security needs, or to participate in peace support or other operations'. The convention also requires that participating states provide detailed information to the ECOWAS Commission on any SALW import.

TRANSPARENCY MECHANISMS

According to a 1991 UN report: There are many types of information of arms transfers that could be included in measures to promote transparency. The most important criteria for the choice of types of information are political acceptability and relevance for the achievement of transparency. Some of the possible characteristics are the following: (a) Supplier and recipient; (b) Final user; (c) Date of agreement and/or date of delivery: (d) Type of arms, components, knowledge or services transferred: (e) Basic performance characteristics of the arms or components transferred; (f) Quantity of arms or components transferred; (g) Financial terms; (h) Technical support and training arrangements.

Since the early 1990s an increasing number of national, regional and international transparency mechanisms in the field of arms exports have been developed. As well as providing the impetus for the P5 to agree a set of guidelines to prevent destabilizing accumulations of arms and conflict, the 1991 Gulf War also boosted efforts within the UN General Assembly to increase the transparency of international arms transfers. Meanwhile, several states, particularly in Europe, have responded to parliamentary and public pressure for greater oversight of national arms export policies and have begun to publish national reports on their arms exports.

The UN Register of Conventional Arms was established in December 1991 'to prevent excessive and destabilizing accumulation of arms... in order to promote stability and strengthen regional or international peace and security [and to] enhance confidence, promote stability, help states to exercise restraint, ease tensions and strengthen regional and international peace and security'. Each year states are requested to submit to UNROCA information on their imports and exports of certain categories of major conventional weapons. For the years 2005–2007, 23 states from Africa, 27 states from the Americas, 39 states from Asia and the Pacific and 44 states from Europe reported. As of 1 January 2009, only 90 states had submitted data on their imports or exports during 2007, almost half of which came from Europe.

As of 1 January 2008, 31 states had published at least one national report on arms exports, compared with 6 states as of January 1998.48 For the most part, the decision to publish these national reports resulted from pressure from parliaments and non-governmental organizations for greater oversight of the governments' implementation of their arms export policies. The force of these demands increased following a spate of arms export related scandals in the 1970s, 1980s and 1990s. The quality of the information contained in these reports varies, but at a minimum the report tend to include information on the number of licences issued, broken down by destination and value. Under the EU Common Rules states are asked to submit data on the financial value of arms export licences issued and actual arms exports, broken down by destination and by EU Military List category. The data on licences and exports, along with aggregated data on denials, is compiled in a publicly available annual report. For the 10th of these annual reports, published in 2008, 16 of the 27 EU member states submitted data for all requested categories.

6

The Humanitarian Challenge of Small Arms Proliferation

INTRODUCTION: EPG WITHIN THE GLOBAL SMALL ARMS CAMPAIGN

The humanitarian, political-economic and security dimensions of excessive and destabilizing accumulations of small arms confront civil and political society with the need for immediate action. With political awareness aroused by the human toll of illicit small arms in Africa, Asia, Europe and the Western Hemisphere, denoting the issue's global dimension, the UN is embarking on the important task to convene, by 2001, an international conference on the illicit trade in small arms in all its aspects.

A nascent global campaign is to be commended for successfully pushing small arms onto the agenda of multilateral arms control. Unlike the international campaign to ban landmines, however, the emerging "movement" is lacking in focus and direction. A plethora of initiatives notwithstanding, concerns persist that economic and political interests of the few may hinder tangible humanitarian results for the many.

The potential for diversion is immense as even basic agreement on how to define the issue remains wanting. Is it, for example, an arms control, disarmament or crime prevention issue; is one to address oneself on the supply or the demand side, the precipitating versus root causes of small arms violence? Too overwhelming, then, the dualism which connects illicit arms to the licit trade, where a majority of them originate, too daunting the interaction between the licit and illicit trade, too challenging the interconnectedness between the root and precipitating causes of civil conflict and small arms violence.

Small arms violence poses as much an arms control challenge as a humanitarian challenge. It can also be said, since a majority of weapons producers are located in the developed world and a majority of weapons recipients in the developing world, the small arms issue is, at its core, a North-South issue. In the North, the global campaign on small arms must be put in the framework of development, demilitarization and peace building. In the South, such a campaign must be put in the context of a broader justice-oriented community and human rights.

Reducing the number of small arms requires a multisectoral and comprehensive approach, encompassing a whole range of measures, both operative and normative, which must be dealt with both within the context of conflict prevention and conflict resolution. Small arms action must address both security, humanitarian and developmental concerns.

Economic development is dependent on a secure and stable political environment. Some refer to this as the "Security First" approach. But the opposite is also true: without economic development, many of the root causes of grievance cannot be properly addressed and there will be no political stability. A more appropriate-nonetheless more daunting-approach instead of "Security First" is "a proportional and integrated approach to security and development." In areas of conflict, both security and development aspects must be integrated into national programs as well as into international cooperation efforts.

Whereas, however, taking a narrow approach "Security First" advances security at the expense of development, the proportional-integrated approach takes too broad a venue with respect both, to the supply of and demand for small arms, existent and future stockpiles and inherent linkages between security and development. It would appear that it strives to achieve too much in too short a period of time.

Recognizing security and development as corollaries in reducing supply the EPG compromise cooperative regulatory approach advances a constructive parallelism between both input functions without establishing ipso facto linkages which, from a bargaining point of view, should lend itself to tangible results within a reasonable time frame. The compromise approach built around a universal, comprehensive and non-discriminatory Small Arms Control Regime which centres on transparency and accountability should not be seen as an alternative, but as a minimalist position concomitant to the integrated-proportional approach.

An independent international commission the Eminent Persons Group strives to make a specific contribution to the emerging global small arms effort. While fully acknowledging the need for a broad approach, EPG pursues a cooperative regulatory approach to the international trade in small arms. As a sub-campaign and integral to the larger small arms campaign being led by the International Action Network on Small Arms (IANSA), EPG undertakes to confront the supply side of the illicit trade by making cross-border arms sales subject to arms control, export and transparency regimes.

Moreover, governments will be encouraged to limit the number of small arms approved for export, to combat illicit transfers of weapons and to assist in extracting surplus weapons which are circulating the global market. In this complex situation, a sincere abhorrence of covert wars and civilian destruction would prove conducive to putting in place the norms that would regulate state behaviour.

The attainment of the goal requires an integrated proportional approach between governments and civil society to advance elements of a realistic plan of action for the 2001 UN conference on small arms trafficking in all its aspects. Within the preparatory process for the conference, this approach consists of two tracks: first, the involvement of EPG on the inter-governmental level and secondly, the participation of EPG within the NGO community. For the two levels of action, the governmental and non-governmental, are co-dependent and mutually enhancing in building momentum for regulatory controls and micro-disarmament.

EPG's ability to remain highly visible at both, the non-governmental and inter-governmental levels of small arms action, defines the Commission's juxtaposition within the global small arms effort. The Commission's uniqueness lies in the special blending of incumbent and former officials at the highest levels of government from around the world. Members of the Commission represent both, weapons-exporting and weapons-importing countries.

This active involvement of decision-makers in the early stages of and throughout the preparatory process is essential to political advances towards curtailing small arms proliferation. It is the high caliber of members of the commission, which provides for the level of credibility and political prestige to assure serious deliberations.

With respect to the governmental level, EPG is in exploratory talks with UN member States, within the Group of Interested States (GIS), to provide for a consultative framework, affiliated with but independent of the eminent persons group. GIS is comprised of foreign ministers of those UN member States which are taking the lead on the small arms issue and which find themselves in conceptual agreement on the cooperative regulatory approach inherent in SACR.

Without prejudice to national bargaining positions, GIS facilitates consultations on a multilateral approach to small arms proliferation both, throughout the preparatory process and at the conference itself. With respect to the non-governmental level EPG is actively cooperating with and working through IANSA. At the same time, as part of its commitment to help raise the profile of small arms proliferation globally, EPG is pursuing a vigorous public diplomacy schedule.

In close consultation with UN member States, the UN Secretariat and other NGOs the group will, within the preparatory committee, advance elements of an action agenda aimed at curtailing illicit small arms by confronting the illicit trade. To be successful such an action agenda must centre on increased transparency and raised common standards and provide concrete and practical measures on the global and regional level. The group will submit to the UN conference a report on the scope and magnitude of the illicit arms trade, ways to curb it and the United Nations role in collecting and disseminating information in this area, prevention and enforcement.

SMALL ARMS VIOLENCE: THE HUMANITARIAN CHALLENGE

The destabilizing accumulation of small arms outside of formal regulatory controls and the resulting toll inflicted on civilian populations in countries around the world poses one of the great humanitarian challenges of our time.

Small arms violence undermines good governance and, in so doing, jeopardizes fundamental human rights, economic development, political stability, social justice and peace. The overabundance of small arms has come to affect nearly all parts of the UN system. In exacerbating armed conflict, violence, crime, social disruption, displacement of peoples and human suffering, and threatening UN peace and relief missions, curtailing the proliferation of small arms will be "one of the key challenges in preventing conflict in the next century."

The qualitative and quantitative nature of post-modern warfare has changed and greatly increased its impact on civilians. There has been a complete elimination of the well-recognized distinction between combatants on the one hand and the civilian population on the other. In many wars, the primary strategy seems to effect maximum civilian casualties by either maiming or outright killing. Indeed, decimation of the opponent's civilian population has become an essential part of the strategy of modern warfare.

Small arms are the weapon of choice in most conflicts and responsible for 90% of casualties; they are the weapons that kill most people in most wars. A majority of the 200,000 deaths annually are civilian, most notably children, with only a minimal decline of casualties (less than 30%) in the post-conflict phase. For these weapons are inexpensive, readily available and easy to operate. In Uganda, for example, an AK-47 automatic rifle, of which there are around 55 million in circulation, and which can be easily carried, maintained and assembled by a ten year old child, can be bought for the price of a chicken and in Northern Kenya for the price of a goat.

In many conflicts, children are forced to engage in open hostilities. UNICEF estimates that a quarter million have ended up as "child combatants" in some 30 recent conflicts. A whole generation of children the world over is being inducted into a culture of violence marked by violent death and injury, with dire psychological consequences. This mental militarization, de-humanisation and transformation of societal values, which lead to the quest of some to solve social problems in a violent manner will, over time, tear apart the last remnants of civil society. In developing countries around the world, ever-expanding small arms and light weapons expenditures aggravate deteriorating domestic conditions. Civil wars disrupt trade, tourism and investment. With more and more resources diverted to maintaining internal order, human rights abuses increase, basic human needs are neglected and democracy and development are put at risk.

The growing control of crime over civil society poses additional dangers to political and economic reform by threatening democratic structures. In many countries, precious natural resources, rather than being means for economic and political empowerment for the many, end up fueling the engines of war and annihilation to enrich the few. The trade in diamonds, oil and precious metals increasingly provides funds for illicit arms purchases and has led to the creation of a dangerous strategic triad of political, criminal and commercial interests. A 1996 World Bank report explains the connection between war and poverty. During the past decade, fifteen of the twenty poorest countries in the world have experienced major conflict. Virtually every low-income country in the world has either undergone major conflict, or borders on one or more countries in conflict. The inability of increasing numbers of governments to redress social iniquities worsens the conditions of the disenfranchised and greatly contributes to frustration and sudden explosions of violence.

The world has seen more conflict in the last twenty years than at any time that century. As a result, about 35 million people are currently displaced, either outside or within their country. While the mere presence of small arms in large numbers and outside formal security structures may not in and of itself generate conflict, it nonetheless increases the likelihood of violent eruptions and increases their scale and lethality. At the same time, their continued presence or improper management during a peace process may prolong conflict. Moreover, increasingly, these weapons are being turned against relief workers, who provide desperately needed social services throughout the world. Beyond threatening intra-state political and economic stability, the ready supply of inexpensive small arms through the illicit arms trade proves conducive to heightening inter-state conflict. Weapons routes crisscross the entire continent and it is no longer necessary to be a neighbor to a conflict area to feel its ill effects. Weapons from Afghanistan, for example, travel eastward to reach China's coastal cities and southwards to feed conflict in Sri Lanka.

With cross-border guerilla groups proliferating and dividing into warring factions capable of outgunning government forces, internal instabilities increasingly tend to evolve into larger regional wars, putting the nation-state system itself in jeopardy. The conflict in Congo-Kinshasa involves the armed forces of eight countries and several militia groups. As a result, of the 22 million refugees globally, 8.1 million are in Africa.

Around the globe, there are at least 20 locations where an armed conflict could occur or recur due largely to an incomplete process of disarmament either of former combatants or civilians, particularly among societies with fragile or fledgling state structures.

SMALL ARMS PROLIFERATION: THE ARMS CONTROL CHALLENGE

Over the course of the past decade small arms have become the primary choice of weapons for political and criminal groups in fueling armed conflicts, wars, massacres, ethnic cleansing and human rights violations. That, in no small measure is due to the fact that small arms are too readily available and too inexpensive, while at the same time requiring only minimal training, logistics and support to maintain and operate. 300 manufacturers in 74 countries produce small arms, of which well over 500,000,000 are believed to be in circulation, inside or outside of state regulatory controls. Between 1985 and 1995, there has been a twenty-five per cent increase in the number of producers. Moreover, low-end sell-offs or give-aways of "surplus" small arms increase supply as well. As a result, there is an overabundance of inexpensive small arms glutting the world market. Yet, to date the international trade in small arms remains largely unregulated.

Principal sources of small arms include: small arms acquired for legal purposes and misused (e.g. human rights violations and external aggression), small arms acquired for legal purposes and sold/stolen; small arms for crime and unintentional injuries (gray market), and illegally manufactured or trafficked small arms (black market). Whatever the perspective, i.e. peace-building versus crime prevention or arms control, draining these supply sources is imperative. Measures must be devised to limit the access to small arms (licensing, storage, embargoes), to reduce the supply of small arms (control of manufacture, identification, tracing etc.) and to reduce the demand for small arms (amnesties, buy-backs). The weapons of violence must be brought back into the control of the state, with the state itself being made accountable for its deeds. This essentially means empowering the state at one level, and using all tools available to induce more responsible behaviour on its part, at another. The two approaches must be mutually compatible.

The permanent members of the UN Security Council alone are responsible for 85% of the global arms trade. 40% of the worldwide flow of small arms is attributed to illicit trafficking and the majority of illicit weapons are proven to originate in the licit trade. Getting these governments to tighten national controls and to accept strengthened international standards for legal arms transfers should lend itself to reducing supply, significantly. Small arms transfer policies should be designed to support transfers that do not destabilize or threaten regional peace and security. With production monitored and limited and exports restricted and tighter controlled a reduced supply should restrict access and decrease overall circulation.

Given that small arms are produced, acquired and exported for legitimate purposes it is not, as opposed to the global campaign to ban landmines, appropriate to seek a ban. Rather, EPG's overall objective is to assist in efforts to curtail the supply of illicit small arms. Such an objective will require a constructive parallelism among a range of politically and legally binding instruments, involving operative and normative measures which pertain both to the licit as well as the illicit trade, and which address both conflict prevention and conflict resolution. As one building block toward this overall objective, the group's goal is to promote a cooperative regulatory approach built around a small arms control regime (SACR), broad in scope and global in reach and to consist of, on the preventive side, (1) a Small Arms Register, (2) strengthened national export controls, and (3) an international code of conduct. On the reduction side, to consist of weapons collection programs as integral to peace agreements and post-conflict demobilization and reconstruction programs as well as to conflict prevention strategies.

Universal, comprehensive and non-discriminatory SACR would integrate current efforts based on a variety of approaches: crime prevention, arms control, firearms regulation, human rights, development, gun safety etc. It should, therefore, not be viewed as detracting from or interfering with ongoing, local, national or regional efforts. Rather, SACR can be said to provide a set of common standards around which these efforts can be harnessed.

Cooperative arms regulation and disarmament must address security and developmental concerns as functional corollaries and must be integrated into national programs as well as into international cooperation efforts. While the task is a daunting one, many international development agencies have already taken steps to incorporate security sector reform and other conflict prevention strategies into their assistance programs. Integral to cooperative disarmament, preventive measures must pursue two objectives: first, to limit and control availability and access to small arms (supply side) and secondly, to reduce the demand for such weapons (demand side). On the supply side such an approach necessitates measures aimed at effectively regulating legal transfers between states based on a principle of responsible restraint, controlling the availability, use and storage of small arms within states, preventing and combating illicit transfers, collecting and removing surplus arms from both civil society and regions of conflict, increasing transparency and accountability, support for research and information sharing.

Correspondingly, on the demand side, the international community must commit to helping reverse cultures of violence through support for the reform of the security sector (both police and military) in affected states as fundamental to good governance, through the promotion of norms of civilian non-possession and of government restraint, by enhancing demobilization and reintegration programs for ex-combatants, by halting the abhorrent use of child fighters and by effectively combating the culture of impunity that fuels the illicit arms trade. Also, reduction measures must be devised to secure, destroy or otherwise responsibly dispose of small arms that are already in circulation, inside or outside of legal possession. The international donor community should establish collection and buy-back programs as well as other mechanisms to identify and promote best practices and to ensure adequate financial support. This is of particular importance with respect to "surplus" military weapons during a peace process. Integral to peace accords, combatants must be demobilized, disarmed and weapons surrendered safely destroyed. There are important lessons to be learned from small arms collection and destruction (Mozambique, Mali, Liberia) reintegration of ex-combatants into productive civilian life (Cambodia, Philippines), post-conflict reconstruction (Cambodia, Bougainville) and the reform of police, judicial and penal systems (Cambodia, Papua New Guinea). Law enforcement efforts in States where the illicit use of small arms is particularly severe should be supported as well.

The international donor community should cooperate with affected states in the establishment of incentive-based weapons collection programs as well as other mechanisms to identify and promote best practices and to ensure adequate financial support. The UN can develop centres for excellence pertaining to certain aspects of the problem area, such as arms collection programs, security sector reform and security arrangements for post-conflict development. Technical and financial resources are needed and the UN can play a role in mobilizing these resources.

AN INTERNATIONAL TRANSPARENCY REGIME

A UN Register on Small Arms could help in addressing the destabilizing consequences of large-scale legal transfers by virtue of improved management and control. Given the overall import of small arms as a destabilizing factor, such an approach would appear preferable in order to address the small arms issue as an arms control issue in its own right, independent of larger conventional weapons. The monitoring of small arms flows as conducive to determining destabilizing accumulations could, in fostering transparency, enhance trust, confidence, security and, by extension, durable peace. The Register would have to be universal, comprehensive and non-discriminatory. Under the Register, governments would be required to submit generalized reports, declaring production, stockpiling and transfer of small arms, to mark small arms and commit themselves not to import nor export unmarked small arms. Such a measure would hold governments to a higher standard of accountability. Within this context, the contentious issue of covert arms shipments could be addressed as well. Special oversight mechanisms could be set-up to protect parochial national security interests.

A UN Register could also furnish details of illicit arms seized, illicit arms destroyed and a list of third party arms brokering agents convicted of illegal brokering activities. A proposed UN yearbook, available to the general public, with the aim of collecting and analyzing data on small arms production and transfers might further advance the objective. There should be generalized reports to the Register as well as to the Yearbook.

Verification and transparency are mutually enhancing. Thus, information gathering and sharing, integral to an intrusive verification process and critical to prevention and enforcement, is both a precondition for and function of transparency. Consequently, cooperation, coordination, training and information sharing among police, intelligence and customs within and between countries must be enhanced. Moreover, UN early warning systems should be set up in order to enhance early detection of proliferation. Points of transfer, such as harbors and supply roads, especially in regions of conflict, must be controlled for. Such could be done by encouraging a "monitoring culture" within which, in countries concerned, UN, embassy personnel, or NGO-fieldworkers, for example, sound alarm the moment they witness small arms accumulations or illicit transfers. Regional organizations, such as the OAU, OAS, and OSCE, for example, will be pivotal to supporting the monitoring capacity in low-income countries.

Also, small arms tracking by improved, simple and cost-effective arms marking techniques, together with the exchange of information on small arms production, stocks, and transfers, should further enhance transparency, be it global or regional in scope. All weapons should be marked (showing for example the year and place of manufacture, as well as current ownership) so that records can be maintained and each movement of each weapons traced. Arms tracking by means of marking holds markets and governments to higher standards of accountability.

NATIONAL EXPORT CONTROLS

National legislation on the manufacture, possession, use, trade, transport and circulation of small arms must be revised and reinforced. Export control norms must be set and concrete and practical measures supporting their implementation developed. Export permits of limited duration should be granted on a case-by-case basis and, consistent with international agreements, arms control initiatives and possibly existent UN embargoes, should be guided by weighing the risk of adverse economic, political, or social impact within the recipient nation, as well as the human rights, terrorism, and proliferation records of the country in question. Governments should be encouraged to exercise unilateral restraint where such action is effective and not impeded by overriding national interests. Restraint must apply to the transfer of "surplus" weapons as well.

A new emphasis must be placed on enforcement at both, the national and regional level, especially in order to confront the globalization of the black market in small arms and new operational linkages between political and criminal groups. Practical control measures must be enhanced at national and international levels, such as police and customs cooperation must be strengthened and border patrols improved. Model regulations on small arms transfers should be developed to confront new transnational threats, including the production, distribution, and abuse of narcotics, illegal arms trafficking and terrorism. Internationally operating criminals, the "merchants of death," must be identified, apprehended and prosecuted to the fullest extent of the law. States must be supported in their serious efforts to restrict the flows of small arms into their countries and sub-regions. Partnerships could be developed to improve the capacity of law enforcement, customs and border patrol to monitor and control arms flows and accumulations. International assistance to help develop national and community capacity to combat illicit trafficking in arms is essential.

Authorizing systems must be established for small arms manufacturers, dealers and, in particular, brokers. Increasingly, as controls on arms brokering are weak in many countries, brokering agents are found responsible for a majority of "illicit" arms shipments into regions of conflict. Too often efforts to control arms brokering are undermined by brokering agents moving offshore, where controls are less stringent or even absent. An international response to the brokering of small arms is necessary. A comprehensive control regime should be put in place to regulate the activities of national and international agents who engage in the business of brokering with respect to the manufacture, export, import or transfer of small arms. There should be government licensing requirements for corporate and individual arms brokering activities. In order to reinforce and strengthen national laws, corporations and individuals should be subject to national jurisdiction for their worldwide arms brokering activities. Such an approach would also help States avoid becoming unwitting parties to illegal arms trafficking; aid in verifying the accuracy of arms export applications both before and after export authorizations, prevent misuse and diversion, help identify and apprehend international criminals and ensure their prosecution to the fullest extent of the law.

AN INTERNATIONAL CODE OF CONDUCT

Governments have foremost responsibility for controlling arms manufacture and transfers. Existing laws and regulations have failed in halting the illicit manufacture and trafficking in small arms. Since small arms tend to flow from unregulated to regulated areas, a purely national response would be of little consequence. Rather, multilateral cooperation is called for on international standards for domestic controls as well as international standards for tracking the flow of weapons. A concrete possibility could be to revise the "Principles Governing Conventional Arms Transfers" to include amendments that specifically address the proliferation of small arms. A more comprehensive approach is, however, in conformity with Art.

26 of the UN Charter, to reach agreement on an effective export control regime based on universal principles for the regulation of small arms transfers. Integral to responsible national export policies, an international code must promote national and multilateral responsibility, restraint, control and transparency.

An international code of conduct must control the legal manufacture, transit and transfer of small arms, including subcomponents, munitions, delivery systems, military and security training, and sensitive military and dual-use-technology, in order to confront illicit diversions from the licit trade. With theft, corruption or neglect contributing significantly to the availability of small arms to the illicit trade, States should be required to undertake greater efforts in ensuring adequate safeguards. In this regard, the UN could provide a focus for sharing vital information on stockpile management and safe management of small arms. At the same time, the illicit manufacture must be addressed.

The International Code should set clear standards for arms transfer eligibility. Governments should be held to free and fair elections, human rights and civil liberties protection and respect for international law. Those governments that have not already done so should be required to integrate respect for humanitarian law and human rights into relevant national systems and international agreements relating to development and arms transfers and their implementation. Moreover, civilian control over the military and transparency in military spending should be assured. At the same time, a government could not be engaged in a civil war, international conflict, or sponsoring international terrorism. Arms transfers must take into account an analysis of their impact on regional and national security. In addition, all nations would be required to participate in the UN Small Arms Register, to respect international arms embargoes and military sanctions. Small arms transfers to States not party to the Code are prohibited. Overall, government to government transfers should be restricted.

In order to enhance export and import licensing standards, the Code should require requests for authorization to contain an authorization manifesto which includes, inter alia, a number which is unique to the country of issuance, the name of the issuing country, date of issuance, identification of authorizing party, identification of importer, quantity, value, type, manufacturer, model and country of manufacture and expiration date. To prevent misuse, unauthorized re-exportation and post-export diversion, increased efforts must be placed on verifying the accuracy of small arms export applications both before and after export authorization. In particular, arms exports should be subject to the provision of a valid end-user certificate.

Should an export license have been rejected by one State party to the international code, then another State issuing the same license should be required to inform on its reasoning in so doing. Moreover, the Code should strengthen licensed arms production standards. Under an approved arms production license, an arms company in one country permits a company in another country to produce weapons on its territory. Unfortunately, as export controls in the second country may prove to be of a lower standard, many weapons designed and initially produced in restrictive countries tend to flow to sensitive destinations from less restrictive countries. Therefore, the same checks that are being applied to direct arms exports must be applied to licensed arms production, as well.

At the same time, obligatory third party liability insurance should be required for every small arm produced or traded. Original owners must be held liable for the damages incurred by their small arms during the illicit phase of their life cycle. It should be irrelevant that the damaging act itself is, by whatever reason, perpetrated by a third person. Such liability insurance would protect victims of gun violence. It would force small arms producers and dealers to act more responsibly and would protect the taxpayer from being shouldered with the bill.

Third party liability should be coupled with clear norms of civilian non-possession. Fully automatic assault rifles, for example, should be barred from civilian use. There must be clear distinction between the kinds of weapons that are legitimately available to military and law enforcement officers and those available to civilians. Advertising for small arms should be restricted. These measures are not aimed at banning appropriate possession and use for sporting or self-defence purposes.

An important element of the Code must be stringent measures to curtail the black market. A lucrative black market, encompassing "non-sanctioned" activities of non-state actors, such as brokers, transportation agents and the like, operating outside the reach of state authority and accepted standards of humanitarian law and often in contravention of existing embargoes, has sprung up to meet an ever growing demand. The black market in small arms cannot be seen in isolation but, if alone from a law enforcement perspective, must be viewed within the context of other illicit markets in commodities, such as drugs and precious stones.

A good approach to curtailing the black market is to increase the cost of trafficking. Towards that end, profits derived from trafficking must be reduced and stiffer penalties imposed. First, there is too much money to be had in small arms trafficking, especially in relation to punishment. Increasing the cost of small arms should have the dual effect of reducing profit margins for traffickers and of making it harder for groups to accumulate them in large quantities. Secondly, illicit small arms trafficking must be punishable, even if it occurs abroad. Nationals of any country even when operating abroad must be subject to national jurisdiction.

The principle of extra-territoriality, which is already enforceable for the trade in human beings, should be extended to the illicit arms trade. It is inadmissible that crossing the borders makes one immune from prosecution. Moreover, illegal trafficking in small arms should be penalized as a treaty crime before the International Criminal Court.

As a significant element of the black market owes its existence to surrogate services, which they extend to governments in covert operations, governments commit themselves to restrict covert arms shipments and to report them to a confidential supervisory panel of the UN Register on Small Arms. For too long, connections between intelligence, law enforcement communities and traffickers have permitted this part of the black market to operate with near impunity.

Finally, the international community should adopt a more systematic approach towards imposing and enforcing arms embargoes or import-export moratoria in regions of violent conflicts, rising tensions or continuing blatant human right violations. Where such embargoes exist, measures have to be taken to ensure their strict implementation. Within this context, the Security Council should give a broader mandate to implement relevant SC resolutions.

IMPACT OF SMALL ARMS PROLIFERATION

The persistence and the complication of wars in Africa are partially due to small arms proliferation. The consequences of small arms on African people due to international conflicts within Africa, rebel group activities, mercenary groups, and armed gang activities have yet to be fully measured. The International Action Network on Small Arms, Saferworld, and Oxfam International put it in perspective when they reported that armed conflict cost Africa $18 billion each year and about US$300 billion between 1990-2005. During this period, 23 African nations experienced war: Algeria, Angola, Burundi, Central Africa Republic, Chad, Democratic Republic of Congo (DRC), Republic of Congo, Cote d'Ivoire, Djibouti, Eritrea, Ethiopia, Ghana, Guinea, Guinea-Bissau, Liberia, Niger, Nigeria, Rwanda, Senegal, Sierra Leone, South Africa, Sudan, and Uganda.

Although proliferation of small arms generates a lot of money for those who manufacture and trade them, African people pay a heavy price due to a lack of accountability or international regulations to address the abuses those products cause. According to the Global Facilitation Network Security Sector Reform, nations such as France, Russia, China, UK and USA – the five permanent members of the UN Security Council – together account for 88 percent of the world's conventional arms exports. These exports contribute regularly to gross abuses of human rights in Africa and elsewhere. Some of these are legal arms sales to irresponsible governments who use them to oppress the people. Other supplies are made available to rebel groups by some countries in an effort to overthrow dictatorial regimes which in many cases become worse or as bad as the previous regime. The United States and France, for example, assisted Chadian President Idriss Deby in removing his predecessor, Hissene Habre, from power. Deby then became another dictator who still has not stabilized his country.

Is violence the only tool we have to bring about change? Whoever said "who wants peace, prepares for war" was wrong in this case. Violence is not the answer to the root causes and triggers of instability in Africa. Nonviolence still stands in the forefront as a means of bringing about true peace. While the root causes of violence in Africa vary, it is unquestionable that small arms are a major challenge to security. The United Nations Security Council's report on small arms, S/2008/258, expresses it well by saying that "[T]he dividing lines between underdevelopment, instability, fragility, crisis, conflict and war are increasingly blurred; the small arms issue is therefore intertwined with the security, development, and human rights preconditions for sustainable peace. Present-day conflict prevention, conflict resolution, and peacebuilding require multidimensional interventions."

In fact, more than ever before, strong measures and appropriate attention must be given to this issue. The United Nation's General Assembly resolution (A/C.1/63/L.39*) on the arms trade treaty aims to establish common international standards for the import, export and transfer of conventional arms. It states that the absence of these standards is "one of the contributory factors to conflict, the displacement of people, crime and terrorism, thereby undermining peace, reconciliation, safety, security, stability and sustainable social and economic development." In addition to finding a solution to the proliferation of small arms, manufacturers and traders of small weapons should bear partial responsibility for the abuses and crimes that are committed as a consequence of use of these arms. Among nations that are culpable, let us single out the United States, as Africa Faith and Justice Network's mission is to advocate for just and fair U.S.-Africa relations. The same way U.S military policies in Africa have promoted dictatorship rather than democracy, the presence of American made weapons on the African continent has hurt the African people more than it has helped. The U.S. is aware that some of their legally transferred weapons contribute to feeding the illegal arms market. It was U.S. made weapons that supported the rebel groups RENAMO in Mozambique, UNITA in Angola, RPF in Rwanda and CNDP in the Democratic Republic of the Congo (DRC). In the UN experts' report on the crisis in the DRC, S/2008/773, paragraph 28 connects the origin of military uniforms shipment destined to the rebel group CNDP from the United

States in these terms: "In October 2008, Rwandan security services seized a shipment of uniforms destined for CNDP at Kanombe airport in Kigali. ... The shipment reportedly originated in Boston, Massachusetts, United States." Although this shipment contained uniquely military uniforms, it does not rule out the possibility that weapons were shipped from the U.S destined to CNDP.

Political instability in Africa continues to create more demand for small arms. Manufacturers of weapons know best the link between politics and weapons markets and are therefore often linked to these political instabilities to take advantage of the weapons business it creates. For example, former Congresswoman Ms. Cynthia McKinney of Georgia, in her opening remarks before the Subcommittee on International Operations and Human Rights of the Committee on International Relations of the US House of Representatives on May 17th, 2001, stated that " [W]hat we do know is that the U.S. Special Forces and U.S funded private military companies have been arming and training Rwandan and Ugandan troops to deadly effect. The U.S. taxpayer should be directly assisting the military efforts of Rwanda and Uganda, the aggressors in this tragic conflict and who are confirmed by Amnesty International and Human Rights Watch as the authors of terrible atrocities against Congolese civilians. Our efforts in Africa have amounted to nothing more than bankrolling belligerent and mass murders." War creates a demand for weapons. This is why manufacturers and traders are opposed to international standards for small arms trade.

In addition to the illegal arms sales network, there is a link between the legal and the illegal trade that consists of illegally selling legally obtained arms. This is the core of the problem of small arms proliferation which violators are not interested in solving. As of September 26, 2008, the United States of America, France, Russia, and permanent members of the UN Security Council had not signed the protocol against the illicit Manufacturing of and Trafficking in Firearms, Their Parts and Components and Ammunition, a supplement to the United Nations convention against Transnational Organized Crimes. Africa Faith and Justice Network, in its advocacy effort to the US government for peace and stability in Africa, calls upon

President Obama's administration to take a leadership role on this long overdue issue. We recommend that the U.S. signs the international Arms Trade Treaty by the United Nations, passes legislation to hold violators accountable, and reforms its arms production and export policy. Such legislation should include ways to track down U.S. weapons wherever they are used to prevent illegal arms trade from the U.S. to Africa and elsewhere.

PROLIFERATION OF SMALL ARMS AND LIGHT WEAPONS

The end of the Cold War removed constraints inherent to superpower rivalry, and contributed to an outbreak of inter-state and intra-state wars and conflicts, often of a religious or ethnic character and often involving unusual violence and cruelty. In addition, some of the proxy wars fuelled during the Cold War decades within states remained unresolved. These wars and conflicts were fought not only by regular armies, but also by militias and armed civilians, in support of the regular forces. They had to be armed and in the process this led to an excessive and uncontrolled proliferation of small arms and light weapons (SALW). The decade of the 90s particularly saw expanding civil wars, in former Yugoslavia, mass starvation in Somalia and so forth, arising out of civil wars enlarging into ethnic cleansing. To control the increasing incidents of regional and inter-state conflicts, Boutros Boutros Ghali, the new Secretary-General of the United Nations at the time, came up with an 'Agenda for Peace' in June 1992, stressing a central role that ought to be played by the UN, and reviewed the various methods for a more effective role of the Security Council in preventing, controlling or resolving disputes through preventive diplomacy, peace-keeping, peace-making and peace-related efforts, as well as for arms control and disarmament. By 1993, the 'Agenda for Peace' was already under criticism for UN's ineffectiveness, given that fratricide grew into ethnic cleansing in Yugoslavia, the peace mission to Somalia failed miserably, there was a political standoff in Haiti, and civil chaos surfaced in Zaire and Tajikistan.

At that point, SALW were considered responsible for deaths and violence in most conflicts and for the collapse of state institutions, especially the police and judiciary, with resulting paralysis of governance, a breakdown of law and order, and general anarchic conditions of banditry and chaos. The SALW used in these conflicts and civil wars were mainly acquired during the Cold War. However, after the Cold War, the SALW used in these conflicts were proliferated through arms black markets, private production, and smuggling. As a result, the full extent of the destabilising consequences of an excessive accumulation, proliferation, transfer and use of small arms and light weapons began to be felt as a major global threat. It led to the re-evaluations of security in international forums such as the UN.

In 1995, in a position paper, entitled 'Supplement to Agenda for Peace' the UN Secretary-General noted that while there were some agreed upon global norms and standards against weapons of mass destruction, there were no such norms or standards that could be used against the excessive and destabilising accumulation of small arms and light weapons. It was then realised that uncontrolled proliferation of small arms and light weapons posed, and continues to pose, a major non-traditional threat to international as well as regional peace and security. The 1995, General Assembly resolution 50/70B first raised the issue of proliferation of SALW. In this resolution, the UNGA, by reaffirming the role of the UN in the field of disarmament stated its realisation regarding SALW in the following words.

'That arms obtained through the illicit arms trade are most likely to be used for violent purposes and that even small arms when so obtained, directly or indirectly, by terrorist groups, drug traffickers or underground organisations can pose a danger to regional and international security, and certainly to the security and political stability of the countries affected.' As a result, the UN Secretary-General established a panel Group of Governmental Experts on Small Arms to report on types of SALW, nature and causes of their proliferation, and the ways and means to prevent and reduce the excessive and destabilising accumulation and transfer of small arms and light weapons, as they cause or exacerbate conflict. At that time many prevailing conflicts inflicted heavy causalities on the people involved, and the victims were mostly women and children. It was estimated that, by 1996, over 35 million people in 23 countries throughout the world were at risk of facing civil strife, either owing to ongoing humanitarian crises, or as a result of a slow recovery from past ones.

The Group of Governmental Experts on Small Arms held a number of different regional and international workshops and finally presented its consolidated report in 1997 on types of SALW, nature and causes of their proliferation, and recommendations to control and prevent their proliferation. In this report, Bangladesh, Sri Lanka, Nepal, Pakistan and India shared the growing concern over the trans-boundary movement of illicit and covert arms trade from Afghanistan, and emphasised on the need for a worldwide campaign to raise global consciousness of the consequences of the inflow to, and outflow of, weapons from Afghanistan. The 1997 report by Governmental Experts on Small Arms acted as a catalyst and placed the issue of SALW on the international agenda. On December 9, 1997, the UNGA endorsed all issues raised by the report in its resolution 52/38J. In 1998, the UNGA established another Group of Governmental Experts on Small Arms to assist the UN Secretary-General to prepare a report on the progress made in the implementation of the recommendations of the 1997 report and further actions recommended to be taken. On August 19, 1999 the UN Secretary-General presented the report of Group of Governmental Experts on Small Arms to the UNGA, in preventing and reducing the excessive and destabilising accumulation of small arms and light weapons. As a result of these efforts the UNGA decided to convene an international conference on the illicit arms trade in all its aspects no later than 2001.

In October 2000, the UN Secretary-General Kofi Annan, in his Millennium Report, 'We the People', presented to the UNGA, attached a special concern to the problems associated with proliferation of SALW. Significantly, Annan described small arms as 'weapons of mass destruction' because the death toll from small arms dwarfed that of all other weapons systems, and in most years greatly exceeded the toll of the atomic bombs that had devastated Hiroshima and Nagasaki. Annan further said that

'The proliferation of small arms, and munitions and explosives has also aggravated the violence associated with terrorism and organised crime. Even in societies not beset by civil war, the easy availability of small arms has in many cases contributed to violence and political instability. These, in turn, have damaged development prospects and imperilled human security in every way. Small arms proliferation is not merely a security issue; it is also an issue of human rights and of development. The proliferation of small arms sustains and exacerbates armed conflicts. It endangers peacekeepers and humanitarian workers. It undermines respect for International Humanitarian Law (IHL). It threatens legitimate but weak governments and it benefits terrorists as well as the perpetrators of organised crime.'

In his Millennium Report, Annan urged the Member States to participate fully in the UN Conference on Small Arms in order to take serious actions to curtail the illicit trade in small arms. From July 9-20, 2001, the UN Conference on the Illicit Trade in Small Arms and Light Weapons in All Its Aspects took place at New York. In order to combat and eradicate the illicit trade in SALW, the States adopted a wide range of political undertakings at the national, regional and global levels. The significant step was the adoption of the Programme of Action (PoA) with consensus by the Member States. The PoA mainly covers the areas of legislation, destruction of weapons that were confiscated, seized, or collected, as well as international cooperation and assistance to strengthen the ability of States in identifying and tracing illicit arms and light weapons. Finally, the Member States agreed to hold a review conference in 2006, as well as biennial meetings along the way. These meetings would allow NGOs and governments to keep the momentum moving forward on the small arms issue under the PoA framework.

On December 23, 2003, the UNGA passed resolution 58/241 and established an open-ended working group to negotiate an international instrument to enable States to identify and trace, in a timely and reliable manner, illicit small arms and light weapons. The working group is making its every effort to ensure that a positive outcome would be achieved.

In February 2005, the United Nations Secretary-General presented its report of 'Small Arms' to the UNSC and recommended that the UNSC and the UNGA should establish a committee to look into how the two organs could work together in the areas of illicit SALW brokering. The UNSC declaring its primary responsibility for maintaining international peace and security, also appealed to the arms-exporting countries 'to exercise the highest responsibility in small arms and light weapons transactions' in accordance with international law.

Currently, more than 640 million items of SALW are in circulation around the world. Around 59% of it are owned or controlled by civilians while the rest are owned by governments, armed forces, police, insurgents and other non-state forces. The annual trade in small arms is about $40 billion. Two-thirds of global arms deliveries go to the developing countries. Small arms are produced by more than 1,000 companies in at least 98 countries, with about 7 million new arms produced annually. Since 1990, more than four million people have been killed, the majority of them were civilians (90%) of whom an overwhelming 80% were women and children. According to a recent report from the UN, 'two million children have been killed in the last ten years in conflicts where small arms have been used; five million have been disabled, and twelve million left homeless.' A 'small arm' thus exists for every twelve persons in the world.

The same is the case with South Asia where proliferation of SALW is very high. In South Asia the proliferation of SALW is linked to insurgencies, ethnic and sectarian violence, organised crimes, political movements and private militias, terrorist activities, inter-state wars, guerrilla warfare and many other violence-related activities. Proliferation of SALW is not only threatening human security, but also impacting on the societal peace, livelihood and economic development of the countries and the communities of the region. It is not an easy task to control the menace of SALW so as to end human misery and sufferings in South Asia.

Since the introduction of the PoA, Pakistan, India, Sri Lanka, and Bangladesh have implemented PoA and submitted their respective national reports on voluntary basis. These reports deal with legal, administrative and procedural measures to combat proliferation of SALW. Despite these measures, the menace of small arms is still prevailing in their respective societies. There is a need to identify weaknesses and problems in these measures to devise a coherent regional approach to address the problems of SALW. There is a growing need that South Asian states should proactively participate in the first UN review conference in 2006 to curb proliferation of SALW, since South Asia itself has such a proliferation of SALW. A coherent regional approach would contribute towards strengthening an international mechanism to curb the proliferation of SALW in all its aspects, because a regional approach is an effective mechanism to curb proliferation of SALW which is a trans-border phenomenon.

Against this background, this paper provides a brief comparative survey of SALW in the South Asian region, and follows that up with an evaluation of the current measures adopted by the South Asian states to address the problems associated with effective legislation, administrative regulations and procedures to curb proliferation of SALW, as signatories to the PoA. It is difficult to have a precise number of small arms users in South Asia. Statistics available from country to country are scarce and not updated enough and yet they present a dismal and a grim picture. Sources of arms proliferation, illegal private ownerships, and illegal smuggling are also additional problems that need to be seriously studied for their impact areas. Lastly the study would discuss the possibilities of regional cooperation in order to develop a more coherent regional solution in line with the international efforts to curb the proliferation of SALW.

PROLIFERATION OF SMALL ARMS AND LIGHT WEAPONS IN SOUTH ASIA

According to the UN Deputy Secretary General, Louise Fréchette, 'No region, no country is immune from the devastating consequences of the proliferation of small arms and light weapons..., [which] severely hampers social and economic development.' South Asia is no exception to how SALW poses a non-traditional security threat. Regardless of age, gender, status or location, all are targets. Moreover, even children can be trained on how to use them. Private ownership of SALW is widespread and they can be obtained very cheaply. The SALW firearms in South Asia mostly originate from western nations. The spread of SALW grew in the wake of Afghan War during the 70s and 80s as refugee communities and volunteers were co-opted along side the regular cadres to fight the Soviet Army, and they had to be armed. Similarly, the end of declared war in Cambodia made available large numbers of small weapons that eventually found their way into Sri Lanka and northeastern India. There are now an estimated 75 million firearms in South Asia, 63 million of which are in civilian hands. India and Pakistan overwhelmingly account for most of the weapons (40 million and 20 million respectively) where there is local production as well, while civilians in Nepal and Sri Lanka own an estimated 3 million weapons. Non-State actors are getting hold of government weapons and re-exporting them to armed groups fighting insurgencies in other countries. The possession of small arms by politicians is also a growing problem across the subcontinent as owning private militia has become both a status symbol, as well as political clout against adversaries. Despite state regulations, several political leaders have not surrendered their arms to their government and still hold unlicensed arms. Politicians use these weapons to intimidate opponents and voters, patronise the underworld and criminal syndicates in order to protect themselves and thus pose a serious threat to the democratic process itself.

In Bangladesh, most of the weapons in circulation are those that were not collected after its 1971 independence war. Bangladesh is also being used as a corridor for smuggling firearms. Currently, Bangladesh has more than 200,000 small arms and most of these are with various organised criminal gangs and their political godfathers. There are about 80 crime syndicates around the country of which more than 28 are active in Dhaka alone. Politicians, too, use armed private militia to protect themselves, as well as to intimidate opponents. Law-makers are also turning a blind eye both to border patrol agents who are poorly equipped and to police officers who rent out their arms to criminals and terrorists. Clandestine manufacturers operate small operations that can be set up, dismantled and relocated overnight. In 2002, Bangladesh introduced tighter controls on firearms, but the problem remains.

Indian's record of small arms is the highest in the region which accounts for around 40 million contraband firearms. In India, all possible problems associated with the proliferation of small arms are to be found: illegal manufacture, theft from State arsenals, licensing loopholes, lax enforcement, cross-border smuggling, political violence, unregulated private security and a movie culture that often glorifies firepower and revenge by those defiant of authority. In India, small arms have eroded human rights, weakened democratic institutions, and polarised ethnic, religious, economic and political differences between citizens. Tensions between Hindu and Muslim groups in India under state patronage are one of the country's major sources of violence. In early 2002, up to 2000 Muslims were massacred in India in state of Gujarat. India also banned 32 organisations under the Prevention of Terrorism Act (POTA) for their activities. Although the Government of India (GoI) has taken several steps it still faces the problems of proliferation of SALW. Currently New Delhi is in the process of drafting a proposal to the United Nations seeking a global ban on small-arms sales to non-state actors. According to reports from a senior Home Ministry official, 'If a global ban is achieved, it would help to improve the security situation in the country.'

Nepal has been suffering from destabilising effects of SALW in the hands of its Maoists. About a decade ago, an aerial fire or the use of tear gas in Nepal would have caused a national hue and cry and national/international coverage of the news. Now, even two digit death statistics have become routine news. Deaths and injuries from small arms have become like an 'epidemic' in Nepal. While the main sources of proliferation of small arms are the Maoist insurgency, criminality and the political elite are no less responsible.

The Maoists rebels have stolen their weapons from police outposts and other government arsenals, while other criminal gangs are engaged in smuggling drugs for guns and money-laundering along the Indian border. Women are often used as carriers of small arms in illicit trafficking. It is estimated that one-third of the Maoist fighters are women. At the community level it is often known who owns arms and where they are kept. After the restoration of democracy in 1993, politicians resorted to all available means to win elections, including armed intimidation. Although a tentative ceasefire agreement was signed between the Government and the Maoists, but the proliferation of SALW remains unabated.

The ratio of SALW proliferation in Pakistan is the second highest in the region. In Pakistan there is a close linkage between organised groups, narcotics, money-laundering, terrorism activities and illicit trade in SALW. The proliferation of SALW and terrorism emerged as one of the main problems after the 1979 Soviet invasion of Afghanistan, when the US covertly armed thousands of 'Mujahedeen' with millions of SALWs, a great number of which eventually found their way into Pakistan along with the refugees who sought asylum. Pakistan's indigenous arms manufacturing cottage industry in the northwest tribal areas named as 'Darra Adamkhel' has fuelled-up the conflict-prone legacy of society with millions of small arms.

Darra's 'father-and-son' arms industry has existed for generations as a family legacy and traditionally, as a cottage arms production industry, has been outside the jurisdiction of central authorities. According to recent estimates, Darra employs more than 400,000 people. Prior to the Soviet invasion of Afghanistan in 1979, these shops produced mainly repeating rifles. The steady influx of weapons from various sources during the war enhanced the local manufacturer's knowledge, skills and production capacities.

The Darra region annually produces approximately 20,000 units of all kinds of weapons, including AK-47. It is estimated that in the past 20 years as a result of on going antagonisms between tribes, sectarianism, ethnicity, terrorism, organised crimes and poor law and order situation have sharpened into ethnic and community divides. Gun-related violence has resulted in more than 500,000 killings around the country. In 2001, the Government of Pakistan (GoP) launched a country-wide anti-arms drive in a bid to curb the 'Kalashnikov culture.' The Government devised a multi-pronged and phased 'de-weaponisation' strategy which includes: banning the display of weapons in public, the buying back of arms, recovering illicit arms and regulating production in the tribal areas. Initially a public awareness campaign was launched with an amnesty period for the surrender of illicit SALWs. After the expiry of the amnesty period, campaign for weapons collection and recovery were launched. Until 2003, around 250,000 illicit SALW firearms of different categories and types were recovered or confiscated, in addition to large amount of ammunition. While this ambitious effort has been praised nationally and internationally, Pakistan civil society is calling for a broader policy framework to address the underlying challenges of under-development which lead to proliferation, namely: the need for economic incentives as an alternative for 'culture of weaponisation'. Despite the official ban on sale and purchase of non-licensed weapons, unauthorised arms and ammunition remain in circulation and the illegal arms trade and gunrunning continues.

The status of proliferation of SALW in Sri Lanka can be attributed to many factors such as the internal armed conflicts, arms and political campaigns, arms held by deserters and criminals, as well as arms owned by private security firms and deteriorating public safety due to criminal activities. One of the main primary sources of SALW proliferation is the internal conflict between Government and the LTTE which has caused more than 65,000 deaths. Although a ceasefire was signed in February 2002, between Government and the LTTE, the circulation of weapons will continue to be a security threat to ordinary Sri Lankans. Meanwhile, it has now become common practice for politicians to raise private armies to literally fight elections for them; and, the generous funding these mercenary armies receive are drawing even government soldiers to join their ranks. Furthermore, politicians offer protection to members of criminal gangs who become allies thus impeding the efforts of police to combat the growing problem of organised crime in the country. According to some rough open source estimates there are more than 2 million firearms in circulation in Sri Lanka. 90% of the illegal arms in circulation are said to come from the Government. Finally, all smuggling from outside Sri Lanka comes by sea routes, and coastal patrols are lacking. The Sri Lankan Government has taken several steps to address the problem through the implementation of relevant legislation, namely amnesty for surrender of illegal arms, registration of existing arms, and attempts to collect weapons and so forth. In January 2002, an amnesty for surrender of illegal arms was offered by the Ministry of Interior but did not produce the expected results. In 2004, disarmament, demobilisation and reintegration (DDR) of ex-combatants, including in many cases child soldiers, started in Sri Lanka which still has to yield its results.

EVALUATION OF MEASURES ADOPTED BY THE SOUTH ASIAN STATES

This section will briefly evaluate the different legal and administrative measures so far taken by South Asian governments to curb the proliferation of SALW in their countries. Four out of six countries have a common legislative history as a colonial legacy which is the Arms Act of 1878. That each country has a legislative framework, rules and regulations regarding issuing of licences and documentation for the legal export and import of firearms and ammunition. All five countries also have provisions regarding domestic production, markings, record-keeping, seizures, penalties and security, safety and management of the stockpiles in custody. However, the scope and stringency of these stipulations varies from country to country.

Bangladesh has made no amendment to its 1878 Act so far, and its current legislation is unable to cope with the present challenges of SALW and, therefore, is considered the weakest in the region. The Sri Lanka Firearms Ordinance has the strictest limitations on exports and imports in South Asia but it does not clearly define what a 'firearm' is and still facing the problems of SALW proliferation from its rebels. Despite provisions for a manufacturing licence, Bangladesh, India and Pakistan have a growing problem with small arms from cottage industries falling into the hands of non-State actors. In Nepal, licensing requirements for manufacturing small arms are very weak. Even a Chief District Officer can issue a licence to favourite persons by his discretionary powers. In India, a police report is not absolutely necessary for the issuing of a permit to own a locally-manufactured firearm. The Government of Sri Lanka, on the other hand, is planning to put a moratorium on the licensing of small arms.

Provisions for the seizures also vary from country to country. In Bangladesh and Pakistan, a magistrate determines if possession is illegal. In India and Nepal, the government has the discretion to seize arms in order to protect public peace and safety. Sri Lanka has the toughest laws, wherein the threshold for seizure is the lowest; any authorised officer can confiscate a weapon on the suspicion that the holder does not have a licence. As far as markings are concerned only the Indian and Sri Lankan gun laws require every firearm made to bear the name of the manufacturer, a serial number and the place of production. Detailed marking allows for weapons to be traced back to the individual manufacturer and serial number, and serves to check illicit possession and to prevent illegal transfers.

All the South Asian countries except India make it mandatory for gun-dealers to maintain proper records of the numbers of firearms in its possession or control. These national laws allow government officers, at least in theory, to ask weapons-dealers to account for the firearms in their inventory at any time. All five South Asian countries' legislation contain penalties for contraventions of restrictions on manufacture, possession and transfer. Punishment ranges from six months imprisonment to death, and the imposition of a fine, alone or concurrently. As a part of their international commitment, the South Asian states also participated in the 2001 UN Conference on Illicit Trade of SALW and agreed to implement the UN PoA, which is a politically binding document endorsed by consensus, as the central global agreement on preventing and reducing trafficking and proliferation of SALW. In practice, the UN PoA establishes an international programme of relatively comprehensive scope, including almost the full range of issues specified in the 1997 and 1999 Reports of the UN Groups of Experts. Thus, it contains substantial agreed-upon norms, standards and programmes on a number of issues, including:

- Preventing and combating illicit SALW production and trafficking;
- Ensuring effective controls on the legal production, holding and transfer of SALW;
- Weapons collection and destruction;
- Management and security of official and authorised SALW stocks;
- SALW control in post-conflict situations; and
- Information exchange and confidence-building.

From a South Asian perspective it is also necessary to have an overview of the implementation of the UN PoA in order to draw a coherent regional approach which in turn would contribute towards building a base for an effective international mechanism to curb problems associated with SALW in all its aspects.

In implementing PoA no coordinated regional action has been taken by the South Asian states. Although attempts were made to implement the PoA at national level, but no major legislative change has been made by any government since the introduction of PoA. However, comparative analysis and evaluation of governmental efforts indicate that in key areas existing laws are not adequate enough in terms of implementation to control the proliferation of SALW in all its aspects. South Asian states are also lacking mechanisms to implement the existing regulations and procedures in order to control illicit trafficking and use. States also lack consistency and coordination to monitor legal trade and enforcing penalties for illicit exchange. Cottage industries are not strictly regulated and as a result smuggled exports to non-state actors are also increasing. The existing framework of the UN PoA is also unable to deal with domestic production. All South Asian states lack standardised export and import licensing and documentation mechanism, especially when corruption is prevalent within the governments and societies. States also lacks control over the political use of SALW. However, Nepal is the only country where legislation explicitly deals with weapons and elections. Above all there is need for a comprehensive regional approach to deal with all theses problems associated with proliferation of SALW in such a way that each state can benefit from its results nationally as well as regionally.

A Coherent Regional Approach

In the field of arms control and disarmament much more needs to be done, not only in the context of nuclear, biological and chemical weapons but also to prevent the proliferation of SALW in all its aspects. In the South Asian context such proliferation of SALW exists mainly due to poor governance and mis-management of law and order as well as the inability or unwillingness of governments to address security-related reforms. South Asian states should take drastic initiatives at national as well as at regional levels to formulate a coherent national and regional approach to curb SALW in all its aspects, in order to assure greater human security. Any future initiatives should be guided by the principles and purposes of the UN Charter, International Humanitarian Law (IHL), human rights, human security, political stability, law enforcement, social and economic development and de-weaponisation of societies. For the success of any regional initiative taken, confidence, trust and understanding, cooperation and information exchange, social and economic development and reduction of poverty are necessary elements. States should collectively identify the hurdles in their way to undertake any interlinked initiatives.

In order to draw a coherent regional approach the following measures should be adopted by South Asian countries to curb problems associated with SALW within their territories;

- Strengthening through modernisation, law-enforcement and intelligence agencies including Police, Customs and Border Control, and enhancement of judicial capacities.
- Establishment of national commissions to check the illicit proliferation of SALW. Such a Commission should serve as a forum for dialogue and discourses among political parties, law-enforcement agencies and civil society to devise and achieve consensus on effective strategies for curbing the proliferation of SALW and related regulations. Furthermore, establishing of a national co-ordination committee would help bring together relevant officials and departments for intra-provincial interactions.
- The unlicensed cottage arms industries could be strictly regulated. However, this has to be done by recognising the prevalent socio-economic conditions and providing viable alternative incentives which would probably work better than taking punitive measures. For example, the domestic producers could be designated the official small arms-makers to complement the bigger manufacturing units, which presently are all government-controlled.
- By making the domestic process more transparent, political influence should be checkmated by which political vested groups resort to the use of small arms

for violence. Political parties should be held responsible for any use of armed militia by its members, or display of weapons.

- Checks on civilian possessions of small arms and control over weapons designed for military should not fall in the hands of civilians.
- South Asian states should re-enact their existing legislations to eliminate loopholes and ensure its proper implementation to reduce the unauthorised use of small arms. Legislation should stipulate registration of brokers, transactions and penalties for illicit activities.
- Proliferation and illicit use of small arms can never be understood in isolation of economic and social development. Therefore, concerted initiatives involving South Asian countries need to be taken.
- All five countries should require legislation for proper markings for both locally manufactured and imported firearms;
- South Asian states blame each other for spreading small arms, however, possibilities of regional cooperation are there but a uniformity of ideas and efforts are needed. Pakistan's seven-stage de-weaponisation campaign is a good example and South Asian states would benefit by adopting similar strategies.
- SAARC is presently unable to discuss SALW concerns in order to avoid any bilateral wrangle. Its role should be expanded to cover problems of SALW. SAARC should evolve an integrated regional action programme for curbing proliferation of SALW. SAARC member states should set up a comprehensive regional convention on small arms and light weapons to investigate, expose and curb illicit arms trade and trafficking across South Asia. All states should be brought under a common legal umbrella for working towards non-proliferation of SALW.
- Collection, safe and secure stockpiling and eventual destruction of small arms should be ensured so that SALW do not get recycled back to criminals, organised groups and non-state actors. States should improve

management of authorised stocks at the point of production, transportation, and storage and record must be kept at every stage. Efficient record-keeping and databases of these stockpiles could serve as a basis for possible future co-operation and information sharing among states. It would be useful for all the countries of the region to extend mandatory record-keeping rules on small arms manufacturers to government agencies and their own stockpiles, as well as to individuals holding licenses to possess guns for private use.

- Money-laundering and safe havens abroad are the main factors behind the proliferation of small arms. In this regard a South Asian police force should be established to stop trafficking of small arms and its widespread use in the region.
- Public awareness and involvement of civil society is also necessary for curbing the element of violence in South Asian societies and prolonged awareness campaigns would serve to source the public apathy into civic action. To this end, informal exchanges, seminars and workshops at the level of non-governmental organisations, academics and media representatives could serve a useful purpose. Governments and civil society need to work together to implement the UN Programme of Action on small arms.
- Member States need to take stock of the challenges of effectively controlling their long porous borders and of associated problems of smuggling, narcotics trade, which in turn are closely linked to the illicit trade in SALWs. In this regard sharing of intelligence on known smuggling networks and illicit arms markets is required. The South Asian states have to muster their will for bilateral and regional co-operation to combat smuggling, the finding and destroying of arms caches.
- Proliferated small arms are mostly manufactured in western countries. There is a need to trace out their routes.
- There is a need to strengthen the Anti-Terrorism Convention adopted by the UN in April 2005. However,

there is the need also to clearly distinguish between legitimate right of self-determination and terrorism for political ends.

- SALW should be redefined to cover other traditional weapons such as knives, swords, machetes and hatchets which have been widely used during civil conflicts and riots by organised crimes. Rwanda and Burundi massacres were done by such weapons.

Strengthening of International Mechanisms

South Asian states are profoundly concerned about the problems associated with SALW and need to devise and adopt international legally-binding mechanisms, based on national, regional and international considerations for curbing proliferation of SALW. The mechanisms should enable South Asian states to control and prohibit the use of millions of SALW circulating in their territories. Any regional, sub-regional agreements and initiatives would in turn complement and reinforce global efforts to prevent, combat, and reduce the proliferation of SALW and their misuse. In this regard South Asian states should take concrete efforts to implement fully the UN PoA, and other related efforts for controlling SALW.

The proposed Draft Framework Convention on International Arms Transfer, 'the Framework Convention', is one example which can provide a legal framework within which further issues can be addressed over time, such as building up a series of interlocking instruments, and subsequent initiatives which could either take the form of protocols to the Convention or self-standing instruments associated with the Convention in some other way.

According to this Draft Convention, international arms transfer should be authorised through licensing. States should ensure that any arms transfer should not violate international law, the Charter of the UN, UNSC resolutions, customary international law, International Humanitarian Law (IHL), human rights, and international norms and treaties. It also states that the use of arms should also be prohibited which are capable of distinguishing between combatants and civilians, or which cause superfluous injury or unnecessary suffering, in serious violation of human rights, for genocides or crimes against humanity, and against violations of IHL. An international registry of international arms transfer should be maintained on an annual basis by the respective national report of every country. Generally this Convention covers almost all kinds of technical, procedural and theoretical aspects to curb proliferation of SALW in all its aspects.

The scope of traditional arms control and disarmament approaches should be extended to cover SALW as weapons of mass destruction, and on a priority basis a strengthened international binding mechanism to control SALW should be established. There is a need to adopt human security-centred policies. Emerging weapon technologies should be analysed as to how they undermine human security and strict state regulations ensure that they do not fall into the hands of non-state actors. Controlling proliferation of SALW is not only a multi-layered work, but also a multi-sectoral effort requiring the formation of partnerships based on national, regional and international levels. The 1997 anti-personnel Land Mines Convention is one such example. Implementation of existing norms, such as the Basic Principles on the Use of Force and Firearms, the UN Code of Conduct for Law Enforcement Officials, and the Firearms Protocol of the Transnational Crime Convention on priority basis is necessary for security and survival of human beings. Curtailment of civilian possession of small arms, security sector reforms, exchange of information between states, inter-regional and intra-regional cooperation, financial and technical help to weak countries are some of the measures which can give strength not only to a legally-binding mechanism, but can also heal the disrupted social fabric.

7

Small Arms Trade and Proliferation in Southeast Asia

INTRODUCTION TO SMALL ARMS PROLIFERATION

The proliferation of small arms is a complex and increasingly international issue. There are important linkages between the non-proliferation, arms control and disarmament dimensions of small arms problems, on the one hand, and firearms regulation (i.e., gun control and criminality) dimensions, on the other. The problems caused by small arms are primarily regional, sub-regional and internal (i.e., within states) in nature. As a result, while useful things may be done on a global level, a primary focus for practical solutions would appear to be in regional, sub-regional and internal action. It is important, therefore, to develop a body of relevant case studies of the impact of small arms proliferation in particular regions as a basis for policy action.

This project will examine the extent of small arms trade and proliferation in two geographical areas of East Asia — Southeast Asia and the Russian Far East. These two areas have significant possibility of experiencing small arms proliferation problems because of ethnic, cultural and political diversity, decades of post-colonial violence, and inadequate policing in both regions, and the emergence of major organized crime in the latter. The general problem of sub-state weaponry is not unique to the two regions, of course, but it is a particular aggravation to government and social order there. From Canada's perspective the problem may become larger as arms sales directly affect maritime trade and state stability in the regions, enter or pass through our territory, or involve criminal organizations within Canada.

The topic of our research is illicit trafficking of small arms and light weapons, as defined by the UN General Assembly. However in some cases it is hard to draw a distinct line between illicit and "legal" arms proliferation, in cases when high-rank state structures are involved in the above activity. The latter cases are also included into the scope of this research.

THE CASE OF SOUTHEAST ASIA

Southeast Asia saw a perverse "peace dividend" of small arms proliferation as early as 1975, with the end of the Vietnam War. An unknown quantity of weapons flowed out of Indo-China at that time into surrounding states, to guerrilla groups and pirates who plied the waters of Southeast Asia. The uneven development between major cities in the region and the more traditional rural regions, combined with the relatively weak presence of state police and military power in rural areas, and the mobility of watercraft, provided opportunities for arms traders to carry on their commerce undisturbed. Reports of rogue Chinese military trading in small arms must also be examined. Fallout from the recent "financial meltdown" in the region may also exacerbate crime growth in the near future. 1 The work for this paper was undertaken with the support of the Verification Research Program of Canada's Department of Foreign Affairs and International Trade. The views expressed in this paper are those of the authors alone.

THE CASE OF THE RUSSIAN FAR EAST

The end of the Cold War has had a direct effect on the phenomenon of small arms proliferation in Asia and elsewhere. The arms buildup in the Soviet Union was both in nuclear and conventional weapons, and with the end of Communism, the rationale for the heavy armaments declined precipitously. Moreover, the demoralization and impoverishment of Russian society and the Red Army has weakened government control over weaponry, which has become a commodity of trade in many cases. The socalled Russian Mafia, which had existed throughout the Soviet period, was lured by the illicit arms trade to facilitate the export of weapons.

IMPLICATIONS

The widespread demand for small weapons has been exacerbated by breakdown of local security and easy access. Relatively simple technology also means that manufacture and assembly does not require advanced industrial techniques. The model of the drug trade may be applicable, and indeed, one of the findings of the research is the linkage of the drug and small arms trade through the same trafficking routes and criminal organizations (not unlike the Latin American experience). Drugs and arms share some of the following characteristics in the two regions under study:

1. Widespread demand for the product;
2. Relatively high value per unit;
3. Relative ease of transportation;
4. Relative difficulty of detection;
5. High profit margin;
6. Corrosive effects on law enforcement within states;
7. Manufacture, shipment, and distribution requires illicit networks, which further undermine law and order; and
8. Long-range harm to society in the diversion of scarce resources to non-productive ventures.

Arms and drugs both have legitimate roles in society, when controlled and used for positive ends – police and defence in the former, and medical purposes in the latter (opiates are used for painkilling and sleep inducement). To the extent that the drug trade model is applicable to small arms proliferation, the above eight characteristics can provide entry points for reducing small arms flows, as follows:

1. Reduce supply and demand for the product;
2. Interdict transportation;
3. Improve detection capability and technology;
4. Clean up police and government corruption; and,
5. Improve enforcement capabilities, including international cooperation.

The Japanese have been successful in practically eliminating small weapons from society, and some lessons for Asia can be learned there. Unless the problem of small arms proliferation is brought under control, civil disorder and violence may become more widespread in the East Asian region. Drugs and small weapons are criminalized because they encourage and facilitate further crimes. Drugs create a dependency which can drive persons to engage in robbery and prostitution to acquire illegal substances, moving out of productive and responsible habits necessary to sustain social integrity. Guns decrease the vulnerability of criminals who undertake greater risks and anti-social actions, knowing that their weapons escalate the cost of challenging their actions.

But drugs also have major differences with small arms. Some trade in the latter is legitimate, as long as there is government sanction, while the illicit drug trade is practically proscribed universally.

Also, illicit drugs have accelerated the spread of diseases such as hepatitis and HIV, affecting individuals far beyond users. The indirect effect of small weapons is much more limited. Finally, the end users of weapons are usually men, and these tend to have profiles of greater criminality and aggressiveness than the average population, while drug users tend to be more passive and of both sexes. Most importantly, the trade in small weapons is an area which lends itself best to detection and reduction in the experience of arms control and verification. The legitimate production, distribution, and deployment of large and small weapons has been the jurisdiction and central interest of the arms control community. Accounting for disposition of large as well as light weapons, for example, has been one of the activities of the Neutral Nations Supervisory Commission (NNSC) under the 1953 Military Armistice Agreement in Korea. Other arms control agreements in other areas of the world have also included small weapons in their provisions.

IMPLICATIONS FOR CANADIAN INTERESTS

Further to the drug trade model, the damage to urban Canada is already visible. If small weapons become widespread, an additional source of civil disorder could challenge our cities, but the likelihood of unchecked small arms entering the country could reinforce criminal networks which find Canada an attractive haven. The Russian Mafia and Chinese Triads are possible candidates in this, and represent a most unsavoury vehicle for one type of globalization. Canada must understand the dimensions and impact of small arms proliferation in Asia and elsewhere in order to prevent large-scale penetration of these activities here.

In the past decade, Canada has identified East Asia as an area of major economic interest, in large part because of rapid growth in trade and immigration. CIDA has targeted the region for development assistance, and so we have growing interest in civil order. We are also dialogue partners with a growing number of countries there on a wide range of subjects. The Canadian navy has been a participant in RIMPAC and has been sending several ships every year on deployment and visits. In the past year (for several years in Japan), the East Asian "economic miracle" has halted, and extended economic problems there will undoubtedly challenge the social fabric and the capacity of governments to insure the domestic safety of their citizens. It is important for Canada to monitor the conditions of civil society, and small arms proliferation may be an excellent measure of social disorder, which correlates with other modes of social pathology including crime, drugs, and corruption.

Our trade, investment and immigration involvement in Asia is highly sensitive to conditions there. The dangers of foreign business in Russia are already legendary, and the same degree of jeopardy could occur in Asian markets with breakdown of governance and economic decline. At the same time, Canadian growing links with the region will mean that problems there will spillover into our own society faster than before, and early warnings are crucial — rather than to wait until small arms coming from or through Asia are a domestic issue here.

Finally, there is the humanitarian issue, most recently addressed in the landmines treaty. All civilians everywhere have a human right of fundamental safety of life and property. The proliferation of small weapons can endanger that right, undermine progress to democracy, and escalate the amount of force governments must use to enforce the law.

TYPES OF WEAPONS

By "small arms" we refer to the list of weapons provided by the Panel of Governmental Experts on Small Arms. The list includes revolvers and pistols, rifles and carbines, assault rifles, sub-machine guns, light and heavy machine-guns, grenade launchers, portable anti-tank and anti-aircraft guns and portable anti-aircraft missile-launchers. Proliferation of ammunition for the above list of weapons, as well as hand-grenades, portable mines and explosives is also included in the sphere of research.

SOUTHEAST ASIA

Scope of Research

The illicit movement of small arms and light weapons into, within and out of Southeast Asia, predominantly through illegal channels and the black market, is a dangerous phenomenon. Borrowing the definition used by the United Nations, illicit trafficking is the movement of weapons that is "contrary to the laws of States and/or international law." This phenomenon is of growing concern because it has the potential to undercut government efforts at establishing stability and order. Also, its potential disruption towards legitimate commercial activities can cause serious harm to economic and social development within the region.

The illicit movement of small arms is a human security concern since it has the potential to fuel increased numbers and levels of violent crimes. This perception mainly arises from the fear that there would be a surge in criminal activities resulting from increased economic hardship, which is induced presently by the region's financial turmoil. Violent crimes, in turn, could present a destabilizing force undermining state sovereignty. Governments in Southeast Asia (and the rest of Asia, in general) are worried about the growing illicit trade in small arms because a number of factors have allowed it to flourish steadily:

- inadequate controls against illicit weapons production, exports and imports at the national level due to poorly trained and/or corrupt officials;
- financial and technological difficulties in implementing effective controls;
- lack of coordination and cooperation among regional states in monitoring the circulation and supply of weapons from within and outside of the region; and,

- non-existence of international or regional agreements on controlling the small arms trade (licit and illicit).

The security impact of illicit small arms movement is not confined to the region. Regional ports are becoming popular sites for transshipping weapons around the world, including destinations in the Middle East and possibly North America. Taking this argument into consideration, the small arms proliferation in Southeast Asia could have significant implications for Canada.

SURVEY OF THE PROBLEM

A. Sources of Proliferation The discussion in this section is based mainly on newspaper and magazine articles as well as press releases about foiled small arms movement within the region. This author relies on such information because documentation on illicit arms trade is not readily available from regional security organizations or think tanks. The illicit nature of small arms movement poses difficulties to attempts at calculating figures. To complicate matters, the task of obtaining data on legal trade in weapons (including small arms) is rather challenging because such data is often considered sensitive material by many East Asian governments. However, this author believes that the collection and analysis of a comprehensive data is conceivable with further research. This section provides an initial step towards achieving such a goal.

China

The People's Republic of China (PRC) may be one of the major sources of small arms proliferation in Southeast Asia. According to media reports, Chinese arms manufacturers are known to be involved in illegal production. The central government determines levels of production for each manufacturer, but many of the factories have produced quantities beyond these levels. Surplus arms are sold through illicit channels for the sake of profits. Officials in Beijing blame this condition on the lack of centralized regulations. However, regulations alone will not solve the problem. Although China recently adopted strong laws against the illicit possession, production and transfer of small arms, such laws may only limit the growth of "cottage" production (which has been growing rapidly). The laws' ability to make an impact against the wellconnected, larger state manufacturers remains doubtful. For example, two firms, Poly Technologies and China Northern Industries (Norinco), are connected to central government officials. The former is a defence conglomerate controlled by the General Staff of the People's Liberation Army (PLA) while the latter reports to the State Council under the Prime Minister. Having entered an era of capitalism, small arms production in China is also increasingly governed by the market — the demand for such weapons within China and in neighbouring states have grown as well as the profits to be had. Current conditions in the arms manufacturing industry contribute to this trend:

- factory managers resort to illicit sales to make up for capital shortages resulting from a decline in "legal" demand for small arms;
- the lack of competitiveness, which result from outdated technology, leads to dumping of weapons; and
- corruption among officials and lack of supervision of surplus weapons result in increased thefts. Beijing attempts to manage the problem through identifying and halting proliferation at its sources, increasing border and port controls as well as launching a campaign to seize banned weapons. Nevertheless, the obstacles are daunting.

North Korea

Weapons from North Korea have also circulated throughout the region and beyond. Some have been confiscated in Hong Kong and most of these were believed to be destined for the Middle East. North Korean weapons range from small arms (machine guns, rifles and grenade launchers) to high tech missile components. Specific information about arms production in the DPRK is scarce, and efforts to assess small arms transfers from North Korea are difficult. North Korea has the additional incentive of needing weapons sales to earn hard currency to buy food to alleviate the ongoing famine as well as other goods.

Russia

Many of the small arms that have been intercepted and confiscated point to Russia as another major source of supply.

Some of these weapons were left over from past conflicts in Indochina (Cambodia and Vietnam), but there are signs that new Russian small arms are also in circulation. Cambodia and Vietnam import Russian weapons for defence purposes, but there is a possibility that theft and corruption among military officials have allowed weapons to fall into non-military hands. Such conditions may be more prevalent in Cambodia, where stability has been uncertain since last year's coup.

Vietnam and Cambodia

Vietnam is another source of small arms in the region. Seizure of weapons from Vietnamese trawlers (some of the Vietnamese "fishermen" appear to be former military personnel) in the South China Sea raises the possibility that Vietnamese military stores are being looted by soldiers and that weapons leftover from past conflicts are making their way into neighbouring states. There is demand for small arms in Vietnam, but the country is increasingly becoming a transshipment area for weapons originating from China and Russia. The weapons enter Vietnam through its porous northern borders and move to its ports before they are loaded onto cargo ships. Russian weapons are also arriving directly at Vietnamese ports where they are further dispersed throughout the region and possibly beyond. Cambodian weapons originate from left over caches of the war against Vietnam as well as continued Khmer Rouge insurgency which had made the country a "killing field" from the mid 1970s until early 1990s. Last year's coup, the ensuing violence and the breakdown of the UN peace-building mission may not have changed these conditions. The demand for small arms has probably risen as the sense of national security diminishes and Cambodians seek personal security through the possession of firearms.

ESTABLISHING PATTERNS OF PROLIFERATION

Patterns of proliferation described in this section should not be assessed as hard data, and are based on analysis of media reports of intercepted small arms movement throughout the region. According to one source, in general the proliferation of small arms is "not random but highly patterned" and it can be controlled effectively through identifying likely channels of supply. Another characteristic of weapons movement through a particular channel is that such a movement often goes in both directions. For example, when illicit Chinese-made machine guns are confiscated in Vietnam, it is apparent that Vietnamese weapons could enter China through the same channel of supply. By keeping these factors in mind, our understanding of the small arms proliferation in the region would be more comprehensive. Small arms proliferation in Southeast Asia is often linked to the drug trade. It is believed that drug cartels in Myanmar are receiving small arms from Chinese sources. This claim may be valid considering that the southwestern corner of China is known as the "Dark Channels" of illicit activities.

It is possible that Chinese weapons are traded for drugs; although information on this remains sketchy. Burmese drug lords have also been receiving small arms from Cambodia. These weapons are usually transported overland through Thailand. The Thai government has attempted to step up controls but high levels of corruption among customs and security officials has undermined such efforts. Chinese weapons are also making their way into Vietnam. However, it is unclear whether the weapons are intended for Vietnamese markets, or if Vietnam is only used as a transshipping site. This is important considering that Vietnam is already saturated with small arms left over from past conflicts as well as those which recently occurred in neighbouring Cambodia. Furthermore, Chinese sources claim that the Vietnamese are smuggling weapons into China, reinforcing the "dual-direction" argument of small arms smuggling.

Small arms from Vietnam have been found on fishing trawlers off the coast of Malaysia on the South China Sea. Malaysian officials argue that these cases do not represent a serious threat because the coastal guards have only confiscated fourteen small weapons from 1990 to 1994. Malaysian optimism is countered by the fact that such confiscations occurred on several occasions, indicating a patterned movement. Actual interception may indicate only the tip of the iceberg. Vietnamese small arms have also been reported circulating in the Philippines, with weapons making their way through methods similar to those in the Malaysian case above. In most cases, illicit weapons were found after the Vietnamese trawlers had been detained for illegal entry. Manila points to rebels in the southern island of Mindanao as the most likely recipients of these weapons. One of the rebel factions, the Moro National Liberation Front (MNLF), admits to obtaining small arms from abroad but has not identified a country source.

These patterns of small arms proliferation do not exhaust those in the region, but do indicate some of the better-known channels of supply.

EAST ASIAN PORTS

The region's ports play a major role in facilitating proliferation. The lack of controls on the movement of goods often allows the ports to be used as sites for transshipping small arms. Arms dealers see these ports as effective channels for dispersing their merchandise throughout the region and beyond. Hong Kong, Taiwan and many of the ports in ASEAN countries share this problem because of the following characteristics:

- the large volume of goods passing through the ports daily;
- frequent corruption and lack of professionalism among customs and security (the military, police, coast guard) officials;
- states' reluctance to impose harsh controls for fear of losing competitiveness;
- financial and technological deficiencies which prevent the development of effective control measures; and
- lack of coordination and cooperation among the region's customs and security officials.

In the case of Hong Kong, former British security officials have noted the problem. Although the demand for small arms in Hong Kong is not high, the territory is a magnet to weapons because its docks are used for licit and illicit transshipment. Hong Kong is strategically located at the crossroads of Northeast and Southeast Asia as well as being the region's gateway to Europe, North America and the Middle East. Although officials claim that Hong Kong's shipping controls are very effective, the port's high volume of traffic is enough reason for arms dealers to take the risk. A tight security net around Hong Kong is neither viable nor seen as desirable because it would severely restrict legitimate trade. The weapons that are transshipped here not only originate from mainland China but also from neighbouring countries such as North Korea. In 1995, a third of the Chinese weapons confiscated originated from PLA sources and have ranged from small arms to high-tech missile components. The situation is worsening because China's harsh internal crackdown on illicit small arms trade has resulted in a surge of weapons movement from the rest of the country to the southern provinces and into Hong Kong. In Guangdong and other areas around Hong Kong violent criminal activities have been on the rise in the last two years.

In addition to Hong Kong, small arms are making their way to Taiwan. Suspected weaponscarrying ships from mainland China have been reported unloading cargoes at several ports on the island. It is still not clear whether Taiwan is the final destination of these weapons or if it simply serves as a transshipping site or both. There have been examples of Taiwan serving as a transit point: the 2,000 AK-47 machine guns that were confiscated in San Francisco about two years ago had been transported by Chinese and Taiwanese citizens. The demand for small arms in Taiwan is high among criminal elements and a report in 1996 also suspects that the Chinese government may be supplying prointegration groups on the island. In addition to the discovery of Chinese weapons, the Taiwanese security apparatus has also found caches of small arms that originate from Sabah, Malaysia. The existence of weapons supplier other than just the Chinese supports the view that Taiwan is a possible hub in a network of illicit small arms trade in the region.

Ports in Southeast Asian countries have been identified as having some of the least effective antismuggling controls in the world (especially against drugs and small arms). The United States has pressured members of the Association of Southeast Asian Nations (ASEAN) to increase control mechanisms at their ports. However, the ASEAN countries have not been responsive. As in the situation in Hong Kong and Taiwan, the lack of effective anti-smuggling controls is a result of the factors described earlier in this section. Most of the ASEAN states, especially Singapore, argue that increased controls would seriously hamper legitimate trade and make their ports unattractive to shipping companies.

THE IMPACT OF ILLICIT SMALL ARMS ON HUMAN SECURITY

Terrorism and Insurgency

The number of insurgency movements in Southeast Asia receiving frequent supplies of small arms is limited. These movements exist in Indonesia, Myanmar and the Philippines. As well, there is continued fighting among different political factions in Cambodia.

The insurgents in Indonesia (Acehnese, East Timorese and West Irian) are among the least likely to receive small arms from abroad. Their numbers are small and they do not have the mechanisms to raise adequate funds for weapons purchase. The Indonesian government and military have been effective in isolating these movements and preventing any contact with the outside. The East Timorese resistance, for example, mainly uses weapons taken from Indonesian soldiers. Therefore, although the demand for small arms may exist in these insurgent areas, the threat of actual acquisition is minimal. This argument is strong especially considering that profits have become the main goal of today's small arms trade. The most likely recipients of small arms in Indonesia are criminal elements. And even this situation is questionable because there is not a network of organized crime, such as the Triad in China or the drug cartels in Myanmar, that have the resources to sustain any form of arms transfer. In the Philippines, separatist groups on Mindanao have engaged in sporadic armed confrontation with central government forces for years. The insurgents have admitted to obtaining weapons from foreign sources. Photographs of rebel soldiers show them to be well equipped with small arms and ammunition, and it is unlikely that these are solely from stealing and confiscating weapons from government forces. Further fighting not only threatens human security in the Philippines, but also could have a significant impact on the country's economic growth.

Since last year's coup in Cambodia, incidents of political violence have been high. "Hundreds of [Hun Sen's] oppositions remain in Thailand in exile or are fighting in the jungles." Although Hun Sen's faction has been accused internationally for committing such violence against Norodom Ranarindh's supporters, the latter often are perpetrators as well. Prior to the coup, during the United Nations sponsored peacebuilding process, it was feared that disarmament efforts would result in small arms moving out of the country and into neighbouring states. However, while the movement of small arms from Cambodia to places such as northern Myanmar is possible, the demand for weapons in Cambodia is rising. Small arms are probably re-circulating within the country and foreign sources may be involved in further re-supply. While Hun Sen's faction could be receiving small arms shipment from Vietnam, Ranarindh loyalists could be receiving theirs from China. To make things even more complicated, the Khmer Rouge is still actively seeking ways to become involved in this political power play.

Criminal Activities

Criminal elements have profited most from easier access to illicit weapons, and there are signs of increasing gun related violence. In China, there is a steady growth in gun-related crimes since 1994 and the government warns of the threat this poses to public security. The problem is intensified by the growing brutality of such crimes. As numbers and levels of criminal violence escalate, citizens seek security through acquiring small arms for personal use. In turn, this trend exacerbates overall conditions as it allows the small arms trade to flourish by raising the demand for such weapons. This becomes the case especially when the government is perceived to be slow and ineffective in implementing measures to manage the problem. Such a situation is not unique to China and can be observed throughout East Asia. The links between small arms proliferation and criminal activities in Southeast Asia is especially problematic when one also factors in the estimated high volume of drug trade in the region. In Myanmar, the sales of small arms to drug lords such as Khun Sa have allowed them to strengthen their power. With easy access to such weapons, the drug cartels have formed well-equipped private armies, which increasingly pose serious threats to state sovereignty. The state monopoly on violence — one of the main characteristics of the modern state system — is increasingly undermined. Through the flourishing illicit trade in small arms, these private armies occasionally appear at least as well equipped and trained than the national security forces. This situation provides drug cartels with the tools to strengthen their grip over communities of peasants who are enslaved by the trade. Small arms proliferation is also associated with the drug trade in the form of common channels of supply.

The transfer of small arms may be different from that of drugs because the former carry more bulk and are easier to trace in their origins. However, the manner in which they are transported is comparable. For example, drugs and small arms transfers across the Thai-Cambodian border are sometimes carried out by concealing these products inside the gas tanks of shipping trucks. In addition to the similarities in methods, these goods are moving through similar patterns of supply channels. This argument is supported by reports claiming that weapons and drugs are often exchanged along such supply lines. The trades in small arms and drugs complement each other; the flourishing of one trade certainly induces growth in the other.

While the small arms/drug trades model also applies to illicit maritime activities, piracy is the more serious problem at sea. The most recent International Maritime Bureau (IMB) report shows that Southeast Asia remains the region with the highest rate of piracy in the world. These criminal activities are frequent in the South China Sea (especially within the Hong Kong-Luzon-Hainan triangle), the Strait of Malacca and the Gulf of Thailand. While trends have been on the rise for the last five years or so, last year's report indicates another problem; the level of violence committed during pirate attacks have dramatically increased.

Acts of piracy in the region are usually carried out using homemade explosives and small arms such as rifles and machine guns. The increasing level of violence during pirate attacks could possibly be linked to the growing availability of small arms. Considering that the number of pirate attacks reported did not increase dramatically, the surge in levels of violence which accompany these acts can only be explained by the widening use of small arms. Consequently, in addition to facing the fear of being robbed, the personal security of ship crews is also increasingly threatened.

Implications for State Sovereignty in the Region

The situations discussed in the previous section indicate that the most predominant threats to security caused by the growth in illicit small arms trafficking are of non-military nature. Insurgency movements, factional fighting and criminal activities flourish with easy access to small arms. While regional states may not see these threats as serious in the short term, their implications in the long run may cause disruption in state legitimacy and stability.

One of the most important features of the modern state is its monopoly on internal violence. However, as non-state, non-military elements gain power, they pose a challenge to the norm. Having just gained their independence from European powers in the latter part of the century (except for Thailand, which was never ruled by a foreign power) countries in Southeast Asia are still undergoing statebuilding processes. Most of them are still concentrating on developing mechanisms against encroachment from other countries (especially considering the existence of historical animosities and unending territorial disputes among the regional countries). As a result, small-scale insurgencies and criminal activities are often overlooked as possible threats to the state.

The growth of drug smuggling and piracy poses threats to the region's economic activities. As the current economic downturn deepens, there is a strong possibility that these activities may grow even faster. For example, the tough anti-drug policies in Thailand, which has been responsible for the declining production of opium on the Thai section of the Golden Triangle, could lose its effectiveness as officials try to relieve their economic hardship through corruption. Also, the hundreds of Indonesians who are fleeing to the Malaysian peninsula could become easy targets for pirates operating in the Malacca Strait. These descriptions are mainly speculative, but they are important considerations for governments in the region. The current economic meltdown represents a tough challenge to statehood in Southeast Asia. The erosion of state legitimacy by internal, non-military, non-state elements renders the task of overcoming the meltdown more difficult. Therefore, it is in these countries interest to attribute more attention to the trafficking of illicit small arms, which enhances the power of these non-state actors.

Implications for Canada

The problem of illicit small arms movement in Southeast Asia could also have repercussions that extend beyond the region's border. Having close relations with most of the countries in the region, there are a number of implications that Canada may suffer if the illicit proliferation of small arms is allowed to grow in Southeast Asia and the rest of Asia in general. These implications can be divided into those that are of a direct nature and those that could affect Canada indirectly.

There has not been any substantial evidence yet that Asian small arms are circulating illicitly on Canadian soil. However, the possibility of this happening is real. The demand for military small arms may not be high, but criminal elements in Canada — as in any country — certainly have some interest in such weapons. Recognizing the *potential* for problem, instead of reacting to it *"after the fact,"* is important considering efforts to extract small arms from society has been proven to be difficult. As Canada becomes more involved in the Asian economies, the volume of transshipment entering the Port of Vancouver is rapidly growing. This expansion could potentially stretch the abilities of Canadian customs officials to monitor the entrance of goods. The experience in Hong Kong indicates that as the volume of transshipment increases, so does the susceptibility of ports to illicit activities. The most recent drug bust at the Vancouver port indicates that criminals are already taking advantage of increased transshipment volume to smuggle illicit goods. Since the channels for drug smuggling are often used for illicit weapons transfer as well, attention should be paid to the possibility of small arms entering Canada through Vancouver and efforts should be taken to avoid this.

In addition to direct shipments of small arms from Asia, Canada should also be on alert for Asian weapons that may have been introduced to North America through U.S. ports. The confiscation of Chinese machine guns at the San Francisco port two years ago indicates the possible existence of a supply channel. Once the weapons have reached North America, they could enter Canada by land in spite of controls along the borders. The Firearms Smuggling Work Group claims that small arms are smuggled into north of the border through means as simple as courier services. Also, gun running from the United States seems to be in association with other types of smuggling such as tobacco, alcohol and drugs. The indirect implications of small arms proliferation to Canada mainly stem from our economic relations with countries of the Asia-Pacific. In 1993, the region was the market for more than $16.6 billion of Canadian exports while imports from the region numbered about $25.1 billion. While Canadian investment in the Asia-Pacific region figured at about $12.2 billion in 1996.[51] Furthermore, Southeast Asian countries such as Indonesia, the Philippines, Singapore and Thailand are among the top 25 most promising markets for Canadian export. The indirect implications of Southeast Asia's growing illicit arms trade can be observed in at least three ways.

First, small arms proliferation has the potential to undermine government legitimacy. As mentioned, the proliferation of small arms has strong destabilizing elements. However, increasing crime and insurgency, fueled by the availability of small arms, is not likely to cause immediate chaos. Instead, the process of undermining government legitimacy will be gradual and in turn, this regression will certainly affect susceptible countries' economic performance. Such a condition would be disadvantageous because Canadian trade and investment interests in the region are high. Second, the rising trend of piracy could present serious obstructions to regular economic activities. The waterways of the region are highly trafficked by ships connecting the region with the rest of the world. The East Asian sea-lanes of communication (SLOC) are the lifelines to the region's economies as well as a major channel for Canadian export and imports. The rising violence related to pirate attacks would hamper the movement of shipping vessels and increase the cost of conducting trade (e.g., higher insurance cost, extra costs for re-routing). Although the negative effects may not be apparent now, their long-term repercussions are reasons enough to become involved in preventative measures such as limiting the flow of illicit small arms in the region. Third, Canada's involvement in humanitarian and development projects in the region is at risk of being undermined by violence caused by the growth in illicit small arms trafficking. For example, the Canadian International Development Agency (CIDA) is funding the six-year, $7.8 million Canada-Cambodia Development Program (CCDP), to aid the process of reconstruction and rehabilitation in this war torn country. This is one of the largest and most active development assistance projects in Cambodia. However, the success of this project could be eroded if political instability and armed violence continue. CIDA and many Canadian Non-Governmental Organizations (NGOs) are also involved in similar development assistance programs in Vietnam and Thailand. In these cases as well, violence caused by easy access to small arms is certainly a factor which limits the accomplishment of these organizations in promoting prosperity, security and Canadian values in the region.

POLICY OPTIONS

UN Based Efforts

The United Nations remains one of the best institutions for promoting efforts to manage the problem of small arms proliferation. Former UN Secretary General Boutros Boutros Ghali's Agenda for Peace was important as a beginning, and last year's Report of the Small Arms Panel provided some guidelines to further treatment of the issue. The greatest advantage to UN based efforts is its inclusiveness, especially when considering that illicit small arms proliferation is a global security problem as much as it is a regional or national one.

One of the most talked about suggestions is the possible expansion of the UN Register of Conventional Weapons to promote transparency about the legal trade in small arms. However, since its creation, the UN Register has had mixed results. Not all states have submitted reports of their weapons acquisitions, but the leading arms exporting countries have responded. The export/import information provided by states often contain discrepancies, but it has revealed some previously unknown data as well as represents a modest step towards enhancing transparency. The expansion of the Register (beyond the seven original weapon categories and to include small arms) seems an efficient and logical progression, however the goal will be difficult to achieve. The creation of the Register in the first place was a difficult enough process and some states are unhappy about its current scope and coverage (hence, the lack of universal participation). For a number of states, the current situation represents the limit of their willingness to cooperate in transparency measures. Although the expansion of the Register may be the most desired goal for countries such as Canada, its actual realization is difficult. Nevertheless, this should not deter attempts to proceed with such an approach.

The UN, through its Centre for International Crime and Prevention, has also increased its activity in the study of domestic firearm regulations. Concerns related to the illicit trafficking of small arms figure prominently in this study.

At the moment, there may be a move towards developing a convention dealing with illicit trafficking within the Commission on Crime Prevention and Criminal Justice. With further development — including more participation among member states — these efforts represent an important step towards a more comprehensive treatment of the illicit small arms trade. The UN's work in this field allows for a multi-dimensional approach (when combined with UN studies on post-conflict disarmament, arms control, norm building and education) to tackling problems related to the small arms phenomenon.

As mentioned in the previous paragraph, the UN is heavily involved in developing effective ways to manage post-conflict disarmament. The provision of disarmament goals in peacekeeping missions is important because they are essential to the creation of lasting peace and stability. This is usually done through the process of norm building as well as educating the people living in post-conflict areas. The UN Disarmament Committee has conducted a series of studies on the role of UN peacekeeping missions in disarming, demobilizing and reintegrating post-conflict societies. These efforts do not necessarily address directly how the movement of small arms affects trends in criminal activities (considering such activities are more predominant in Southeast Asia). However, they provide insights on how small arms originating from countries such as Cambodia, Myanmar and Vietnam can be stemmed.

Regional Based Efforts

In order to complement the achievements of the UN, the Panel on Small Arms also suggested in its report the development of regional initiatives. The ASEAN Regional Forum (ARF) has emerged as a forum for discussions on security, although it is not a formal regional security structure. With the lack of a structured regional security mechanism, the ARF has become an important body for the promotion of policies aimed at managing the illicit trade in small arms. For example, one of the confidence building measures (CBMs) listed for discussion within the ARF and its sub-bodies is "preventing and combating illicit trafficking in conventional small arms." By introducing ideas in the ARF and working within this framework of thinking, regional efforts would most likely be debated and pursued in a more productive fashion.

One of the initiatives could be the creation of regional small arms registers. To ensure efficient exchanges of ideas, policies and information, registers from different regions would be interconnected through a forum within the UN body. In Southeast Asia, Malaysia has indicated a desire to initiate the development of such a register for the purposes of tackling the illicit trade in small arms as well as enhancing regional confidence-building. Since Malaysia is one of the core members of the ARF, there is a possibility that it may decide to introduce such an initiative through this forum. Another idea that seems feasible is the creation of a regional convention against the illicit trafficking of small arms, as we have seen occur in the Organization of American States (OAS). There appears to be common features between small arms proliferation in the Americas and Southeast Asia. These include:

- criminal uses of illicit small arms;
- close relations between the small arms and drug trades (e.g., the cases of Myanmar and Colombia);
- possible proliferation of small arms as a result of post-conflict conditions (e.g., the cases of El Salvador, Nicaragua and Cambodia);
- organized insurgent and separatist movements (e.g., the Shining Path in Peru and Bolivia, the Zapatistas in Mexico and the MNLF/MILF in the Philippines; and,

- existence of relatively stable governments.

These similarities suggest that important lessons can be learned from the OAS experience. In the OAS Convention, there are a number of elements which deserve to be highlighted because of their potential applicability to conditions in Southeast Asia and possibly the rest of East Asia. These include:

- marking of small arms during production to enable increased facility in tracing the origins and movement of weapons;
- strengthening export controls by identifying destination of small arms transfers;
- enhancing cooperation, coordination and exchange of information and monitoring technologies among regional states; and,
- establishing of national bodies that would serve as contact points among the regional states.

The development of a regional convention on the illicit trafficking of small arms would certainly complement similar efforts at the UN level.

Regional countries that face difficulties controlling the inflow of illicit small arms may be interested in pursuing the above suggestions. Thailand, for example, has indicated in the past that it is willing to accept suggestions on how to manage trans-border criminal activities. Importantly, such a convention addresses the problems related to illicit proliferation but does not interfere with legal government-to-government trade in small arms. The ARF might act as a forum for initial discussions on the topic, after which regular multi-lateral discussions would be set up to ensure that focused deliberations evolve.

THE DEVELOPMENT OF A SMALL ARMS DATABASE

There is no comprehensive database of small arms acquisitions and inventories available that is comparable to the one on large conventional weapons maintained by the Stockholm International Peace Research Institute (SIPRI). An attempt to develop such a database would be challenging but not impossible. Some countries in Asia are still hesitant about the confidence-building values of transparency and consider such an act disadvantageous because it supposedly would expose their military weaknesses. However, this view may be changing as precedents, such as declaring weapon acquisitions to the UN Register, instills trust and confidence in military transparency. If the legal trade in small arms becomes more transparent, the task of developing a comprehensive database would become less challenging. In turn, the development of such a database would allow better assessments of policies implemented to counter the illicit proliferation of small arms.

Further Exploration of the ARF Option

ARF considerations might consist of giving more attention to developing a regional convention against the illicit trafficking of small arms, as well as researching the possibility of establishing a regional small arms register. Although a small arms register is often seen as an arms control mechanism, it is also an effective way to approach concerns related to illicit trafficking. Some Southeast Asian countries may react coolly to such a proposal because they may perceive it as a “foreign/western” construct. However, the development of an arms register appears to suit the countries’ preference for confidence-building measures (CBMs) as well as consensus building and nonconfrontational approaches to security relations. The ARF itself would not be responsible for creating and running the register. Instead, it would act as forum in which the topic can be deliberated. Although the ARF meets only once a year, members have observed the value of this forum and therefore, have created several inter-sessional meetings to deal with specific security topics. The forming of an ARF inter-sessional group to address illicit small arms trafficking will indeed enhance regional cooperation. The trans-border nature of illicit movement of small arms has rendered the issue a regional problem. Thus, cooperation through frequent dialogues and workshops would bring the region closer to understanding the small arms phenomenon comprehensively.

The ARF is important in that it is the only forum in which Southeast Asian countries as well as major regional players are able to gather and discuss security issues. In short, getting the countries to sit and talk about the feasibility of a small arms register (its pros and cons) or other actions to address the small arms problem is the most important step of the process.

Since its creation, ASEAN countries have dominated the ARF agenda. Therefore, in order to allow the small arms concern to be included in the agenda of the forum, at least one of the ASEAN members will have to recognize the importance of addressing the issue. It is in Canada's interest that small arms proliferation be discussed within the forum, given the issue's implications for North America. Canada is in a strategic position to suggest some of the paths that could be followed to address the problem adequately. However, Canada must not do so in a patronizing way. As Canadian diplomats already know, Southeast Asian officials are sensitive about incorporating "foreign" ideas into regional policies. Nonetheless, small arms proliferation is too important of an issue for Canada to be left out of the ARF discussions. The creation of a regional small arms register seems feasible as long as Canada introduces the idea to the forum with previous support from the ASEAN members. Only then will the discussion be taken more seriously (once they realize the seriousness of the problem). The manner in which such an idea is packaged matters a great deal.

Concluding Remarks

Past studies on small arms proliferation and its impacts on societies have indicated Central-South America, Central-Southern Africa and South Asia as the most problematic areas. However, this study indicates that the problem is also affecting Southeast Asia. The illicit trafficking of small arms in the region has a security character that is distinct from that in some of the other regions (except for Central-South America, where there are similar features). The implications of illicit trade in such weapons are linked closer to criminal activities than they are related to issues of post-conflict peacebuilding. The exception to this may be Cambodia. But even there the impact of small arms proliferation has not led to the chaos seen in parts of South Asia and Southern Africa. Nonetheless, security conditions in Southeast Asia are of considerable concern to Canada because of its possible implications.

Countries in the region have taken some steps to control the illicit movement of small arms at the national level through methods such as imposing strict laws, increasing border surveillance and training officials. Bilateral approaches such as joint maritime patrols have also taken place among Indonesia, Malaysia and Singapore. However, as the study indicates, overcoming the problem effectively would require more cooperation and coordination among the countries in the region. Acting as a neutral third party (yet having great interest in the situation within the region), Canada may be in a position to help catalyse such cooperation. There may be a lack of interest among some of the Southeast Asian countries because of their inability to project a long-term view of non-military/ human security in the region. Canada could play a role in raising awareness of the concerns related to illicit trafficking of small arms and small arms proliferation in general. In any case, it is not in Canada's best interest to remain idle and wait for the regional countries to come to their senses.

This study shows that a number of approaches can be pursued to achieve regional cooperation in tackling the small arms problem. As reports demonstrate a trend of increasing illicit small arms transfers, countries cannot afford to wait longer in reacting if the problem is to be managed effectively. The conditions will not improve by themselves. This is important to bear in mind, especially considering that small arms are harder to retrieve once they have entered a society.

THE RUSSIAN FAR EAST, EASTERN SIBERIA

In this section, the problem of small arms proliferation will be examined in the region of East Siberia and the Russian Far East, including the Russian-Chinese and Russian-Korean frontiers. This area includes:

- Russian Federation: Irkutsk, Chita, Amur, Magadan, Kamchatka and Sakhalin provinces (oblasts); Krasnoyarsk, Amur and Maritim (Primorskij) territories (krais); Ethnic republics of Sakha-Yakutia and Buryatia.
- China Provinces: Heilongjiang, Jilin, Liaoning, Hebei, Beijing and Tjanjin; "Autonomous Regions"; Inner Mongolia (Nei Menggu)
- North Korea (Chongjin-Najin border area)

However, detailed coverage of political and financial aspects of the problem require some reference to the Moscow area, because major movements of small arms at the Russian-Chinese and Russian-Korean Frontiers hardly occur without decisions of major military, political, business and criminal centres of Russia, most of them in Moscow city/Moscow province area. The Tula province and Urals area of Russia (especially the two provinces of Chelyabinsk and Yekaterinburg) are also mentioned in the research as major centres of arms production of Russia. The Russian Far East, Siberia and Russian-Chinese/Russian-Korean Frontier should be regarded as an area of special concern. Small arms are proliferating there because of the weakened national systems of control on small arms production, exports and imports, particularly at extreme distances. Of major concern among neighbours is that the illicit/semi-illicit proliferation of small arms in the region may be exacerbating crime. At the same time, criminal organizations are also interested in involvement in the small arms trade.

Sources of Small Arms

China and North Korea are the countries reported to be sources of small arms proliferation in the region. In the post-Communist era, there is practically no official control over small arms production and trade. The strict ban on the owning and trade of small arms that existed before 1991 has been lifted. But even during the last decade of the Communist rule, the law banning small arms ownership was not fully enforced for all social groups. Obtaining a license to own and carry small weapons was no longer a complicated process after 1992. Now, many Russian companies and organizations have their own arsenals of small weapons without any license. Millions of private citizens of the Russian Federation are also purchasing firearms in order to protect themselves and their families from the social chaos of crime expansion in contemporary Russia.

Small Arms and the Russian Defence Industry

East Siberia and the Russian Far East have been traditionally reported as areas of increased concentration of unlicensed firearms among private citizens. Since the end of the 1970s most of the families and individuals residing in the underpopulated northern sector of the area owned from one to several rifles, revolvers, pistols or even automatic rifles. Even the Communist authorities tended to tolerate that situation keeping in mind the isolation of rural communities and individual settlements, the vital necessity of hunting and self-defence (including self-defence from wild animals), and finally restricted capability of law enforcement structures to control sparse population scattered across the vast mountainous and forested territory.

The Russian state military industry has been in crisis since the end of the Cold War. Budget cuts, in combination with gradual reduction of federal military forces, led to the degradation of its traditional internal constituency. Trying to improve their financial situation, many state enterprises are looking for new markets to sell their production. Current legal regulations make the legal, large-scale sales of Russian-made firearms to Russian consumers a difficult task, so the military industry looks to the development of small arms exports. In East Asia, Russian military industry still remains a traditional supplier of the armed forces of China, Vietnam and Cambodia. China mainly concentrates on purchasing heavy weapons, aircraft and submarines. Nevertheless, small amounts of Russian small arms are regularly purchased by China. During the last two years Russian arms dealers have been repeatedly visiting other countries of the region (among them Indonesia, Malaysia, Singapore and Thailand) trying to explore and develop new markets.

The state military industry in Russia is backed by government and parliamentary circles, making it easy for the industry to boost small arms exports to traditional partners, as well as to search for new markets. Widespread corruption and corporate protectionism in modern Russian society make it difficult to draw a distinct line between legal and illegal export of arms produced by Russian military industry (in spite of the government declarations about its "strict adherence to norms of international law"). It is also worth mentioning that human rights violations in such countries of Asia such as the PRC or Vietnam never influence the delivery of Russian arms to those countries.

All arms trading in Russia is formally controlled by the federal arms export agency, or "Rosvooruzhenije" (from the Russian: Rus[sian]/Arms). The head of Rosvooruzhenije is Yevgenij Ananev. The second main figure is Rear Admiral Oleg Belavintsev who serves as its deputy general director. Since

December 1997, one of Ananev's chief advisors has been former Russian Defence Minister Pavel Grachev, who is reportedly involved in corruption scandals. (Grachev and Belavintsev are reported to be close personal friends.)

Reorganization of the Defence Industry

In February 1998, a new government commission for the financial recovery of the defence industry was formed in Moscow. On 23 February, in accordance with the resolution signed by Prime Minister Chernomyrdin, First Deputy Prime Minister Anatolij Chubais was appointed as its chairman with Deputy Prime Minister and Economics Minister Yakov Urinson appointed as deputy chairman. Chubais announced on 20 February that the government was aiming at revision of its procedure for concluding contracts with defence enterprises, as well as at reduction of the number of such enterprises receiving state orders from 1,700 to 600.

Several powerful Russian opposition leaders, holding a majority in Russian Parliament (among them Vladimir Zhirinovski), have declared the arms trade one of Russia's economic goals. They strongly believe, and try to convince the Russian public, that the arms trade is a good and reliable business which should be developed to bring cash to the country, as well as to keep military industry jobs. A number of former state enterprises in Russia specializing in small arms production (exact data not available) have sold some of their shares to private structures and citizens. As a result of this, many of them fell into the sphere of the activity of "Russian Mafia" and became sources of totally uncontrolled production and trade of small arms both for Russian and foreign markets.

The Russian Mafia

Well organized criminal groups started forming in Russia (USSR) at the end of the Civil War (1918-1922). After more than fifty years of evolution and transformation, they have managed to preserve their viability and coordination, have accumulated significant funds and have found ways to integrate themselves with the power structures of the Soviet Empire including high-ranking officials of the Communist Party of the USSR and the KGB. The processes of disintegration of the Soviet State during the period of "Perestroyka" and "Glasnost"

(1986-1991) further reinforced the above-mentioned alliance between "professional mobsters" and a part of communist "Nomenclatura," thus creating a special form of organized crime which is often called "Russian Mafia." Modern structures of "Russian Mafia" operating in the sphere of arms production and sales are represented by several powerful groups consisting of criminal syndicates (sometimes called "brotherhoods") working in close cooperation with certain industrial, financial and political groups, recruiting agents in law enforcement structures and involving foreign companies and individual citizens in their network. Severe discipline, conspiracy, excellent equipment, well developed "intelligence" and "counter-intelligence" and relatively professional approach towards marketing and business — all make modern criminal groups of Russia strong and dangerous, as well as, to a greater or lesser extent, unknown and invisible to Western countries (including Canadian and American observers).

Organized criminal "syndicates" and "brotherhoods" of the Russian Federation with their headquarters in the cities of Moscow, St. Petersburg, Yekaterinburg, Chelyabinsk, Khabarovsk and Vladivostok (the latter two in the Russian Far East), were reported to be involved in small arms exports to other countries of East Asia.

By "involvement" is meant various degrees of control over the above sphere of business mainly resulting in accumulating considerable commissions from international arms deals. Smaller criminal groups operating between East Siberia and the Urals tend to control the trafficking of small arms through the provinces of Tyumen, Omsk, and Kemerovo, and through Krasnoyarsk territory, in order to obtain small commissions from the deals. The local transport police (GAI) is often involved in controlling small arms trafficking for the benefit of criminal groups.

The process of rapid decay of the Soviet Army (now Russian Federal Army) started at least at the end of the 1970s with the period of 1993-98 as its culmination. Openly corrupt top brass, an underpaid officer corps, starving soldiers, undermanned and under-equipped regiments — all these factors have resulted in massive thefts of military property, including firearms, which can be easily sold on the black market or used for private purposes such as self-defence or work in private security structures. (Many sergeants and officers combine military service with part-time or freelance work in commercial companies, often as security officers. Strictly banned until 1992, this practice is nowadays widely tolerated).

Defining the Region

The area of current research includes the territory of Transbaykal Military District embracing Chita and Irkutsk provinces and ethnic republics of Sakha-Yakutia and Buryat-Mongolia (approximately 80,000 military personnel at present) and Maritime (Primorskij) Military District embracing the provinces of Magadan, Kamchatka, and Sakhalin Island, territories of Maritim and Amur, and Chukotka (Chukchi) Autonomous District (approximately 77,000 military personnel at present).

The two Military Districts officially contain at least 60 divisions, which were originally supposed to be manned with at least 300,000 military personnel) However most of those divisions are 25 to 75% undermanned leaving thousands of small arms in stores and subject to regular misappropriation by officers, sergeants and private soldiers. The Russian Far East is also the area of Russian Pacific Fleet basing (Magadan, Petropavlovsk-Kamchatsky, Yuzhno-Sakhalinsk, Vanino, Nakhodka, Vladivostok). The above-mentioned problems of the two military districts are typical for the Pacific Fleet as well. Chinese and to some extent North Korean state-owned military industries also serve as sources of both legal and semi-illegal small arms proliferation in the area of research. In China, military industry is not controlled by organized criminal groups to the extent to which it has become in Russia (at least for the reason that in modern China there do not seem to exist well organized criminal structures similar to "Russian Mafia").73 However, corruption is well-developed in the Chinese military industry, which in combination with insufficient control over resources and production makes it possible to produce thousands of firearms for further sale, bypassing official export channels.

MAJOR ROUTES OF SMALL ARMS PROLIFERATION

Russian weapons are systematically moving to Vietnam, Cambodia and Laos by sea from Vladivostok and Nakhodka to

Haiphong and Saigon (Ho Chi Min City) and further through Vietnamese territory. It is also reported that they are often resold by Vietnamese and Cambodian authorities. Certain amounts of firearms might also be transported from Russia to Vietnam by air. We can suppose that some quantities of Russian weapons might be transported from the Russian Far East to Vietnam via Chinese territory, but as of today, no reports on that possible route have been seen.

Considerable numbers of Chinese-made light weapons are regularly passing across the Chinese-Russian border to Russia through two major points:

- Zabaikal'sk (Chita province)/Manchouli (Inner Mongolia) border crossing placed astride Hailar-Chita highway. Since March 1, 1998 (after revamping), this crossing has 14 lanes and is capable of handling 10,000 to 20,000 people and 1,500 cars daily. As of today, about 60 percent of trade between Russia and China passes through this point.
- Blagoveschensk (Amur territory) border crossing astride the Qiqihar-Blagoveschensk highway. This crossing has only eight lanes handling daily not more than 10,000 people and 950 cars. Most Chinese-made firearms are brought to Russia from China by commercial trailers, often accompanied by false papers indicating other types of goods (for example, mechanical toys). Certain amounts of firearms are smuggled by Chinese and Russian private citizens (the so-called "Chelnoks" or "Shuttle-traders"). Actual forms of Russian-Chinese border trade and smuggling in combination with corrupt and under-equipped custom officers and border guards do not permit even approximate calculations of the amount of Chinese-made arms smuggled into Russian federation within the last three years.

We should also mention the secondary direction of small arms (both Russian-and Chinese-made) proliferation in East Siberia and the Far East. This direction runs from south to the north down the rivers Lena, Aldan, Nizhnaya Tunguska, Angara and Yenisey to the cities lying along these rivers and to small rural communities and settlements scattered in their basins.

Some high-quality Russian-made light weapons might be sold to North Korea (at least until 1991 this was one of the regular routes of Russian weapons). Several reported cases of drug smuggling across the Russian-North Korean border (from Korean side) suggest that this might also be one of the routes of small arms trade. (Experience has shown that drug smuggling routes are in most cases the routes of small arms smuggling as well). It is possible that an arms-smuggling route might run through the tiny section of Russian-Korean border Najin-Ungghi (N. Korean side) — Khasan-Posyette (Russian side), limited by the Sea of Japan on the south and the "Kyonghung sack" of Chinese territory on the north.74 One of the possible sea routes of small arms proliferation might lead from Russian Far East (Vladivostok-Nakhodka) to Central and South America. Another reported sea route goes from Vladivostok to Japanese ports — possibly Osaka, Kobe and Yokohama.

Russian-made assault rifles and submachine guns, as well as ammunition have been reported in Nicaragua, El-Salvador and Colombia. As of today, we have discovered no materials tracing the delivery of the above mentioned arms across the Pacific Ocean. However this assumption does not seem unreasonable. We could also assume that if that delivery really took place, some amounts might be reloaded and stored in some ports at the Pacific coast of the USA and Canada.

MAJOR RECIPIENTS OF SMALL ARMS IN THE AREA

In Siberia and the Russian Far East, there are at least four groups of regular recipients of small arms coming from both foreign and domestic sources:

- criminals belonging both to highly organized "Mafia" groups ("syndicates" and "brotherhoods") and to smaller, spontaneously organized gangs;
- private citizens interested in purchasing firearms predominantly for self-defence;
- private security formations; and,
- different opposition and separatist groups.

Russian criminal groups in Siberia and the Far East, with their major headquarters in the cities of Vladivostok, Nakhodka, Khabarovsk, Blagoveschensk, Irkutsk and Yakutsk, (as well as criminal groups scattered all over Russian Federation) prefer Russian-and Western-made (American, German, and Israeli) weapons for permanent use and storage.

Those groups regularly purchase a considerable amounts of Russian-made firearms and ammunition which comes either directly from the military plants (from Tula province, the Urals and other arms-producing areas of the country), or is stolen from army barracks and stores. Some small amounts of Western-made (predominantly American and German) firearms have also been detected in possession of criminals in Siberia and the Far East. These weapons, as well as the ammunition they acquire might be sporadically coming from North America (predominantly via Vladivostok and Nakhodka) and/or from Western Europe (probably through the Trans-Siberian railway).

However, for contract killings and for arming the lowest-class recruits, organized mobsters of Russia tend to use Chinese products mainly because of their low price. According to information provided by the Moscow Nizam Research Group, the black-market price for the latest model of Russianmade AKM assault rifles may vary from $US 1000 to $US 1200 depending on the area and season, while Chinese-made AKM assault rifles are sold in the range of $US 400 to $US 600. The similar ratio ($US 6 for one box of 20 Russian-made AKM cartridges to $US 4 for the similar but made in China one) exists for ammunition.

For contract killings, acts of terror and property destruction, the "Russian Mafia" also uses various sorts of mines and explosives, most of which are produced by specialists working in state laboratories and using state equipment. However, some parts and elements are partially stolen from the stores of the Russian Army, or imported from abroad.

Millions of private citizens of the Russian Federation not involved in organized criminal activities, are also regular purchasers of Russian-and Chinese-made firearms. Often illegally, they acquire firearms at their own risk believing that it might protect their lives, their families and property. Urban residents tend to purchase pistols and revolvers, while rural residents prefer to buy rifles, automatic and even assault rifles. Since the end of the nineteenth century, wearing firearms was a tradition and part of a way of life for rural residents of the Russian-Chinese frontier and remote northern areas of East Siberia and the Far East (both descendants of settlers from European Russia/Eastern Europe and Native Siberians). The main reasons for this tradition were:

- hunting as one of the important means of survival;
- the need to protect human lives from wild animals;
- dangerous atmosphere of the frontier with often and unexpected attacks from China;
- petty and high criminal activity, and regular escapes of inmates from prisons and concentration camps; and,
- low density of population in combination with poor activity of law enforcement structures.

After the end of Civil War (1917-1922), the Communists tried to ban the private ownership of small arms in the area, but that policy was not effective, and semi-illegal possession of small arms by private citizens finally became tolerated by the authorities. Thus almost every family residing in the area keeps and regularly updates its own small arsenal of small arms. Although it is absolutely obligatory that every small arm in the country should be registered, most Siberians tend to neglect this legal prescription. In most cases, residents of frontier and northern areas tend to acquire Russian or Chinese arms (depending on the purchasers' wealth), but some copies of American rifles have also been noted. A similar situation is observed with respect to small arms acquisition and registration by various private security and detective companies in the area, as well as in numerous prospectors' and explorers' teams operating in the remote northern territories.

The Russian and international media have been regularly reporting the presence of small arms in the arsenals of various paramilitary opposition groups. Among those groups worthy of mention are several right-wing and nationalist organizations having branches in Siberia and the Russian Far East, namely: Kossacks, Pamyat', Russian National Union, Skinheads, Young Patriots of Russia, and the leftist terrorist "Revvoyensovet RSFSR" ("Revolutionary Council of Russian Soviet Socialist Republic.") Several representatives of other radical organizations, among them the Liberal Democratic Party, leftist

Union of Russian Communists and different associations of Afghan War veterans, have also mentioned in their public speeches that their branches might also have small arms arsenals. Separatist movements in some autonomous areas of Russian Siberia and Far East, namely the Republics of Sakha-Yakoutia and Tannu-Tuva might be also recipients of small arms both from Russian Army stores and from China. Vietnam and Cambodia are still the main recipients of Russian weapons in East Asia. They acquire Russian weapons for their domestic army and police use, as well as for further sale to Myanmar, Malaysia and the Philippines. The North Korean Army might still be one of the recipients of some highquality Russian weapons, including small arms.

Certain amounts of Russian-made firearms are exported from the Russian Maritim Territory to Japan in exchange for Japanese cars. This "business" has been organized by the Kovalsky Mafia Syndicate (with its headquarters in Vladivostok) and supposedly the Yakuza. We can assume that various separatist movements of China — among them Uigur and Tibetan separatists, as well as guerilla movements in Myanmar, Thailand, Indonesia and Philippines — might have been, or will be, explored and approached by Russian arms traders looking for new markets.

Some Tibetan tribes and communities in remote areas of the Tibetan "Autonomous Region" and the province of Qinghai (for example the tribe of Golog which officially has still not surrendered to Chinese communist troops) have been reported to possess arsenals of Chinese-made firearms, including assault rifles, and to purchase ammunition on a regular basis.

At present, there are about 157,000 Russian troops deployed in the area (the forces of Trans-Baykal and Maritim military districts). Keeping in mind the equipment saved for tactical and strategic reserves, together with some out-of-date weapons, there should be deployed at least 1.5-2 million units of small arms at various military stores. Widespread embezzlement of small arms belonging to the army may have resulted in the transfer of at least 5 to 10% of the above amounts to underground stores of criminal groups, as well as into the hands of private citizens. About 350,000 units of small arms (pistols, submachine guns and assault rifles) should be deployed at MVD (Federal

Police), OMON (Special Police Forces) and FSB (Federal Security Service) stores in the area.

In spite of widespread corruption and collaboration with criminal structures typical of Russian law enforcement structures within the last years, the stores of the above forces have never been reported as objects of embezzlement. Private citizens (both involved and relatively non-involved in criminal activity) residing in the research area, are expected to hold at least 2,000,000 small arms (rifles, automatic rifles, carbines, assault rifles pistols and revolvers). The possible number of small arms in underground ("Mafia"-controlled) arsenals in the area is estimated at 3,000 to 10,000 items including Kalashnikov assault rifles and machine guns, TT and TM pistols, Uzi rifles and submachine guns, as well as antitank weapons and grenade launchers (RPG-22-1 "Mukha").

POSSIBLE CONSEQUENCES

Further development of small arms proliferation in the area might boost further escalation of crime and organized crime in Siberia and the Russian Far East, especially regarding new wars between different criminal groups.79 It may also boost crime in China. As of writing, kept under relative control by Chinese law enforcement structures, criminal activity might strongly escalate in the face of economic reforms, corruption and small arms proliferation. The process of proliferation may also escalate criminal activity in Mongolia, situated between Russia and China and dependent on both neighbours.

Escalation of Corruption

Most salaries paid to Russian policemen, customs officials, etc., do not exceed $US 400 per month while purely subsistence wages for one person are at least $US 800. Further escalation of criminal activity in the Russian Far East and Siberia, in combination with ongoing underpayment of law enforcement officers, makes it necessary for them either to look for additional part-time jobs, or to take bribes and cooperate with criminals. The latter variant tends to seem more attractive to the increasing percentage of Russian law enforcement officers and leading to the formation of what Russian criminologist A. Gurov calls "the Criminal State."

Export of Crime

Further proliferation of small arms in the area together with the escalation of corruption and helplessness of law enforcement structures, leads to accumulation of funds in the hands of organized criminal groups in Russia and China, as well as the growth of their members. As a result, criminal groups are already exploring such prospective "business areas" as Japan, Singapore, USA and Canada. During the last five years, numerous representatives of Russian and Chinese organized criminal groups have penetrated Canada and USA and have started building networks here. Within the next ten years, their influence in North America could significantly increase and drastically worsen the criminal situation here. Canada has already been used by Russian and Chinese criminal structures as a place for moneylaundering and permanent residence. This process might develop further if not brought under control, and turn Canada into a springboard for Russian criminal groups used for penetrating the USA.80

Terrorism and Insurgent Groups

Concentration of small arms in the arsenals of the "Russian Mafia" has made contract killings and other acts of terror typical elements of modern Russian life. If not brought under control, this process may expand into new countries and areas. Concentration of small arms in the arsenals of rightist and leftist opposition parties and organizations might provoke political violence, in turn increasing the flow of political refugees to North American countries.

Illicit trade in small arms in Siberia might facilitate separatism and violence in some ethnic "republics" of Russian Federation (mainly Sakha-Yakoutia and Tannu-Tuva). Accumulation of small arms in the hands of citizens might eventually provoke high-scale ethnic violence between native and Russian Siberians on one hand, and Chinese and Korean settlers on the other. This scenario might also create refugee problems.

Accumulations of small arms in the area might activate so-called "Siberian separatism." At the moment, this sentiment is popular among a relatively small number of Slavonic-speaking Siberians, but However it is most likely that small arms acquired by mobsters for their "actions" will lead to an increase in violence when used. the idea of an independent Siberia might someday cause political and even military confrontation in the area.

POSSIBLE POLICY OPTIONS

The challenge of small arms proliferation facing national governments requires international cooperation and coordination. Some of the general tasks which must be addressed, include the following:

- collection and regular updating of accurate information on small arms flows — both legitimate and illicit;
- monitoring the traffic routes;
- locating and confiscation illegal stores and depots; and,
- identifying the leaders of criminal and paracriminal groups involved and interested in illicit proliferation of small arms.

More international coordination in the field of exchange information and tracing, as well as the intercept of the illicit movement of small arms are among possible options. However, experience suggests that these options do not work well either in China, or in Russia because of corruption and traditional mistrust towards foreigners/westerners in both countries.

Accumulation of information and tracing might work better if a considerable number of competent law-enforcement officers in the area would serve as direct sources of information for law enforcement structures of Canada and USA. This might work well in Russia for two reasons: In spite of traditional mistrust, there exists a stereotype of a "Mighty American Cop" among Russians including Russian law enforcement officers, and that stereotypical figure is respected. Russian law enforcement officers are underpaid and open to part-time jobs for other employers (among them criminal gangs). Thus many of them might also work for non-criminal employers overseas representing, for example, Canadian or American law enforcement structures. It is presently an opportune time to recruit them, as they are relatively free of old communist ideology, while new radical nationalist ideology is still not strong enough to prevent them from being hired by foreign structures. Other East European backgrounds, i.e., the descendants of "white settlers" who first came to Siberia at the end of the 16th century.

SMALL ARMS IN SOUTH ASIA

The proliferation and illicit use of small arms in South Asia can never be understood in isolation. This is as much a theoretical position, as it is a practical one. In view of recent developments at the local and global levels, particularly with the arrival and reproduction of globalisation, small arms had a qualitative transformation with respect to its proliferation and use. Never did the world see such an easy availability and at the same time grandeur yet demonic use of weapons that have been conventionally categorised as 'small.' It seems that the humane call of Bhupen Hazarika that 'We are in the same boat, brother!' has come to haunt us-from Chicago to Chittagong, from Jaffna to Johannesburg, from Bosnia to Baghdad-indeed, more dramatically yet more painfully. But lest we make a mistake in understanding the dynamics informing, influencing and reproducing the proliferation and illicit use of small arms, it is important that we take a critical account of the meaning of globalisation and its practical implications locally, nationally, regionally, and of course, internationally.

Globalisation, mainly because of its birth from a complex combination of multiple interactions, has given rise to a multiversity or multiple universes of knowledge and practices. Three precise modes could easily be identified. First is economic globalisation, second is reverse globalisation, and the third is subaltern globalisation. In each of these modes small arms play a precise and distinctive role. A closer exposition will make this clear.

ECONOMIC GLOBALISATION

The Globalisation meaning has been best captured by an OECD publication which, while crediting the term to Theodore Levitt who first used it in 1985 in his book, The Globalisation of Markets, sees globalisation as 'a seamless or borderless, global economy.' More concretely, it is informed by precise sets of economic activities with precise characteristics on a world scale. There exists a subtle difference between the 'internationalisation of economy' and 'globalisation' according to this perspective. While the former primarily refers to the internationalisation of trade and later on, the internationalisation of finance and investment, each coming in the wake of precise historical moments of capitalism, globalisation refers to the complex combination of all these but more importantly one that is inclusive of a thoroughly transformed production structure. The latter can be best described as the organisation and development of a denationalised form of production.

That is, multi-national or rather transnational companies now collect resources in several countries, process them in another several countries and finally, export the finished products to the rest of the world. A fully finished product, therefore, no longer has one single birthmark; it has multiple birthmarks since several countries have gone to produce it. A Compaq computer, in that sense, is no longer entirely American, or a Toyota car fully Japanese. The final product of both these items will have components made in several countries of the world. Put differently, unlike the previous internationalisation of things, in the globalisation phase of capitalism the thing itself is the product of the international or global market.

In this newer configuration, the non-state enterprises are often more critical than the state-oriented or state enterprises in the reproduction of capitalism. The need for safeguarding the non-state enterprises, therefore, is as vital as protecting the state enterprises. The outcome has been greater policing and diffusion of licit weapons, which often for reasons of pilferage and structural leakage end up in the market as illicit commodities.

Reverse Globalisation

The second meaning of globalisation is very much intrinsic to the developing country's craze for modernity, principally the organisation of the (post-colonial) nation state in the image of the modern 'Western' state. In some respect this has been well described by Nirad C. Chaudhuri as early as 1926 when Chaudhuri, while referring to 'a clash of civilisation' between the East and West, sarcastically noted that 'the real cultural role of the (colonised Indians) is to assimilate the ways of Europe' (1996:1,5). Put differently, if OECD's definition could be referred to as economic globalisation, the modernist aspirations of the developing or less developed countries could be referred to as reverse globalisation.

The global reach of Bollywood (India's film industry) and Indian restaurants are good examples of reverse globalisation, where the non-state forces of the East or that of the South are no less critical in channelising the development of the (culturally and intellectually colonised) less developed or developing countries. One critical outcome of reverse globalisation has been to develop militarily in the image of the modern West, bringing with it not only the military hardware, including small arms, developed in the West but also the impetus to produce such weapons at home. Often this has taken the form of joint collaboration between developed and developing countries with many of the small arms like AK-47, M16, G3, and even grenades produced and marketed as globalised items. Again, for reasons of pilferage and structural leakage many of these weapons end up in the market as illicit commodities.

Subaltern Globalisation

There is yet another type of interaction informing and reproducing globalisation. This is a complex mode and therefore requires greater care in its exposition. Critics have already referred to the mushrooming of global networks resisting economic globalisation as 'globalisation from below'. The latter includes a diverse group of people environmentalists, NGOs, religious groups, small farmers, labour unions (incidentally of both the developed and developing countries), women's movement, consumerists, African debt relief campaigners, anti-sweatshop activists, and the like, all one way or another either critical of or directly suffering from and struggling against the impact of economic globalisation. Here the forces of the seemingly disempowered non-state have creatively joined hands to overcome the exploitation of the empowered non-state, i.e. the forces of economic globalisation. The subaltern nature of the resistance movements, particularly the networking, can hardly be minimised.

But then, there is a further subaltern variant to the whole notion of globalisation from below. This refers to the deepening of relationship between and amongst the 'dubious groups' and 'shadowy activities' ranging from smuggling of goods and people, illicit production and trading of small arms, money laundering, narco-production and trading, terrorism, and the like, and that again, across and beyond national, ethnic, racial, and even religious affiliations. The subalterns, particularly the poverty-ridden and marginalised population, become easy target of such groups and activities, but more importantly the state of being itself becomes a factor for certain groups of (relatively well off) people to rally support and even clandestinely work for their cause.

A protracted nature of poverty and marginality and a lack of substantive global concern also push them to seek informal or even criminal means to reproduce their lives or redress the situation. The complex networking at this level and in combination with the resistance movements against economic globalisation could be best referred to as subaltern globalisation. Here the subalterns, including their ardent supporters and sympathisers, are no less creative and empowered when it comes to organising and reproducing their activities at the global level, and that too often by challenging the overly empowered forces of economic globalisation.

Two things are worth pointing out here. First is the subtle connivance of the state machineries with the dubious forces in reproducing subaltern globalisation. In fact, the state machineries go on to empower the subaltern networks almost to their own peril, which brings us to the second point. Indeed, if economic globalisation is in the business of weakening the power of the state, the practices of subaltern globalisation are no less menacing and destructive to the state. According to Mittelman (2000: 214): '(Criminal) groups are alternative social organisations that, in some respects, challenge the power and authority of the state to impose its standards, codified as law. These groups constitute an alternative system by offering commerce and banking in black and gray markets that operate outside the regulatory framework of the state; buying, selling, and distributing controlled or prohibited commodities, such as narcotics; providing swift and usually discreet dispute resolution and debt collection without resorting to the courts; creating and maintaining cartels when state laws proscribe them; and arranging security for the so-called protection of businesses, as well as sheltering them from competitors, the state and rival criminals. There is no reason to doubt the destructive potential of subaltern globalisation. Even those resisting economic globalisation and joining ranks with the subalterns may find themselves at risk if and when the destructive potential of subaltern globalisation is played out with full ferocity and demonic intent. The use of small arms can hardly be underestimated here. A quick look at some of the practices of subaltern globalisation would provide credence to our contention.

SUBALTERN GLOBALISATION AND THE ARMING OF THE NON-STATE

The element of subalternity in the resistance movements against economic globalisation (and the case could also be stretched to reverse globalisation) cannot be denied. The anti-globalisation protests in Seattle, Rome, Prague or Washington all tend to indicate that the subalterns or marginalised forces have been put into a dire situation because of economic globalisation. The protests are otherwise meant to highlight the grievances of the subalterns worldwide.

The resistance movements however in and by themselves do not reproduce the life and living of the subalterns. Mittelman has already indicated that 'where poverty is severe, criminal gangs flourish' (2000: 209). The link between poverty and criminality is less linear than what is seemingly suggested here. A state of subalternity in fact creates conditions that make people disinterested in the business of reproducing the power of the state. Mis-governance otherwise becomes the (dis)order of the day. People, particularly the subalterns, increasingly start depending on informal, often criminal, means for reproducing their livelihood. Even when requiring business or personal security they fall back on the power of the 'godfathers,' hired goons, mastans, and the like, than on the otherwise inept, often corrupt, governmental machineries.

A shadowy network of things and transactions gets reproduced and in the process destabilises not only the power of the state but also the power of the subalterns, indeed, making them more vulnerable and disempowered. This further creates grounds for fresh recruits and creative but demonic ventures for organising and reproducing subaltern globalisation.

Narco-terrorism

Narco-production and trading is a lucrative business in this region. In 2001 Myanmar surpassed Afghanistan as the largest producer of illicit opium and heroin in the world. To provide some knowledge of the amount, 865 metric tons of opium was produced in Myanmar in 2001, almost all of which were processed into heroin and sold to the illicit market both within and outside the region (BCB, 2002:1). This is more than double the amount of illicit opium that is available in other heroin-producing countries, such as India, Columbia, Mexico, or Laos (ICB, 2002:2). It may be mentioned that there exists a vibrant but complex relationship between opium growers and heroin producers, drug dealers and consumers, security and custom officials, high-risk investors and money launderers, and that again, not only nationally but also regionally and globally. As the following U.S. Drug Enforcement Agency report suggests (BCB, 2002:1):

'Opium poppy cultivation and heroin refining take place in remote, mountainous border regions. Armed ethnic groups such as, the United Wa State Army, the Kokang Chinese, and the Myanmar National Democratic Alliance Army control the cultivation areas, refine opium into heroin, and also produce methamphetamine. Associates of these organisations from other Asian nations have shipped tons of heroin from Burma to the United States within the past decade. The largest single heroin seizure in the United States consisted of 486 kilograms of Burma-produced heroin that the US Customs Service discovered in a containerised shipment of plastic bags from Southeast Asia, via Taiwan, en route to a warehouse in Hayward, California, in May 1991'.

But Myanmar, apart from being a member of the infamous 'Golden Triangle', is also close to yet another major narco-producing region, the 'Golden Crescent.' In smuggling heroin from Myanmar beyond the region and the continent both India and Bangladesh are used as transit points (BCB, 2002:4). This further exacerbates problems related to narco-terrorism in the region. In fact, one critical problem arising out of the confluence of two major narco-producing and trading regions is the cementing of a diabolic relationship between insurgent groups, arms dealers and narco-terrorism. Such a relationship is quite common in and around Thai-Myanmar, Indo-Myanmar and Bangladesh-Myanmar borders. Not that all the insurgent groups engage in narco-production or narco-trafficking but it has been found that almost all of them have regularly taxed and exhorted money from the traffickers while providing protection to the latter for conducting trafficking in drugs. There are several critical implications of this.

Firstly, the transnational narco-networks, now backed by armed insurgents, make anti-narco-production or anti-narco-trafficking drive immensely difficult. And given the terrain (both physical and topographical) in which the insurgents and the traffickers operate there is now all the more reason to believe that the nationally-organised military or coercive solutions may not be the correct way of overcoming the menace of narco-terrorism.

Secondly, weapons, particularly small arms, in the hands of both the insurgents and traffickers become more rampant, indeed, to the point of threatening the law and order situation in the vicinity. A large portion of the money received from taxing and extorting the narco-traffickers goes on to purchase small, at times sophisticated, arms for the insurgents.

Finally, subaltern aspirations get entwined between insurgency and narco-terrorism, almost to the point of blurring the distinction between the two. While this becomes handy for the state machineries in the strategy of depicting the insurgents as narco-traders and winning back the support of the members of the dissenting communities, it often leads them to quick-fix remedies with little or no results. As the World Bank-sponsored study on Indo-Bangladesh border smuggling once pointed out that 'Ordinary men, women and even children participate in smuggling as couriers, porters and rickshaw pullers' (Nandy, 1995), which only indicates that the subalternity of smuggling or even narco-terrorism is far more complex than what is readily understood. There is therefore no guarantee that the narco-menace would discourage the subalterns from joining the trade.

Money Laundering

Narco-terrorism would not make much headway without the practice of money laundering. It is the latter that provides the required funds for the production and later on, shipments of the narcotics across regions and continents. The weakness and corruption prevalent in the banking system of the region remain easily susceptible to money laundering. Often drug traffickers invest their drug profits in the country's infrastructure and legitimate businesses (BCB, 2002:11). The drug trafficker cum money launderer otherwise with the connivance of the bank and the state end up running legal businesses! When such a structure comes into being it becomes impossible to eradicate narco-trafficking and all the corroborating agencies, including money laundering and terrorism, unless and until the state itself goes through a sustained period of reforms and restructuring.

At times certain other structural factors are also responsible in reproducing money laundering, as is the case with the stateless but relatively well off Rohingyas living abroad. As stateless and few licit areas to invest, these Rohingyas have no option but to launder money to various Rohingya nationalist or insurgent groups, mainly to fulfil their subaltern aspirations in the northern Arakan region of Myanmar. That a part of this money would be used in purchasing arms and later on in insurgent or terrorist activities can never be ruled out.

Let me at this stage clarify one point. Once a subaltern struggle takes a military or violent turn, it cannot escape from being linked to the various networks of subaltern globalisation. This is because in order to sustain the subaltern movement through military means there is a dire need for both cash and arms, indeed, over and above the committed recruits of fighters. Often the funds as well as the arms come via the network of dubious groups and shadowy activities.

In recent times, more so in the post-cold war era, this has been the case practically with all the militant groups, including those directly involved in subaltern movements. Tamil Tigers is a good instance, which despite having being funded by the Tamil diaspora, did not hesitate to enter into the business of selling heroin and hashish for financing arms purchases (Shah, 1998:515). Again, take the case of Kachin Independence Organisation, a militant group fighting for the interests of the Kachin people within Myanmar, which with five thousand regular 'armed' soldiers remains 'heavily involved in the heroin trade' (FAS, 2003). This is not something unexpected in view of the protracted nature of these movements and the cost that is involved in sustaining them. Even a modest costing will show that the need for cash is quite substantial. For instance, if we take that a militant group is made up of 3000 fighters or terrorists and that each is paid a monthly allowance of Rs. 5000, the need for cash just for paying the terrorists every month comes to Rs. 15,000,000 (or USD 319,148 at the current exchange rate), which is quite substantial in local standards (Swami, 2003:7). Often the militant groups for the sake of maintaining their freedom and this is more so in the aftermath of the cold war shy away from a particular source of funding. Instead, they now prefer diversifying fund-raising, which at times includes money from taxing the narco-traders or even joining in the business of selling drugs and arms. The following report is a good indicator of the militant groups' involvement in arms trafficking and making money from it (TDS, 2002:12):

Around 100 AK-47 rifles reached different gangs of criminals in the port city (of Chittagong) and its surrounding areas from the insurgents of Arakan state of Myanmar staying in deep forests across the Bangladesh border.... Arakan insurgents sold the rifles and some other sophisticated weapons to these gangs through a clandestine channel of local kingpins of arms dealers and smugglers on various occasions in the past few years. This brings us to the third and final area, the issue of illicit small arms.

Illicit Small Arms

If anything that has empowered the terrorists and mastans lately, it has been the proliferation and use of illegal small arms. In April 1996 the Bangladesh military seized the following weapons from the vessels off Cox's Bazar (Nepram, 2002:99), a place incidentally not very far from the Bangladesh-Myanmar border:

List of Illegal Small Arms

AK-47 Rifles............................	500
Machine guns........................	80
Rocket launchers.................	50
Grenades................................	2000

It is difficult to imagine that these weapons, including many in the pipeline, enter Bangladesh without some connivance of the state machineries, particularly police and customs departments. But even the knowledge of possible 'helpers' does not provide a clear picture as to who received the arms and more importantly who supplied them. The best we can do in this kind of circumstances is consult Jane's Infantry Weapons, a book of notable distinction, and find out the names of the countries manufacturing these weapons. According to Jane's 1996 edition, the following countries, both developed and developing, were listed as the main producers or suppliers of small arms: Argentina, Austria, Belgium, Brazil, Britain, Chile, China, France, Germany, India, Iran, Iraq, Israel, North Korea, Pakistan, Russia, Singapore, South Africa, South Korea, Spain, Switzerland, Turkey, USA, Venezuela and many more. But this does not help much unless we identify the birthmark (i.e. the original manufacturer) of the small arms that are found and used in terrorist activities. But since the public had no access to the seized weapons mentioned above, there was no way to find out the birthmark of these weapons. But then a survey conducted at Dhaka University in 1995-1996, supplemented by various newspaper reports, helped to trace the type, birthmark and cost of small arms found in the hands of student political cadres and in-campus mastans. The following is the list:

Small Arms Used by Mastans in Dhaka University

Type	*Birthmark/Manufacturer*	*Price (Taka in Thousand)*
Saddam Pistol	India	40-50
9 mm bore pistol	Italy	50-60
22 bore pistol	Spain, Italy, Brazil	30
7.65 mm bore pistol	Italy	60
Chinese rifle	China	80
303 cut rifle	Britain	25
.45 revolver	USA	60
German revolver	Germany	n.a.
.324 revolver	Pakistan	15-22
Pipe gun	Local	3-5
Shutter gun	India	n.a.

The type and birthmark of the small arms indicate that the bulk of them were produced in developed countries but then it does not tell us how they made it to the University. It is unlikely that these weapons were directly shipped or airlifted from the manufacturing countries to their destination in Dhaka. What is more likely is that these weapons entered Bangladesh from various border points (Bangladesh-Myanmar as well as Indo-Bangladesh) via a vibrant subaltern network (both dubious and political) that possibly included at various stages of their shipments members of both developed and developing countries. On this issue, a national daily of Bangladesh reported (TDS, 2000:10): 'Sixteen northern districts of the country, especially the frontier ones are flooded with illegal arms and ammunition, posing a threat to law and order situation. These arms are mostly possessed by political activists, outlawed extremists, terrorists, extortionists and miscreants. The illegal arms include both foreign and local sten gun, SMG, sawed-off rifle, SLR, revolver and pipe gun. Most of the firearms are in the hands of activists of 'three political parties' who have separate hideouts in different places in this region including frontiers of Natore, Pabna, Sirajganj and Bogra districts'.

The subaltern nature of the network cannot be denied, although the flow of small arms has gone beyond those adhering to some form of subaltern aspirations. In fact, the flow has become so acute and extensive that even the former Indian High Commissioner to Bangladesh, Deb Mukherjee, publicly noted that 'It is possible that firearms are among the items smuggled from India into Bangladesh' (TDS, 2000:12; Husain, 2002). Put differently, without an extensive subaltern network, it is impossible to imagine the flow of small arms, whether to Cox's Bazaar or Dhaka University. At times, however, not only the arms flow but also the network could prove deadly. Let me cite an example by quoting Singh (1995:59):

'A large number of terrorist groups are believed to be in possession of man-portable SAMs now.... The whereabouts of the unaccounted 560 Stinger missiles (out of the stock supplied to Afghan Mujahideen) are unknown, and all efforts to recover them have failed so far. A few had appeared in Iran, having been sold by the Mujahideen. Another 312 were reportedly sold in the open market at Landi Kotal (Pakistan) in January 1993. Earlier this year (1995) the LTTE shot down two Sri Lanka

Air Force aircraft carrying passengers'. What we have here is a subaltern network consisting of Afghans, Iranians, Pakistanis, and in so for as the missiles making it to the hands of the Tamil Tigers, Indians and Sri Lankans. But then, an American made weapon changing hands in Afghanistan, Iran, Pakistan, India and finally reaching Sri Lanka can only make everyone culpable when the said weapon is finally used against the Sri Lankans. Similar is the case with the weapons that are used in Bombay, Karachi, Dhaka, Delhi, Colombo or any other place in South Asia. Indeed, if there is an element of subaltern bonding among the users of small arms, there is also a bonding, albeit more social, among those killed by these weapons. This is because most of the victims turn out to be disempowered, marginalised subalterns!

What is To be Done?

The activities arising out of subaltern globalisation, particularly of the shadowy and dubious variants, are not so easy to overcome, and this is more so when access to and returns from them are overwhelming and easy. Indeed, in the backdrop of poverty, polarised politics and poor policing, there is less urgency on the part of the common masses to help locate and seize illicit small arms. The return (physical, mental as well as financial) from doing so, and this is at the level of both the community and the individual, must be higher than those provided by the various networks of subaltern globalisation. In this respect, if there is a need for macro-intervention, reforming and even reformulating age-old institutions and laws and covenants, there is also the need for micro-intervention, with the locality and the individual actively participating in the process and benefiting from it. In the case of South Asia the macro-micro interventions may be initiated at three levels.

Reforming the police is the first. The group that is responsible for tracing, seizing and destroying illicit small arms is thoroughly inadequate. This is not so much for the lack of efficiency as for the deliberate disinterestedness in the task. Some policemen even do not have a chair to sit at their respective offices! If that is the case, and added with the poor pay and uncertain future, there is little hope that the police could challenge the shadowy and dubious networks of subaltern globalisation. As is the case, often the latter buys them up. In this respect, police reforms would be no less ‘a revolution’ for it would weaken a critical part of the network through which illicit small arms enter the market and reproduce subaltern globalisation. This reform must be substantial inclusive of the population as a whole.

Empowering civil society is the second. Creative micro interventions are required in this area. One could think of activities ranging from ‘civil watch groups on small arms’ to forming local, national, regional, even international ‘associations of the victims of small arms.’ Insofar as the latter is concerned, the role of the American mothers during the Vietnam War. As mothers of the victims they were at the forefront in anti-war demonstrations. In fact, their contributions were no less in bringing sense to the government and putting an end to the U.S. military role in Vietnam. Given the number of killing in South Asia from illegal small arms, it would be quite worthwhile for the mothers (or even fathers, sisters and brothers) of the victims, irrespective of their national, sub-national, religious, ethnic, ideological and communal affiliations, to come together and share their pain and bereavements. This could even lead to novel initiatives, including voicing in greater numbers a global disarmament of small arms.

Finally, insofar as the proliferation and use of illicit small arms is beyond national boundaries, a South Asian civil-police force ought to be creatively nurtured and established. In this region, policing has been an absolute prerogative of the government and the coercive forces, namely the police and the military. There has been virtually no role for the civic population or the civil society on matters related to security. But there is more civil content than military when it comes to narco-terrorism, money laundering and illicit small arms. Indeed, these are critical sectors in the nexus that is responsible for reproducing contemporary terrorism and the demonic use of small arms. Beefing up the power of the police or the military to contain and resolve these issues would take us nowhere. A combined civil-police force and that again South Asian in scale would have the effect of not only de-governmentalising but also de-policing security issues, indeed, to a point where civic population would be engaged in the task of creatively challenging and combating the shadowy and dubious networks within and beyond national borders.

8

Towards a Negotiating Mandate for an Arms Trade Treaty

The second session of the UN Open-Ended Working Group (OEWG) on an Arms Trade Treaty (ATT), held from 13-17 July 2009 at the United Nations in New York, has moved the possibility of a negotiating mandate for the treaty a step closer, but divisions remain as some states, including many of the major arms exporters, continue to question the feasibility of an arms trade treaty.

Chaired by Ambassador Garcia Moritan of Argentina, in its final hours the OEWG was able to incorporate some language on substantive elements into its final report, following efforts by Mexico in particular. Due to insufficient time, however, the OEWG was compelled to drop several key elements from the text-including elements previously agreed by the 2008 Group of Government Experts (GGE).

The relatively weak language in the brief substantive portion of the Group's report disappointed many ATT proponents, who fear that the weakened positions could lock future work into a less comprehensive and less effective treaty. They argue such a treaty would add little to the existing patchwork of national and regional regulations on arms transfers.

Despite this the mood of the meeting was optimistic. The most notable outcome of the second session of the OEWG was the achievement of consensus, for the first time, on the need for "international action" to address the problem of the unregulated trade in conventional arms. As a result there is growing expectation that some governments might push for early adoption of a negotiating mandate perhaps as soon as the upcoming 64th (2009) session of the UN First Committee.

Areas for Discussion

To pave the way for negotiations, the broad objective of the OEWG is to narrow differences on four areas of an ATT: goals and objectives; feasibility; scope; and parameters.

Goals and objectives refer to what the problems the treaty is meant to solve at the broadest level. They can be as narrow as preventing the illicit transfer of arms to terrorists or as broad as establishing rules and criteria affecting all arms transfers. They could also be anywhere in between, for example, prohibiting transfer of arms to abusers of human rights or international humanitarian law. With a wide range of divergent views on the table, many opponents of the Treaty have sought to delay negotiations by demanding that governments broadly agree on the goals and objectives of a potential treaty before consenting to any negotiating process. Feasibility refers to the objective that an ATT be universal, objective and non-political, non-discriminatory, and include clear definitions. Several key governments continue to maintain that an ATT is not feasible, though the number of overt sceptics has dropped considerably since 2006.

Scope refers to the type of weapons and activities or transactions an ATT would cover. Activities and transactions potentially encompasses the full range of acts related to the transfer of weapons, from licensing and brokering to export, transshipment, and import, etc. Parameters refers to the real substance of the treaty. For example, the potential range of principles or criteria that would give an exporter a presumption to deny an export, such as violation of human rights or the potential for the arms to be used to commit crimes or to violate international humanitarian law. They also cover the operational mechanism by which any such principles will be applied to arms transfer decisions.

NGO pressure for an ATT

Current efforts to establish an ATT can be traced back to the efforts made by Non-Governmental Organizations (NGOs) from the mid-1990s onwards. In 1997, a group of Nobel Peace Laureates, led by then former Costa Rican President Oscar Arias, published a draft International Code of Conduct on Arms Transfers. The basic object of that effort was to create criteria for the transfer of all types of weapons based on promotion of democracy, protection of human rights and transparency in military spending. It sought to prohibit arms transfers to states that support terrorism or that are engaged in aggression against nations or peoples. The work of the Arias Foundation in the 1990s was instrumental in creating momentum for an ATT.

This effort was followed years later by the European Union's adoption of a Code of Conduct on Arms Exports, approved by EU foreign ministers on 25 May 1998. The EU code established eight criteria for the approval of arms transfers, including relevant international commitments or treaties, respect for human rights in the destination country, the existence of armed conflict in the destination country, the risk the arms will be used in aggression or to bolster a territorial claim, the national security of EU states, the destination country's support for terrorism, the risk of re-export, and the compatibility of the transfer with the economic capacity of the recipient.

The work of the Arias Foundation and the Nobel Laureates picked up momentum in the 2000s. In 2000, a group of NGOs revised the 1997 Nobel Laureates' Code of Conduct. As part of this effort, in 2003 the group circulated a draft Framework Convention on International Arms Transfers to the First Biennial Meeting of States to the UN Programme of Action on Small Arms. The object of the draft Convention was to prevent the transfer of arms in violation of international law or obligations, or if the exporting state has reason to believe the weapons will be used to violate human rights or international humanitarian law or to commit crimes against humanity or genocide.

In 2003, the International Action Network Against Small Arms, Amnesty International, and Oxfam launched the Control Arms campaign, intended to establish a binding international agreement to control the arms trade according to established principles of human rights, humanitarian law, sustainable development, and peaceful international relations. In 2004 the governments of Brazil, Cambodia, Costa Rica, Finland, Kenya, Iceland, Macedonia, Mali, the Netherlands, and the United Kingdom pledged to work toward an ATT. The largest arms exporter of this group, the United Kingdom, became a key driver of this effort after 2004.

At a meeting from 20-22 February 2005 in Dar Es Salaam, 31 governments agreed to move forward a process to establish global principles on arms transfers based on existing international law. The foreign ministers of the states of the Great Lakes and Horn regions of Africa announced their support for an ATT at the third Ministerial Review Conference of the Nairobi Declaration. More governments announced their support for an ATT at the second biennial meetings of states to consider implementation of the UN Programme of Action to Prevent, Combat and Eradicate the Illicit Trade in Small Arms and Light Weapons in All Its Aspects (UN Programme of Action on SALW). The EU Council announced its support for the effort during its meeting in Luxembourg in October 2005.

THE ATT PROCESS MOVES TO THE UN

At the 61st session of the UN General Assembly (UNGA) First Committee, seven states, Argentina, Australia, Costa Rica, Finland, Japan, Kenya and the United Kingdom, introduced a draft resolution to the First Committee, entitled "Towards an arms trade treaty: establishing common international standards for the import, export and transfer of conventional arms." The central element of the draft resolution was to request establishment of a group of governmental experts (GGE) in 2008 to examine the feasibility of such a treaty. The resolution also requested UN member states to submit their views to the UN Secretary-General by 30 April 2007.

The First Committee adopted the resolution, co-sponsored by 116 states, with 139 governments voting in favour. The United States was the only government to vote against and 24 governments abstained. States that opposed the resolution and a prospective treaty generally focused on the necessity of a GGE, rather than directly expressing opposition to a treaty. The UN General Assembly subsequently adopted the text in December 2006 as resolution 61/89, with 153 states voting in favour.

In September 2007, the UN Secretary-General appointed the GGE, which included experts from 28 countries. The GGE met in three sessions between February and August 2008 and adopted a final report by consensus. The GGE included nearly all major arms exporters, including many of whom had expressed doubts about feasibility of the ATT. Due to these difficult dynamics and the complexity of the issue, the GGE was recommended a slower, "step by step" process. Its major recommendation was for further consideration of the issue within the UN in an open and transparent manner on the basis of consensus-meaning through a process including the entire UN membership. The GGE report, as well as an analysis of states' views by the United Nations Institute for Disarmament Research (UNIDIR), has also made plain the extent of disagreement on feasibility, scope, and parameters.

UNIDIR noted seven members of the Group held the view that an ATT was not feasible-China, Egypt, India, Israel, Pakistan, Russia, and Venezuela. For sceptics, feasibility ATT rested on the definition of its goals and objectives. As a result the OEWG took up the task of discussing goals and objectives. The Group agreed that a feasible treaty would contain objective and agreed criteria that reflect the (separate) responsibilities of importers and exporters.

The GGE was unable to come to any agreement on scope, either on the weapons or activities to be covered. Some states focused on the categories of weapons used by the UN Register of Conventional Arms, with many governments suggesting the addition of small arms and light weapons and their ammunition. Some governments also advocated for coverage of parts and components, manufacturing technology, dual-use technology, explosives and new types of weapons or technology.

The GGE also agreed little on parameters except for that an ATT should be based on the principles of the UN Charter with governments tending to emphasize Charter provisions on: excluding the threat or use of force; non-interference in the domestic relations of states; the right to individual or collective self defence, including the right to acquire arms; and the obligation to carry out the decisions of the Security Council, including arms embargoes. Related to common standards for arms transfers, states tended to favour criteria dealing with the risk or end-use of specific transfers and disfavour country-based assessments.

Enter the Open-Ended Working Group

At the 2008 First Committee, the seven original sponsors of the ATT resolution tabled a new draft text, following closely on resolution 61/89. Following on aspects of the GGE report, the new resolution included a decision to establish an Open-Ended Working Group, open to all states, to meet in six one-week sessions between 2009 and 2011 to consider where consensus can be found on a prospective treaty.

The resolution picked up eight more votes in favour than the 2006 resolution and it shed six abstentions. Though this resolution faced some difficulties when the UN revealed it might not be able to finance the meetings, governments were able to work through this impasse, thereby allowing the UNGA to adopt the draft as resolution 63/240 in January 2009. Only the United States voted against. Nineteen states abstained, including a number of Arab states, China, India, Iran, Israel, Pakistan, and Russia.

The mandate of the 2009 OEWG meetings was to consider elements from the GGE report where consensus could be developed for inclusion in an ATT, "which provides a balance giving benefit to all, with the principles of the Charter of the United Nations and other existing international obligations at the centre of such considerations." The second session was also tasked with sending a report to the 64th (2009) General Assembly.

Goals and Objectives

If the first step toward articulating the goals and objectives of an ATT is identifying the problem, then the OEWG remains in a troubling condition. Though delegations made real progress in narrowing differences, fundamental issues remain unresolved. The OEWG was unable to move past the work of the GGE in clearly articulating what the goals and objectives of ATT would be.

Delegations continued to disagree over the problems caused by the unregulated arms trade, though the OEWG did inch forward slightly on a broader, common understanding of the dilemma. Whereas the GGE report recognized only the problems of international organized crime and terrorism, the OEWG added instability to this list. Some governments would have liked to see other problems specifically linked to the unregulated arms trade, such as its contribution to armed conflict-a connection that continues to be blocked by some major arms-exporting states.

On identifying goals, the OEWG was unable move past the lowest common denominator consensus of the GGE. Its report recognizes "the need to address the problems relating to unregulated trade in conventional weapons and their diversion to the illicit market." Thus, states agree an ATT should prevent the diversion of arms to unauthorized users. As pointed out by several delegations, preventing diversion is the responsibility of both arms exporters and importers. Some governments also want ATT to include standards on end use, focusing also on the unique responsibilities of importers. The OEWG was unable to move past the GGE's recognition that both importers and exporters have responsibilities to address the problems related to the illicit trade in conventional arms.

The OEWG did not attempt to articulate any language dealing with the objectives. The majority of delegations continued to envisage the primary objective as establishing common international standards for export controls that are implemented through national legislation. Many delegations recognize the need to construct a Treaty that is resistant to political abuse, though some are sceptical that this can be achieved in a treaty that relies exclusively on national assessments of criteria. Consensus is unlikely to form around any type of external or UN-based verification or assessment mechanism. The Indian delegation continued to insist that a binding treaty is not the best way to create global export control standards. The Indian delegation said that it would like to see an ATT that is broader than just export controls. One of India's central arguments is the problem that some key governments hold national law as supreme over international norms. Other delegations, such as France, rejected this reasoning as an argument against a binding treaty.

The Russian delegation suggested that enhancing national control over conventional arms should be an objective. Russia and Egypt have both suggested that defining the objective of the Treaty is necessary before moving on to the issues of scope and parameters. Their argument is that the provisions of an ATT can only flow from its objectives.

Questioning Feasibility

The GGE had achieved consensus that, "To be feasible, a potential arms trade treaty would need clear definitions and be fair, objective, balanced, non-political, non-discriminatory and universal within the framework of the United Nations." Though this language is not reflected in the OEWG's report, in statements made during the July session, delegations did not vary from these criteria.

Compared to the GGE, fewer governments in the OEWG explicitly or implicitly questioned feasibility, though China, India, Iran, and Russia expressed continuing scepticism. The Russian delegation aired the strongest reservations, continuing to question the wisdom of a global treaty and calling for an analysis of why existing regional and sub-regional mechanisms are insufficient to address the problems of an unregulated arms trade. Iran also described a legally-binding instrument as "premature". In addition, some delegations suggested working towards an intermediate step. India and Japan made separate suggestions that a non-binding normative framework could help guide further negotiations. In India's view, such an endeavour would satisfy its requirement for a step-by-step process toward an ATT.

Disagreements on Scope

Delegations to the OEWG continued to express a wide range of divergent views on which weapons and activities are to be covered by an ATT. Like the GGE report, the report of the OEWG reflects the lack of substantive agreement.

Categories of Weapons: The majority of governments continues to advocate for a comprehensive Treaty that covers all types of conventional weapons. Such advocates generally agree that an ATT should cover the seven categories of weapons contained in the UN Register of Conventional Arms (UNRCA) plus small arms and light weapons (SALW), the so-called 7+1 formula. Supporters of 7+1 include Cuba, Indonesia, and

Singapore. A larger number of delegations, including Argentina, Brazil, Bulgaria, Guatemala, Japan, Norway, South Africa, and Paraguay, support including ammunition as well and have dubbed this approach 7+1+1. Generally excluding use of UNRCA, several other delegations also called for specific inclusion of SALW and their ammunition, including Australia, Bulgaria, Canada, the Netherlands, New Zealand, Romania, and Uruguay.

A number of delegations and NGOs, especially those who see the ATT as a means to address the humanitarian and human rights problems related to the unregulated arms trade, cautioned that UNRCA should only be considered a starting point for discussion. They note that UNRCA, intended as a post-Cold War transparency measure relating primarily to the accumulation of major conventional weapon systems, omits "an extensive range of conventional weapons... that are widely used in conflict and human rights crisis zones." Such weapons include: military helicopters and aircraft other than those designated for "combat"; naval vessels with displacements of less than 500 tonnes; unarmoured military vehicles; artillery with a calibre of 75 mm or less; and some types of unmanned aerial vehicles.

In addition, some have called for the inclusion of specific items not covered by UNRCA, including explosives, spare parts, new types of arms, dual-use items, technical expertise, and the financing of the illicit arms trade. Complicating the matter further, some delegations have taken stands against incorporating both the UNRCA and many of the aforementioned items. Egypt has been particularly vocal in its opposition to using the UNRCA categories. Brazil, Egypt, and Indonesia argued against inclusion of dual-use items. Egypt argued against coverage of either expertise or new types of arms. Western states, such as the United Kingdom and the United States, have been keen to exclude sports weapons, though a few delegations have called for them to at least be taken into account.

The Russian delegation cautioned against a comprehensive scope, arguing that it would be impractical and infeasible to go from a situation where no global regulation exists to an all-encompassing treaty. The Russians called for a more targeted approach, perhaps focusing on SALW. The International Committee for the Red Cross (ICRC) suggested that instead of compiling competing lists of items to be included, states should focus on what weapons should be *excluded* from a treaty. ICRC takes the view that an ATT should cover all conventional arms and negotiations should evaluate if there is reason to not include any given weapon system.

Treaty Coverage: Delegations also remained divided on the actions to be covered. The majority continued to advocate for an ATT to cover comprehensively all types of transfers, including: import; export; re-transfer; loans; transshipment or transiting; and brokering. India cautioned that arms transfers within military alliances should not be exempt from coverage.

Some delegations still argue that a narrow, targeted, or selective approach would lead to a more effective treaty. Egypt was the most vocal, arguing that an ATT should focus on preventing illicit brokering rather than trying to regulate or impose restrictions on activities that are presently permitted.

Some delegations also called for a Treaty to cover actions not strictly related to arms transfers. India and Pakistan made arguments for the inclusion of specific aspects of arms production and the accumulation of arms. Such a provision would not be entirely without precedent as the UN Register of Conventional Arms, *inter alia*, requests states to provide information on arms holdings and procurement through national production.

Top 20 Arms Suppliers 2003-2008

Rank	*State*	*% of total*	*US$ (mil)*
1	United States	30.51	34,901
2	Russia	24.95	28,536
3	Germany	10.01	11,450
4	France	8.40	9,607
5	United Kingdom	4.49	5,132
6	Netherlands	3.32	3,803
7	Italy	2.41	2,761
8	Spain	1.86	2,123
9	Ukraine	1.82	2,083
10	Sweden	1.76	2,012

11	Israel	1.75	2,007
12	China	1.67	1,908
13	Canada	1.16	1,322
14	Switzerland	1.10	1,262
15	Belgium	0.62	704
16	Poland	0.48	549
17	South Korea	0.39	450
18	South Africa	0.37	427
19	Finland	0.21	244
20	Montenegro	0.18	208
	All others	2.53	2,889
	Total	100	114,386

Source: SIPRI Arms Transfers Database.

Figures are expressed in USD (millions) at constant 1990 prices and may not add up due to rounding.

Parameters

The issue of parameters also continued to be highly divisive with governments still unable to agree to more than a baseline of placing the principles of the UN Charter at the centre of an ATT. The OEWG discussions focused on two primary areas: what principles should be applied; and how principles could or should be applied.

The OEWG sought to make progress towards identifying a common set of standards where governments would have a presumption to deny an arms transfer. Delegations agreed that any such criteria should be drawn from existing international law and that an ATT would not create any new international norms. The chair noted a general view that any parameters must be objective, non-discriminatory, and politically stable.

The discussions continued to reveal a widely divergent, but not necessarily irreconcilable, range of views regarding applying the principles of the UN Charter, international humanitarian law, human rights law, or other existing international principles to arms transfer decisions. The Indian delegation opined that the Group's inability to agree on parameters was closely linked to the lack of consensus over the goals and objectives of an ATT.

Consistency with UN Charter

There continued to be consensus on the bottom line that any ATT should be based on, or at least not inconsistent with, the principles of the UN Charter, which should be applied in a non-discriminatory way. A number of governments cited the need to ensure adherence to the Charter's provisions barring the threat or use of force, non-interference in the domestic affairs of states, implementation of UN Security Council decisions including arms embargoes and the right to individual or collective self-defence. Beyond the UN Charter, the only principle that enjoys consensus is that governments should prevent arms transfers that risk diversion to terrorist or organized criminal use.

International Humanitarian Law

Statements to the OEWG expressed broad, cross-regional support for incorporating international humanitarian law (IHL), though few identified specific principles. In a compilation of global principles for an ATT, a group of NGOs argued that arms transfers should be denied when they are likely to be used to commit: gross violations of IHL; serious violations of IHL; or genocide and crimes against humanity. A number of delegations also expressed support for using an ATT to deal with humanitarian issues stemming from armed conflict. Potential provisions dealing with armed conflict include preventing arms transfers to conflict regions or preventing arms transfers to users that national authorities assess might engage in humanitarian offences.

Human Rights

Inclusion of human rights standards also continued to see cross-regional support, though with less widespread enthusiasm than IHL. Pakistan spoke out against inclusion of human rights standards, arguing that, in a treaty based on national-based implementation, such national assessments would be subject to political abuse. A number of delegations also called for incorporation of human, social, or economic development needs-likely in the form of some criteria that mandate an exporting state to assess whether or not the importing state is diverting resources from the needs of its population through arms purchases. Others called for arms transfer decisions to take into account regional stability.

Few delegations spoke against inclusion of IHL and human rights standards in an ATT-China, however, did remark the subjects should be "handled with caution". It is clear from the lack of consensus-aside from the anodyne recognition that both importers and exporters have responsibilities-that some continue to stand against inclusion of such standards, at least until greater clarity is achieved on identifying the principles and objectives.

Other Issues

Perhaps crucial to securing and maintaining support for an ATT, a number of governments have cautioned that a Treaty must not overrule existing national or international export control standards. Norway suggested the treaty should allow for states to adopt and maintain standards that are more stringent than that imposed by an ATT. The United States echoed this sentiment, warning that it would not be interested in any effort that undercut its existing export controls or that permitted arms transfers to "destabilizing users".

Several delegations, including developed and developing states, recognized the need for cooperation and assistance to small states in implementing the treaty. France specified such measures must be voluntary. A number of delegations cited the need for transparency and reporting provisions and no one spoke against such measures. Some delegations called for some form of verification and compliance mechanism, though Italy argued it would not be feasible to empower some international body with the authority to overrule national decisions to deny an arms export. As noted by the UK Ambassador, there is no right to receive an arms import.

Applicability

Governments must also decide how any such standards are to be applied to arms transfer decisions. Most governments and NGOs continued to focus on the approach of assessing whether the risk of a given transfer might be used or diverted to illicit use-a risk assessment approach-rather than making decisions based solely on the record of the recipient. This approach is broadly consistent with that advocated by the ICRC, as well as that taken by the Nairobi Protocol, ECOWAS Convention on SALW, and proposals of the Control Arms Campaign.

The risk assessment approach differs from the standard enacted by the EU in its Code of Conduct, which requires members to assess the IHL record of the recipient, though the United Kingdom has advocated for risk assessment in the context of the ATT. Amnesty International has advocated for a multi-tracked assessment including both the risk a transfer might be used or diverted to commit human rights violations and the recipient's respect for-or its attitude towards-human rights law.

Action and Next Steps

The most notable outcome of the second session of the OEWG was its expression of support for "international action" to address the problem of the unregulated trade in conventional arms. For ATT supporters, such an acknowledgment represented a major victory in that it signals consensus within the UN system for some form of action, though without specifying what form that action might take.

A few governments and many NGOs expressed optimism that the upcoming session of the UN General Assembly might be able to contemplate a negotiating mandate. Statements delivered by a few delegations, however, seemed to flatly preclude this possibility, signalling that no action would be conceivable until the OEWG concludes the full term of its mandate in 2011. Given the large number of major differences on nearly every aspect of an ATT, the remaining sessions of the OEWG, representing only four weeks of meetings spread over two years, might be hard pressed to achieve consensus on any of the items on its agenda. Support for more substantive discussions came from surprising places, however. The United States, offering an "administrative point of caution," argued that the one-week format of the OEWG was insufficient and appealed to states to consider ways to adjust its mandate.

Conclusions

Since the conclusion of the GGE, opposition to an ATT *per se* has all but evaporated and all governments now agree some form of international action should be taken. Despite this, doubts about feasibility remain amongst several key arms exporting and importing governments, most vocally Egypt, India, and Russia. There is also still no consensus on whether international action should take the form of a legally-binding treaty-the type of action favoured by the overwhelming majority of states.

One-third of the way through its three-year mandate, the OEWG still finds itself in discussion mode, rather than in drafting mode, as it has yet to attempt to work out agreements over the basic goals and objectives, scope, and parameters of an ATT. In the upcoming session of the UN General Assembly, it is possible that ATT proponents may be able to leverage the consensus on the need for international action into agreement for steps beyond the OEWG. Some may still find it premature for a preparatory committee for an international conference to conclude an instrument; an expanded discussion format with a stronger negotiating mandate may be possible.

Absent agreement on the basic elements, rushing the process, may run the risk of failing to secure agreement on key features of an effective Treaty-particularly giving it a legally-binding character and ensuring its scope is sufficient to actually deal with the humanitarian and human rights concerns that gave rise to this initiative. In the end, getting it right should prove to be more important than doing it fast.

It might be fruitful to make progress first toward identifying the problem. The Russian delegation continues to hold a firm position on the necessity of gaining a better understanding of the failing points of regional and sub-regional approaches. In the context of SALW, in 1995 the General Assembly agreed to establish a government expert panel to explore and agree to the nature of the problem first as governments and NGOs built momentum toward what eventually become to the UN Programme of Action. After agreeing to the nature of the problem in 1997, states were able to secure agreement in the next year on both a follow-up process and on a deadline for achieving agreement on action.

The result of the 2008 GGE was especially disappointing in that it was particularly weak on reaching agreement on the problems to be solved, citing only diversion to unauthorized users, transnational crime, and terrorism. For the OWEG, coming to a common understanding of the goals and objectives may go a long way toward settling the feasibility issues and perhaps even breaking down the final barriers of resistance toward negotiating some form of binding treaty. NGOs have clearly articulated their visions for the principles and objectives of an ATT. Governments should use the upcoming sessions of the OWEG to achieve such a vision as well.

CAMPAIGN AGAINST ARMS TRADE

Campaign Against Arms Trade (CAAT) is a UK-based NGO and campaigning organisation working towards the abolition of the international arms trade. Founded in 1974 by a broad coalition of peace groups, CAAT is united in opposition to the military industrial complex and the growth of the private military industry. It argues that these organisations reinforce global militarism whilst undermining attempts by civil society and the United Nations to resolve disputes peacefully. CAAT's main focus is to end the influence of arms companies over the UK government, and works together with similar organisations in other countries to the same end. CAAT has grown in stature in recent years as a result of several high profile campaigns, particularly its legal challenge against the Serious Fraud Office's decision to suspend a corruption investigation into BAE Systems in 2007.

Current Issues

BAE Systems and Saudi Arabia Corruption Inquiry

BAE Systems formerly British Aerospace, is the world's third largest weapons trader. In September 1985 BAE was a signatory to the UK's largest ever arms deal, the Al Yamamah contract to provide military planes as well as servicing provisions to the government of Saudi Arabia. This ongoing contact has evolved through several phases to the present day and has thus made the company £43 billion pounds.

Shortly after the contract was signed however, corruption allegations began to surface concerning bribes paid to Saudi officials through a £60 million pound slush fund. On 12 September 2003 the Serious Fraud Office began an investigation into possible corruption. BAE are also the subject of four active SFO investigations for its dealings in Romania, the Czech Republic, South Africa and Tanzania, calling into question the general operating conduct of its agents. However on the 14th December 2006 the Government discontinued the Al Yamamah probe on the grounds that its conclusions may embarrass the Kingdom of Saudi Arabia and threaten Britain's national security.

CAAT in conjunction with the Corner House, an anti-corruption NGO, mounted a legal challenge to this decision, to assess if in curtailing the Serious Fraud Office's investigation the Government had acted illegally. Thus on 9 November 2007 the High Court in London granted a request for a judicial review of the decision. Subsequently, on the 10 April the conclusion of this review stated that the Government had indeed acted illegally in stopping the corruption investigation. Lord Justice Moses and Mr Justice Sullivan ruled that the Government had capitulated under intimidation from the government of Saudi Arabia and that "no-one whether within this country or outside, is entitled to interfere with the course of justice." BAE Systems continue to deny any impropriety stating the court had failed "to distinguish between a commission and a bribe."

Subsequently the SFO launched an appeal that was heard before the Appellate committee of the House of Lords on 7 and 8 July 2008. On the 30th July the House of Lords overturned the High Courts' ruling, and decreed that the SFO had acted lawfully in the interest of national security. Senior Peer Lord Bingham of Cornwall stated that "the director's decision was one he was lawfully entitled to make" but the ruling incited a chorus of condemnation from Nick Clegg in the House of Commons. The leader of the Liberal Democrats characterised the verdict as "a legal licence for international blackmail." The ruling also provoked considerable ire among anti-corruption campaigners and a string of NGO's. CAAT spokesman Symon Hill commented "BAE and the government will be quickly disappointed if they think that this ruling will bring an end to public criticism. Throughout this case we have been overwhelmed with support from people in all walks of life. There has been a sharp rise in opposition to BAE's influence in the corridors of power. Fewer people are now taken in by exaggerated claims about British jobs dependent on the arms trade. The government has been judged in the court of public opinion."

In response to the judicial review the Government has drafted a controversial clause of the Constitutional Reform Bill. This will grant the attorney-general the power to quash any further such investigations with immunity from judicial interference. CAAT and the Corner House have both condemned any such legislation as a perversion of justice which will erode the accountability of the executive and threaten the rule of law.

Closure of DESO

The Defence Export Services Organisation was an adjunct of the Ministry of Defence concerned with procuring contracts for private military companies to export arms to foreign governments. The closure of DESO had been a core campaigning aim of CAAT since its inception in 1974, and was their main focus in 2006. CAAT brought considerable pressure on the government concerning the ethics of some such trading, given that in 2004, UK arms export licenses were granted to 13 of the 20 'major countries of concern' identified by the Foreign and Commonwealth Office in its 2005 Human Rights Annual Report. CAAT also alleged that DESO unfairly privileged the interests of the arms companies and helped facilitate bribes to foreign officials. In response to this on 25 July 2007 Gordon Brown announced that DESO would indeed be shut down.

Chief Executive of BAE Systems Mike Turner condemned the decision by citing the damage it would do to Britain's export trade. CAAT argued that the closure of DESO is a step forward in transparency for the government. As a result it will be less hamstrung by lobbyists seeking to manipulate its human rights and budgetary policies.

In future export promotion will be the responsibility of UK Trade and Investment, the body that supports all UK exports. On 1 April 2008 the UKTI Defence and Security Organisation, which will be responsible for some of DESO's previous functions, was formed. The current head of UKTI DSO is Richard Paniguian CBE, a former BP executive. CAAT has pledged to monitor UKTI to make sure that military exports, (less than

2% of total UK exports in 2004), do not monopolise a disproportionate amount of its resources.

DSEi: Reed Elsevier Campaign

Defence Systems and Equipment International is one of the largest arms fairs in the world which takes place in London bi-annually, the last occurring in September 2007. From 2003 to May 2008 the DSEi was organised by Reed Elsevier, a publishing and information company, who acquired the previous organisers Spearhead in 2003. As CAAT is opposed to the existence of arms fairs, it campaigned to encourage Reed Elsevier to extricate itself from the arms industry. There followed a sustained and concerted effort from academics, doctors and writers that use the company's products, who demanded they end their involvement with arms fairs on ethical grounds. This culminated in Reed's decision to sell its arms fairs to Clarion Events in June2007, a sale which was completed in May 2008.

However, CAAT intends to continue campaigning for the overall closure of DSEi and other arms fairs.

Clean Investment Campaign

From universities to local authorities CAAT has consistently sought to highlight areas where public bodies hold shares in companies trading in arms. On 9 July CAAT released research that 75 local authorities in the UK held such investments through their pension funds. It has argued that many council employees reject the notion that they should help to prop up such companies and continues to advocate a more ethical investment strategy. The long standing Clean Investment campaign has had many successes in the past, one of the most significant occurring in 2001. In response to pressure from the CAAT Christian Network the Church of England redefined its investment criteria and confirmed it will no longer invest in arms companies. Despite excluding arms company holdings, the Church remained, in 2005, the second best performer of more than 1,000 funds over the previous decade.

Furthermore, from 2005 the CAAT Universities Network has met with considerable success in its campaign to advocate ethical investment across the UK. A report entitled 'Study War

No More' has highlighted military funding and involvement within 26 British universities. CAAT facilitates research into the details of university investment portfolios which has helped students to mount their own campaigns for clean investment. This has resulted in many universities divesting their shares in the arms industry, whilst many more campuses continue to campaign for similar action to be taken.

Private military companies

Since the invasion of Iraq in March 2003, the use of 'private military companies' has become standard practice for countries such as the UK and the US. CAAT considers these contractors to be modern-day mercenaries.

The Geneva Convention may classify as a mercenary a civilian contractor who is "motivated to take part in the hostilities essentially by the desire for private gain and, in fact, is promised, by or on behalf of a party to the conflict, material compensation substantially in excess of that promised or paid to combatants of similar ranks and functions in the armed forces of that Party". Private military companies have become big business, with an estimated turnover world wide of $100 billion, and their use is set to rise.

The UK Government's Green Paper of 2002 on Private Military Companies prompted a debate on the privatisation of a whole range of military services which has been taking place with little comment, high profile cases such as Sandline in Sierra Leone notwithstanding. CAAT seeks an end to all mercenary activities. If this cannot be achieved at this point, the following controls are its minimum immediate requirements:

- a ban on all combat activities
- all dealings between Government departments and agencies and the military companies, other than operational details, to be in the public domain
- any contract entered into between a military company and a foreign government to stipulate a cash fee and no other benefit. No other business sharing directors or offices with the providers of security should be allowed to have any dealings with the foreign government concerned for a period of, say, five years. The ownership of the military companies should be made transparent.

- companies to be made responsible under UK law for any breaches of human rights or the laws of war that may be committed by their employees

CAAT is also committed to publishing research on the issue in order to raise public awareness of the ever increasing role mercenaries play in modern conflict zones.

Structure and Funding Network

CAAT has no formal membership structure. Individuals and affiliated groups (local branches of peace organisations, trade unions, churches, etc.), donate whatever they can afford towards the cost of running the campaign and receiving *CAAT News*, a bi-monthly magazine. There are also sponsoring groups who either took part in founding CAAT or have taken a major supporting role since. However 80% of CAAT's funding comes from individual donations.

CAAT is made up of grass-roots groups who come together to campaign for a variety of causes and issues surrounding its overall aims. In addition to local groups, CAAT also has a Christian Network, which looks at arms trade issues involving churches and mobilises Christians against the arms trade, (although CAAT as a whole includes members from many diverse faiths and those of no faiths). CAAT also has a Universities Network which involves students and university staff in campus-based campaigning. Potentially, other new networks can be formed at any time.

9

Taxation of the Arms Trade

INTRODUCTION

The idea of taxing the arms trade has been around for some time. It seemed attractive to several authors, including some very eminent ones, for a number of reasons, including that it might provide additional funds for development. However, there are major practical and also principal problems connected with an arms trade tax. It therefore was never close to being seriously negotiated, let alone implemented. There has been a revival, since the late 1990s in the form of an "insurance" on small arms with limited objectives but some potential to arouse political interest.

Earlier suggestions

The idea of an arms trade tax first gained international prominence through its place as one of the major recommendations fur further consideration in the „Brandt"-Report (Independent Commission on International Development, 1980). The commissioners argued that a tax on the arms trade would have the effect of increasing the price of arms and thereby reduce arms transfers. This was deemed to be beneficial for development as arms imports were seen both as a financial impediment to development as well as a factor in fueling conflicts. However, the Commission also felt that the tax could rake in income that could be used for development purposes. The Brandt-Commission's suggestion of an arms trade tax was picked up by both non-governmental organizations and some governments. However, there was also major criticism and opposition for reasons discussed below. In the end, there was little follow-on to the suggestion and the arms trade tax met a similar fate as the bulk of the "Brandt-Report", which had been asked for by the then-President of the World Bank, Robert McNamara. Reduction of the negative effects of the arms trade, including through some kind of tax, was also an issue in the discussions of the later Palme-Report (Independent Commission on Disarmament and Security, 1982).

In the late 1980s and early 1990s the idea of an arms trade tax was predominantly kept alive by Oscar Arias, former President of Costa Rica and winner of the Nobel Peace Prize. Arias variously advocated to use the income gained from a substantial tax on the arms trade to feed a development fund, or to use the money to support disarmament activities in developing countries. He also contributed, in this vain, to the Human Development Report of 1994 which addressed military-related issues and where the later influential concept of 'human development' was developed (UNDP, 1994). Recently, a variant of an arms trade tax has been debated within NGO circles concerned about the widespread suffering stemming from the use of small arms. The German researcher Peter Lock proposed to levy a tax on ammunition exports and to require producers and traders of small arms to pay for compulsory third party damage liability insurance. The income from these compulsory insurance premiums, which can be thought of as a tax, should be used to compensate victims of small arms use. The suggestion of a compulsory third party damage liability insurance was reiterated by the "group of eminent persons" on small armed chaired by former French Prime Minister Michel Rocard. While it has not found its way into the documents to be negotiated at the United Nations Conference on the Illict Arms Trade in All its Aspects, scheduled for July 2001, it remains on the agenda of NGO and some states, such as Mali.

OBJECTIVES OF AN ARMS TRADE TAX

Proposals on an arms trade tax have vented a number of objectives:

- Reduce the volume of the trade (and, in turn, production) in arms. The rationale here is that arms are traded 'too cheaply'. Fewer weapons will, so it is assumed, reduce the incidence and costs of wars, especially those fought by insurgents with little financial backup. In addition, it has been argued that an increase in price might reduce the volume of arms imports and thus save money which could be spent for development purposes.

- Raise money. The original proposal contained in the Brandt-Report included the consideration of an arms trade tax as a source of 'fresh' money for economic development. As mentioned, Oscar Arias has, in several contributions, focused on this objective and called for the funds raised through an arms tax to be spent on economic development and disarmament measures.
- Compensate victims of wars. The idea of a compulsory insurance on arms sales (currently limited to small arms, but covering domestic and export sales) combines the objectives of lowering sales volumes and raising money, albeit for a very specific purpose. It draws on principles of causation, such as 'polluter pays', by holding producers and users of weapons responsible for the damage done by the use of weapons. In some proposals it is envisaged that private insurance companies will be involved in administering such a compulsory insurance scheme. However, it may be more realistic, in view of the risks involved, to provide for some mixture of private administration and public guarantee, or an independent fund for the compensation of victims.

VOLUME AND PRICE EFFECTS OF AN ARMS TRADE TAX

The level of possible revenues from an arms trade tax has not been seriously estimated. There are several reasons for this lacuna. One is that the proposal has never gained much international support, but there are also serious methodological problems. The volume of the arms trade is not well established. Furthermore, it is difficult to estimate what will happen to prices and volumes after a tax on the arms trade has been introduced. Such an estimation is however necessary as both sellers and buyers will adopt their behaviour to the new circumstances.

Arms trade volume

The volume of the global arms trade is not known. Traditional methods to determine the trade in specific goods do not yield results. International trade statistics, such as those published by the United Nations or the International Monetary Fund, probably include most of the trade in arms, but mostly in categories that do not distinguish between military and civilian goods.

Neither the Standard International Trade Classification (SITC) nor the Brussels Tariff Nomenclature (BTN), the two most widely used international trade classification schemes, provide for sufficient detail to separate the trade in arms. Only a few national statistical offices differentiate further than recommended and publish comprehensive data on their exports and imports of arms.

Those that do provide statistics that are not fully comparable, as different statistical standards of what goods to include are applied (Brzoska, 1985). Estimates of the volume of trade therefore have to rely on other methods. Generally the approach is to find about the physical transfer of goods. The most ambitious of these efforts is the UN's Register of Conventional Arms. It came about in 1993 in order to increase transparency of cases of threatening accumulations of weapons. The reporting record on the exporter side has been good, though not comprehensive. However the Register only contains data on the number of weapon systems transferred and no financial data.

Other sources provide estimates of the volume and value of the arms trade. The two best known are the US Department of State (United States, 2000) and the Stockholm International Peace Research Institute (SIPRI 2000). Methodological basis for estimates and coverage differ among these sources. A rough estimate would put the trade in major weapons (aircraft, armored vehicles, artillery, ground radar, missiles, ships) at about $30 bn in the late 1990s. Including other types of weapons (light weapons, ammunition) and spare parts brings the trade volume up to about $50 bn. These rough estimates do not include the illegal trade whose volume, by definition, is not known.

Arms trade price elasticities

What would happen in the case of a 10 percent arms trade tax? Will it affect the quantity of weapons traded, the price of weapons? How much would this reduce the income from such a tax? Will the arms trade volume (producer price plus tax times quantity) increase or decrease with a tax? And who will actually pay the tax, the producers, or the buyers? In order to provide answers to these questions, some basic economics of the arms trade is necessary.

Few studies of the effects of price on demand and supply – the price elasticities of demand and supply-in the weapons trade exist, most of these are theoretical or based on studies of single cases.

There is no agreement on the price elasticity of supply. Standard economic reasoning, based on decreasing marginal product, assumes that price increases with quantity. However, there are good reasons to surmise that price actually decreases with longer production runs. One major factor are the high up-front costs of weapon systems, which are often borne by the national procurement authorities and are not recovered in later exports to third countries. A second factor is steep learning costs, resulting in increasing economies of scale. A third factor is competition among suppliers. Especially since the end of the Cold War overcapacities of production in many countries have resulted in fierce competition on world arms markets, often subsidized by national governments of the producer countries. For simplicity, in the following discussion, two cases of supply curves are distinguished: one where supply increase with prices, the other where supply is perfectly elastic, that is not dependent on prices (constant economies of scales). The demand curve seems to be more standard. Levine and others found, in a crossectional comparison of arms trade statistics from different sources, a price elasticity of about –0.5 (the only other significant determinant of quantity in their regressions estimation was military expenditures of importers, which was positively related to quantities, Levine, Mouzakis and Smith, 1998 p. 232). However there is reason to believe, that the price elastiticity of demand is lower, and may even become inelastic for countries in crisis or at war. In such cases, a certain amount or weapons may be demanded, whatever the price.

Here is a brief summary of the effects of a tax, depending on price elasticities of demand and supply:

- With standard price elasticities, the effects of a tax are split between a decrease in quantities and an increase in price, depending on particular elasticities. With a given demand curve, the volume of tax (marked by the gray area) decreases with the reduction of quantities in equilibrium. The total volume of the arms trade (including tax) would rise or fall, depending on the elasticities of supply and demand. Income for arms producers (prices times quantities) would decrease.
- With a perfectly elastic supply of weapons, the price rises by the full amount of the tax, while quantities are also reduced. Tax volume is lower than in the first case. The total volume of the arms trade (including taxes) would likely fall, depending on the price elasticity of demand. Income of arms producers (income times quantities) would decrease.
- With perfectly inelastic demand quantities with respect to prices, the prices also rise by the full amount of the tax. As quantities are not affected, this results in the maximum possible tax revenue. At the same time, the volume of the arms trade (including taxes). Income of arms producers would remain constant.

Incidence of an arms trade tax In some of the proposals for an arms trade tax it seems to be assumed that this more or less automatically would lead to a North-South transfer, from arms producers to beneficiaries of the income from such a tax. However, an arms trade tax is a typical consumer tax. The burden of consumer taxes is generally shared among producers and consumers, depending on price elasticities of supply and demand.

Structure of the arms trade

The trade in arms is predominantly a North-South trade, a trade from industrialized countries to developing countries. An initial impression therefore would be that a tax on arms transfers would predominantly be a tax on industrialized countries. This assumption seems to be behind ideas to use an arms trade tax as a fund for development purposes.

A simple argument could go like this: As the volume of the arms trade is about US $50 billion, a 10 percent tax would result in income of about $5 billion. This money could then be used for development purposes. As indicated above this tax volume would only come about in a situation of perfectly inelastic demand. In all other cases, the volume of trade, and correspondingly the tax income, would be reduced. The actual reduction would depend on the exact shape of the supply and demand curves, but it would likely not be substantial.

Who pays?

Taxes can be raised at the level of the supplier or the buyer. While this may make a difference with respect to the practicalities of raising the tax, it does not do so with respect to the basic economics of a tax. The incidence of the tax, who is actually paying in the end, is not affected.

The earlier discussion of effects of a tax can be extended to cover the basics of the incidence of such a tax:

- In the 'normal' case, with 'standard' elasticities, the tax is split between buyers and sellers: buyers have to pay more, but, with reduced quantities, producers also get less.
- In the case of perfectly elastic supply, the price rises by the full amount of the tax. The tax has to be entirely borne by the buyers. Quantities are reduced, but by definition this has no effect on the price of supply.
- In the case of perfectly inelastic demand, the entire tax burden is also borne by the buyers. This, obviously basic, discussion of the incidence of an arms trade tax indicates that it certainly cannot be assumed that the burden will be borne exclusively, and most likely not even predominantly, by producers. Rather, it is more likely that a good, if not the major, part would be borne by buyers.

Tax incidence and tax objectives

Obviously only buyers of weapons would pay the tax. But these would likely contribute a major chunk of the tax income. If this income was fed into a fund, whether for development as originally suggested by the Brandt Commission, of for disarmament, as suggested by Oscar Arias, or for war victims, as suggested by Peter Lock, it would be, to a major extent, coming from the buyers who are predominantly in the developing world. Still, unless their demand for weapons was perfectly inelastic, another objective of an arms trade tax, namely a reduction in the quantities of arms imports, would be achieved. However, again depending on the elasticities, they might pay more for the fewer weapons they get.

COMPLIANCE ISSUES

Supplier participation

A standard objection to an arms trade tax – as well as to any other global tax, is that it is unlikely that all, or even the major, supplier governments would participate. There are several issues involved:

- Incentives to export arms. Arms producing countries have, as outlined above, strong economic incentives to export arms. They therefore need to expect substantial political or economic benefits from reducing arms exports and feeding an international fund.
- Strategic behaviour. Unless it is assured that at least the major supplier states are participating, an individual arms producing country going along with an arms trade tax will lose overproportionally. Other, non-complying producing will gain market shares. As this is known to all major suppliers, it is likely that no one will agree to raise the tax unless it is fairly safe that all major suppliers will agree (unless a country has strong national incentives to do so).
- Absence of an enforcer. Without a world government, or a similar authority to level such a tax, it would be difficult to bring individual countries to comply. For instance, if the tax was raised at the level of producers, there would have to be a mechanism to ensure that producers raise the tax and transfer it to a fund, or whatever is foreseen to be sourced by the tax.

Illicit trade

Another problem of an arms trade tax that is fairly frequent also in other areas of taxation is that of tax avoidance through illegal trade. Already a good part of the international arms trade is illicit. The illicit arms trade encompasses not only the perfectly black market, where stolen or otherwise illegally acquired weapons are sold, but also various types of "gray" markets, for instance covert sales by governments, illegal resales of used weapons, sales of weapons as dual-use goods etc. A tax on arms transfers would likely increase the incentives for trading illicitly, for producers, traders as well as governments. It is however unlikely that this would become a major new problem at least as long as the major arms exporting countries were willing to enforce such a tax.

The high-cost end of the internal arms market is regulated fairly well, not in the least because it is difficult to hide the transfer of 'bigticket' items. An arms export tax would not change this situation. On the other end of the market, small arms and light weapons, very substantial illicit trading is already occurring. This may increase. However, as trade volumes involved are not very large, this would not affect the tax income in a major way. It might lead to an even lesser degree of public oversight and control in an area that is already widely out of control (Lumpe, 2000).

Increased transparency

One major precondition for participation of a sufficient number of governments would be greater transparency in the arms trade. While the level achieved with respect to heavy weapons, for instance through the UN Register of Conventional Weapons, is encouraging, it is not sufficient. For instance, there is no reliable information on prices and volumes. Much more problematic is the situation with respect to small arms and light weapons. Here some NGOs and like-minded governments started a major initiative which is, in 2001, culminating in the mentioned United Nations conference. However, much more work will need to be done before transparency in this part of the arms trade is sufficient for a verifiable arms trade tax.

Stimulating domestic production

A tax on trade would very likely stimulate tax avoidance through non-taxed domestic production. It is well established, that restrictions on the arms trade stimulated domestic production. However, domestic arms production in countries that do not have a very diversified industrial infrastructure tends to be comparatively expensive. A tax with a low rate will therefore not have major effects on domestic arms production.

PRACTICAL ASPECTS OF ARMS TRADE TAXATION

Tax collection

An arms export tax would best be collected at the point of export. While in theory there is no difference whether the tax was collected at the point of production, export or import, practical considerations make it more plausible to focus on exports. One reason is that the number of exporting countries is considerably smaller than the number of importing countries (about half as many countries). A second reason is that exporting countries are predominantly industrialized countries which in general have more experience in collecting export taxes and more effective customs services.

Tax basis

While national definitions of weapons differ and international trade statistics do not cover weapons comprehensively (Brzoska, 1995), there exist a number of definitions of weapons which would be readily available for taxation purposes. Two definitions, for heavy weapons and for light weapons have been developed within the UN system. In addition, the Wassenaar Arrangement, an informal information mechanism which includes more then 30 countries responsible to close to 95 percent of all arms exports has developed a comprehensive munitions list. The European Union has adopted a list which is very similar to the Wassenaar munitions list.

Reexports

The implementation of an arms trade tax would face a number of specific issues that would need to be addressed. One such issue is reexports. It lies in the logic of an arms export tax that all exports of arms should be taxed, whether they are exports of new or old weapons. On the other hand, exports of parts (which are classified as weapons) within coproduction projects should not be taxed, rather the export of the completed should be taxed.

Principal issues

The idea of an arms trade tax has also been questioned from more fundamental points of view. Singling out the trade in weapons While several observers found it very attractive to tax specifically the trade in weapons, others have objected. Proponents of an arms trade tax have highlighted the detrimental effects that weapon imports can have. Thus Oscar Arias has argued that spending on weapons has been detrimental for development and that excessive transfers of arms have been a major factor in the escalation of conflict into wars, their prolongation and human costs (Arias, 1995). Opponents, on the other hand have argued that the links between arms transfers and wars are weak, and that it is a solemn right of governments to import arms, indirectly guaranteed through Article 51 of the UN Charter on the right to individual and collective selfdefense.

As usual, there is some truth in all these observations. Arms imports are reducing import capacities and growth prospects of developing countries. They have contributed to the escalation and prolongation of some, but not all, conflicts (Brzoska and Pearson, 1994). It is a solemn right of countries to import arms for their defence, but not for purposes of aggression. On balance, it seems that there are good reasons for singling out and demeritorizing weapons. In fact this is already done in several ways. For instance, as was mentioned above, the UN maintains the Register of Conventional Weapons, an instrument of early warning of excessive accumulation of arms put into place after Iraq's armaments programs of the late 1980s had help make it into an aggressive military power. Arms exports restrictions are also the major form of sanctions under Chapter VII of the UN Charter exercised by the UN Security Council in the 1990s (Brzoska, 2001). Finally, a UN conference has been organized to address specifically the trade in small arms.

An arms trade tax would be a further, though not radically new, step in differentiating arms from other goods. It would signal, similar to specific consumption taxes in many countries that there are social costs which are not covered in market prices.

CORRECTING MARKET DISTORTIONS THROUGH SUBSIDIES

Arms exports are heavily subsidized by exporter countries. Export subsidies include the following forms:

- Direct subsidies. A number of suppliers financially support buyer countries, or buy weapons from producers and sell them, below production costs, to allies. An example of such a subsidy is the grant portion of the United States' Foreign Military Financing program. The US government plans to spent US $3.7 billion under this program in Fiscal Year 2002, predominantly for arms transfers to Israel (US $2 billion) and Egypt (US $1.3 billion).
- Indirect subsidy. A form of indirect subsidy results from the transfer of partly fungible resources to buyer governments which than use these resources, or their own resources freed by these transfers, to purchase weapons. The US government for instance plans to provide, in Fiscal Year 2002, US $2.3 billion of foreign aid under the Economic Support Fund, which predominantly is used to help Egypt and Israel defray the costs of weapons bought from US companies. Another, form of indirect subsidy is the linking of military and civilian projects. The UK government, for instance, funded the Pergau Dam in Malaysia with the tacit understanding that the Malaysian government would buy British Hawk aircraft. A High Court ruled this an illegal use of development aid money in October 1994.
- Export financing schemes. A number of countries maintain subsidized export credit schemes that regularly also cover arms sales. In addition, major supplier governments also give direct credit. The German government, for instance, is directly covering sales of submarines to Turkey at a concessional rate of interest. Military exports are explicitly exempted from the OECD's Guidelines for Officially Supported Export Credits as well as from the authority of the World Trade Organization.
- Marketing subsidies. Marketing or arms is often supported at government level, in the British case, for

instance, by the Defence Export Services Organization. Centralized government marketing can be an instrument to ensure that the seller government receives a part of the proceeds from arms exports, such as in the case of Russia's Rosoboronexport, in other cases, however, the government subsidizes sales through government agencies.

- Operational support. In many cases, governments are willing to provide training support to purchaser of weapons, either in their own countries, as a form of military aid, or in the buyer country. Sweden, for instance, has trained Indian officers to use Bofors guns sold to the country.
- Payment of initial research and development. Exports of weapons are often calculated on the basis of variable unit costs, not total costs. Initial research and development costs, which often are a large chunk of total costs are predominantly borne by the original producer government and not charged to export customers.

There are a number of estimates of arms export subsidies for individual countries which range between a few percent of the total value to more than a third of the value. The global amount of dedicated aid for military exports has declined drastically since the Cold War (Brzoska, 1992) but it is still substantial. The United States alone is planning close to US $6 billion to support arms transfers. Not included in the data on arms trade subsidies are generally cases of defaults by customers. Arms trade debts are not separated from other forms of debt and are, if need be, rescheduled as part of general debt relief. However, it is known that around the time of the Gulf War the US and other industrialized countries canceled close to $10 billion of debt outstanding from arms imports by coalition countries. Iraq, on the other hand, continues to have a similar debt to France and Russia for arms deliveries prior to the Gulf War (Brzoska, 1992). An arm s trade tax could correct for the general market distortion brought about by these subsidies. However, as mentioned, subsidies vary considerably among suppliers. A flat tax rate would not eliminate the distortion among suppliers (and, to the extent that they buy predominantly from one supplier, recipients) but could reduce the effective demand for weapons.

DIFFERENT TREATMENT OF PRODUCTION FOR DOMESTIC PURPOSES AND INTERNATIONAL TRADE

Another fundamental problem of an arms trade tax is that it privileges domestic production over trade. While the financial effects of such tax are not likely to be very large, it raises fundamental issues related to the equality and sovereignty of countries.

Countries which are importing weapons will be disadvantaged compared with those producing them domestically. It has been argued that this is against the spirit of the UN Charter, which, as mentioned, guarantees the right to self-defence. Restrictions to weapon imports, including special taxes, should therefore not be arbitrary but based on good reasons. An obvious counter-argument is that countries are free to produce weapons domestically and thus evade the tax. However, this argument is somewhat disingenuous, as such a strategy would most likely result in increasing expenditures on arms, and would thus be detrimental to the objectives of an arms trade tax.

Another argument is that there are already numerous taxes on arms exports of many countries – value added tax, export tax or administrative surcharges. The US government, for instance, routinely charges commercial arms producers when it processes exports. Still, it remains questionable to only tax the trade and not domestic production. The main reason for only choosing trade in earlier proposals seems to have been practicality. It would be even more difficult to comprehensively tax production than trade. It should be noted that the later proposal of an insurance premium covers production and trade.

Windfall profits for illicit traders

Another fundamental issue raised by some opponents to an arms trade tax is that it would benefit black and gray market arms dealers (Lock, 1999). These would be able to charge prices which included the tax without paying the tax. Again, the financial aspect seems to be less of a concern than the principal problem. This again is a problem with any consumer tax and not particular to an arms trade tax. The best way to deal with this issue would be to reduce the amount of illicit trade. The international community has been trying to do just this for some time, and is currently focusing on the trade in small arms. An arms trade tax would contribute to these efforts as it would raise the level of transparency in the international arms market.

Paying for arms imports

A particular concern is that of indirectly funding weapons imports through an arms trade tax. In general, an increase in the amount of resources available to a government will result in higher weapon imports (Brzoska, 1992). A transfer from a development fund to an arms buying government which is spending this extra-money as it spent those resources available to it earlier, will stimulate arms imports. As this government also at least partly paid the arms trade tax, it is also compensated for paying this tax. Care should therefore be taken that funds from an arms trade tax are not going to countries who are buying weapons in large quantities. Giving money to governments which are buying weapons would counter the major objectives of an arms trade tax, namely a reduction in the trade volume and making money available for development. Also, funds should not be fully fungible. It would be better, it they were paid our for specific projects which are clearly benefiting development. Alternatively, one could foresee, as Oscar Arias has done in some of his contributions, that the money should go to disarmament related projects, such as the demobilization and reintegration of armed forces, the destruction of weaponry or the conversion of defence industries.

10

The Development of South Africa's Arms Industry

South African society became increasingly militarised during the Total Strategy era of the 1970s and 1980s. At an economic level, militarisation included increasing levels of military spending, the development of a domestic arms industry and growing institutional links between the state, the military and private industry. The militarisation of the South African economy, which took place between 1961 and 1989, is reflected in the trends in the country's militarisation indicators.

'When human security needs are not met, we foster a cycle of violence. When we allow militaries to grow in power to control increasingly desperate populations, we have failed to address the root causes of conflict. Too many poor countries spend their limited resources on militaries that serve only to oppress their people. Unless we put an end to the arms trade, we will never put an end to violence.' – Dr Oscar Arias, 1987 winner of the Nobel Peace Prize

The development of a domestic arms industry was one of the most significant aspects of the militarisation of the apartheid economy. South Africa's arms industry was established with British aid just prior to the Second World War, when training aircraft were assembled locally and the Pretoria branch of the Royal Mint manufactured small arms ammunition. During the war, the arms industry manufactured a substantial amount of basic weaponry for the Union Defence Force and the Allied forces, including armoured cars, bombs and ammunition. After the war, most of the wartime arms factories converted to their pre-war civilian activities. During the 1950s and early 1960s, South Africa relied heavily on arms imports (mainly from Britain). However, South Africa's withdrawal from the Commonwealth in 1961, and the imposition of a voluntary United Nations arms embargo in 1963, provided the impetus for a shift towards the establishment of a domestic arms industry. The Armaments Production Board was established in 1964 to control the manufacture, procurement and supply of all armaments for the South African Defence Force. The board also took over the Department of Defence's workshops and the ammunition section of the South African Mint, and was authorised to co-ordinate arms production in the private sector. By the mid-1960s, nearly a thousand private sector firms were involved in various aspects of domestic arms production.

In 1967, the UN Security Council passed a resolution calling on all states to stop supplying arms to South Africa. In 1968, the Armaments Production Board's name was changed to the Armaments Board. It was tasked with the procurement of armaments for the SADF and ensuring the optimal utilisation of the private sector for arms production (Simpson, 1989:222). In the same year, the government established the Armaments Development and Production Corporation (Armscor). The Defence Ordnance Workshop and the Ammunition Section of the South African Mint became its first full subsidiaries. Over the next few years, Armscor took over various private sector companies, such as Atlas Aircraft Corporation, and established a number of new production and R&D facilities.

In 1973, the government established the Defence Advisory Council (DAC) to co-ordinate the private sector's involvement in domestic arms production. DAC was chaired by the then

THE SOUTH AFRICAN ARMS INDUSTRY

The South African arms industry was born in secrecy and its purpose was to facilitate the wars of destabilisation – the armed contras of Angola and the third force units like Vlakplaas. The lines between unconditional war and criminality were blurred and associated with bribery, corruption and murder. R130 billion was squandered in defence of apartheid and it is shocking that this industry is not being phased out in the new South Africa. The current Ministry of Defence even shares offices with Armscor. The cabinet seems to have a perverse fascination with this industry as a form of jobs and finances–despite the embarrassment caused by deals like those with Syria and Rwanda. Our arms deals have unfailingly brought us into disrepute. It is argued that South Africa has a right to self-defence even though we have never been attacked by another country. To argue that an arms industry is necessary for self-defence is nonsense, other countries manage fine without one. We need to sell 70 per cent of arms produced to be financially viable; one can't have an arms industry without selling weapons. Everyone working in this industry is one less person working in development in South Africa. South Africa still has a chance to do things differently.

Minister of Defence, P.W. Botha, and included the president of the Armaments Board and representatives from many of the country's major private sector companies (for example, Anglo American, Barlow Rand, Tongaat and South African Breweries). The establishment of DAC represented the growing institutional links between the state, the military and private industry.

Increasing international opposition to apartheid, and world-wide demands for a mandatory arms embargo against South Africa, prompted the government to embark on a major reorganisation and expansion of the arms industry during the mid-1970s. In 1976, the Armaments Board and the Armaments Development and Production Corporation merged to form the Armaments Corporation of South Africa (Armscor). The restructuring and expansion of Armscor was funded by a secret government grant of R1 200 million. The 'new' Armscor assumed responsibility for the procurement and production of armaments for the SADF. It was no coincidence that the reorganisation and establishment of the 'new' Armscor occurred in the same year as the United Nations mandatory arms embargo against South Africa.

During the 1980s, the domestic arms industry expanded considerably in response to South Africa's increasing involvement in regional conflicts, which required a guaranteed supply of weapons of ever-increasing sophistication, and the growing militarisation of the state.

New state-owned research, development and arms production facilities were established, and the private sector became increasingly involved in domestic arms production. By 1984, more than 2 000 private sector firms were involved in domestic arms production, either as contractors or suppliers of military technology and equipment to the SADF.

In the early 1980s, the arms industry began to experience economic problems as a result of increasing production costs, excess capacities and declining domestic demand. Drastic staff cuts were made at Armscor, several defence contracts with private sector firms were cancelled, some of Armscor's production activities were rationalised, and a government commission was set up in 1984 to investigate Armscor's financial problems. These problems were exacerbated by the embargo which forced the industry to adopt uneconomical practices, such as tooling-up for short production runs and stockpiling items which were not readily available in South Africa.

By the end of the 1980s, the arms industry had reached a relatively high level of self-sufficiency and could meet most of the equipment requirements of the SADF. However, because of the country's limited research and development (R&D) resources, and the presence of the United Nations arms embargo, the local arms industry did not try to reproduce or emulate the R&D which had already been carried out by the major Western arms producers. Instead, it concentrated on upgrading, modifying and modernising existing armaments and weapons systems. One of the ways in which South Africa became increasingly self-sufficient in arms production was through its ability to continue to obtain foreign inputs (technology, personnel, components) in circumvention of the United Nations arms embargo.

Economic significance of South Africa's arms industry

The establishment and development of a domestic arms industry necessitated massive investment by the state and large-scale private sector involvement. By the late 1980s, the arms industry had developed into one of the most significant 'sectors' of the country's industrial economy, in terms of both employment and its contribution to the national economy. However, its expansion and increasing economic significance during the 1970s and 1980s occurred when the economy was performing poorly, and there is evidence to suggest that the development of a domestic arms industry imposed a substantial burden on the national economy and was a contributing factor to the country's deteriorating economic performance in the 1970s and 1980s.

The arms industry emerged as a significant creator of jobs during the 1970s and 1980s. By 1989, over 150 000 were employed in the arms industry. Total arms industry employment as a percentage of total manufacturing employment increased from less than 1 per cent in 1961 to 10 per cent in 1989, while arms industry employment as a percentage of total employment in the formal sector increased from less than 1 per cent in 1961 to over 2 per cent in 1989.

Although the arms industry emerged as a significant provider of jobs during the 1970s and 1980s, most were highly capital-and skill-intensive and reserved for whites, given the strategic concerns of the industry. Thus the employment benefits of domestic arms production perpetuated the racist structure of the labour market and were inappropriate for a country such as South Africa with scarce capital and an abundance of unskilled labour. The arms industry also absorbed a disproportionate share of the country's skilled labour at the expense of the civilian economy, thereby inhibiting the development of the more productive sectors of the civilian economy. By 1989, Armscor employed nearly 2 000 scientists and engineers – over 10 per cent of the total number of R&D personnel in the national economy.

The use of scarce national resources for investment in arms production had negative consequences for investment in the civilian sectors of the economy. It has been suggested that the excessive share of state investment in strategic industries (for example, Armscor and Sasol) during the 1970s and 1980s represented a form of 'misinvestment', in that large amounts of scarce resources were invested in the wrong (capital-intensive) sectors and the wrong types of technology (for example, synthetic fuels) because of strategic considerations.

While the establishment of a domestic arms industry was intended to reduce the cost of arms imports, by the end of the 1980s it was estimated that South Africa was still spending nearly R2 billion on arms imports per annum. The value of arms imports peaked in the years before the imposition of the United Nations arms embargo in 1977, then declined quite substantially throughout the 1980s, with marginal increases in the late 19805. While South Africa became less dependent upon imports of completed weapons systems after 1977, it remained highly dependent upon imports of machinery, technology and components which it needed for arms production. Thus, the development of a domestic arms production capability created new forms of dependency on foreign sources of technology and machinery, and ended up absorbing increasing amounts of scarce foreign exchange sources. South Africa's arms industry entered the international arms market in the early 1980s as a result of rising overhead costs, excess capacities and declining domestic demand. Armscor launched a massive international marketing drive in 1982, and by 1989 the value of South Africa's arms exports had increased by nearly 400 per cent.

Despite the increases in the value of arms exports between 1982 and 1989, the contribution to the national economy was fairly insignificant if one includes the costs of export subsidies, marketing (paid for by Armscor from the defence budget), and the fact that much of the R&D and production costs of export products were subsidised by the domestic procurement budget. South Africa's trade balance in armaments remained negative between 1982 and 1989, despite the positive contribution of arms exports. The arms industry remained a net user of foreign exchange throughout the 1980s.

The evidence presented in this section suggests that the increasing militarisation of the South African economy, and particularly the development of a domestic arms industry, imposed costs on the national economy. The fact that the arms industry absorbed scarce resources (capital, labour, foreign exchange) at the expense of other sectors not only exacerbated many of the existing structural problems in the apartheid economy (for example, shortages of skilled black labour) but also contributed to the underdevelopment of civilian sectors.

Defence cuts and disarmament measures

South Africa's external strategic environment changed dramatically after 1989. The end of the Cold War and the break-up of the former Soviet Union effectively put an end to superpower rivalry in many parts of the Third World, including southern Africa. The cessation of East-West contestation was accompanied by a reduction in ideological tensions within and among African countries, and by significant moves towards political pluralism in southern Africa (for example, Zambia and Malawi). These developments contributed to the resolution of most of the region's historical conflicts (for example, Namibia and Mozambique) and provided opportunities for countries to reduce their levels of military spending and implement disarmament measures.

The interlinked processes of democratisation and disarmament which occurred had a positive impact on the South African state's external threat perceptions, and led to dramatic changes in the country's defence and foreign policies. South Africa withdrew its armed forces from Namibia and Angola in 1989, formally abandoned its policy of military aggression and regional destabilisation (for example, covert support for Unita and Renamo), and embarked on an ambitious programme of diplomatic and economic outreach to African states. These developments, together with the ending of apartheid, removed the dominant source of instability and antagonism in the region and led to a dramatic improvement in inter-state relations.

As a result of these positive developments, and in response to severe budgetary constraints and changing government spending priorities, the De Klerk government cut South Africa's defence budget dramatically after 1989. Between 1989 and 1995, the defence budget declined by more than 50 per cent. With the defence cuts, the share of defence spending in GDP declined from over 4 per cent to just over 2 per cent between 1989 and 1995; the share of defence in total government expenditure declined from over 15 per cent to 7 per cent during the same period.

The structure of the defence budget exhibited significant changes between 1989 and 1995. The share of personnel and operating costs increased at the expense of procurement and R&D spending. The increasing share of personnel costs during the pre-election period was related to the SADF's internal deployment in support of the police, particularly as a result of the increasing political violence which accompanied the final stages of the constitutional negotiations. The share of personnel and operating costs continued to increase after 1994 as a result of the integration process and the formation of the South African National Defence Force (SANDF). The dramatic decline in the share of procurement spending was related to the cancellation and postponement of several armaments projects.

Despite the significant cuts in South Africa's defence budget between 1989 and 1995, the country remained the largest military spender on the continent in absolute terms. In 1995, it accounted for nearly 65 per cent of total military spending in southern Africa, and 27 per cent of total military spending in Africa (SIPRI, 1995).

The defence cuts implemented after 1989 were achieved as a result of, and in conjunction with, a variety of disarmament measures. These included:

- the rationalisation and restructuring of the SADF, including the disbanding of various SADF units and the closure and scaling-down of various bases and installations;
- ending compulsory conscription for white males at the end of 1993;
- the cancellation and postponement of major weapons projects;
- retrenchments of SADF and Armscor personnel;
- the withdrawal or sale of redundant and surplus military equipment;
- the termination of the country's nuclear weapons programme.

The cuts in defence spending were accompanied by the restructuring of the public sector arms industry. As part of a policy of 'commercialising' public enterprises, the government restructured Armscor into two organisations in April 1992. A new state-owned industrial company called Denel was formed under the Ministry of Public Enterprises, and inherited most of Armscor's R&D and production facilities. Armscor remained part of the Ministry of Defence and retained responsibility for the acquisition of armaments for the SADF.

The economic impact of defence cuts and disarmament

Defence cuts, although desirable for a number of moral, political and economic reasons, can have short-term adjustment costs. These costs are normally felt in terms of job losses and the impact on towns and regions dependent on defence spending. The defence cuts and disarmament measures implemented in South Africa after 1989 had a dramatic impact on the domestic arms industry. Many defence firms went out of business or exited from the defence market, and the industry as a whole underwent a process of downsizing and restructuring. The value of arms production (including exports) declined by over 40 per cent between 1989 and 1995. The contribution of the arms industry to the national economy also declined after 1989, and the value of domestic arms production in total manufacturing output declined from nearly 8 per cent in 1989 to around 4 per cent in 1995 and, as a share of GDP, from nearly 2 per cent in 1989 to under 1 per cent in 1995.

The cuts in defence spending had a significant impact on employment in the domestic arms industry. Total employment declined by over 90 000 between 1989 and 1995, including over 10 000 in the public sector arms industry. Arms industry employment as a percentage of manufacturing employment declined from over 10 per cent in 1989 to 4 per cent in 1995. As a percentage of total employment, it declined from over 2 per cent in 1989 to just over 1 per cent in 1995. The declines in arms industry employment occurred within the context of a severe recession and corresponded to declines in manufacturing employment and total employment in South Africa generally. The job losses in the arms industry after 1989 were not offset by compensating increases in employment in other civilian sectors of the economy, and may have contributed to increasing unemployment in the economy as a whole. While it is possible that the lack of job creation in the civilian sector was linked to the presence of a severe domestic economic recession, the De Klerk government at no point used the savings from defence cuts to fund retraining schemes for defence workers or to create new civilian markets. Occupation categories, such as engineers, scientists and labourers, bore the brunt of the retrenchments in the arms industry and there is evidence to suggest that many found it difficult to find work in civilian sectors.

The negative impact of the defence cuts and disarmament was felt most acutely in those towns or regions which were heavily dependent on defence spending as a result of the location of military bases or arms production facilities (for example, Simon's Town). The bulk of Armscor's retrenchments (nearly 80 per cent) after 1989 were concentrated in the Pretoria-Witwatersrand-Vereeniging (PWV) region, compared to the 20 per cent in the Western Cape, and less than 1 per cent in the Free State (Batchelor, 1996). These retrenchments corresponded to the geographical location of Armscor production facilities and the private sector arms industry (Rogerson, 1990). Although defence cuts were concentrated in the PWV region, the size and diversity of the region's economy meant that it was more able to absorb the impact than some of the country's other regional economies.

A GLOBAL PERSPECTIVE ON LIGHT WEAPONS

The twentieth century has been marked by a global scattering of violence and the material vehicles of violence – light weapons. Increased intergroup violence is a major characteristic of the contemporary world, with particularly harsh outbreaks in Bosnia, Burundi, Croatia, Kashmir, Nagorno-Karabakh, Georgia, Rwanda, Sri Lanka, Somalia, Sudan, Yemen and the Kurdish areas of Iraq and Turkey. This violence is often explained by essentialist arguments about a primordial ethnic identity. The dangers of the reliance on a primordialist theory of ethnicity are illustrated in the case of Rwanda. The theory assumes that people are born into particular cultural identities which command their deepest loyalties. The violence in Rwanda between the Hutus and Tutsis – and the violence in former Yugoslavia between Serbs and Croats – is explained in terms of fixed, inherited identities. However, many scholars have emphasised that ethnic antagonism did not cause the 1994 Rwandan genocide, although the form it took involved the systematic manipulation of ethnic identities for political ends.

The 1994 Rwandan genocide also illustrates the impact of the systematic accumulation of modern weaponry. It shows how the growing global diffusion of small arms is contributing to the incidence and intensity of violence in the post-Cold War era. 'Western journalists have made much of the fact that a good deal of the killing was performed with knives and machetes, giving this episode a distinctive air of primitive savagery. It should be noted, however, that the killings began in a relatively systematic fashion . . . and that the earliest massacres were conducted by the army and organised militias equipped with grenades and assault rifles imported from France, Egypt and South Africa by the Rwandan (Hutu) government' (Klare, 1995:36). There is evidence that some of the mass murders – for example, of 20 000 people in a stadium – were carried out using machine-guns. This is an item South Africa exported to Rwanda in 1992, but the managing director of Armscor, in a letter to Amnesty International, also used arguments about machetes and ethnicity to minimise South African responsibility.

The Rwandan case is part of a larger pattern; since 1989 there have been global changes in the nature of violence and armed conflict. There has been a shift away from war between states involving major weapon systems, to intra-state war involving light weapons. Instead of wars being fought between states with well-organised armies equipped with major weapons systems confronting each other across defined geographic boundaries, today's violent conflict is usually an internal struggle with irregular forces using light weapons. This set of changes 'constitutes a remarkable break with the past'. The international disarmament agenda has focused on weapons of mass destruction and neglected light weapons. The threat of nuclear war has not disappeared – a threat captured in E.P. Thompson's warning of 'exterminism' – but it is one that has diminished, while light weapons proliferate.

The global diffusion of light weapons is part of recent changes in the global arms trade pattern. Michael Klare has conceptualised these changes as a shift from the 'proliferation/arms race' model that focused on the transfer of arms and technology involved in major weapons systems from one state to another, to what he terms the 'diffusion/global violence' model. The proliferation model was concerned largely with state-to-state transfers of major weapon systems from six or seven major industrial powers; under the diffusion model, there are more actors involved in the transfer of light weapons. The changes in the nature of armed conflict in the post-Cold War world have led not only to shifts in the global flow of weapons but to dramatic changes in the social organisation of violence. In intra-state conflicts involving light weapons 'it is members of the opposing group who are seen as the enemy, not the armed forces of a hostile state'. The boundaries of opposing group identities are socially constructed and defined.

The current predominance of light weapons has reversed the trajectory whereby warfare was becoming increasingly impersonal: a process of killing and maiming by pushing a button or moving a lever. The technology of major weapons systems made its victims invisible 'as people ... seen through the sights of firearms could not be'.

Small arms are responsible for most of the deaths in current conflicts, the most common being the automatic assault rifle. The majority of actors in these conflicts are sub-state groupings. All the violent conflict under way in the world involves violence between internal groups, often ethnically defined, rather than states. According to one estimate, 'only 4 of the 82 armed conflicts recorded in 1989-92 were of a classic inter-state character, while all of the remainder entailed some degree of internal warfare, usually along ethnic and religious lines'. Instead of the 'cats paw' wars of the Cold War era fought by the superpowers using proxy forces, there are civil wars taking place within failed states, in what have been termed 'teacup wars' (Gelb, 1994:36). States are losing their monopoly of legitimate violence. 'The key narrative of the new world order is the disintegration of states' and the 'key language of that dissolution is ethnic nationalism'. This implies the reversal of another historic trend: the disarmament of civilians in the process of Western state formation. 'Well-armed groups of citizens are forming all over the world' (Tilly, 1991: 7) and this process threatens to subvert democracy.

SDUs were initially armed with knobkieries, spears and homemade weapons, but later obtained access to a variety of firearms including AK-47s and R4 rifles (Rosenthal, 1994). Rosenthal found that SDUs were not armed by MK, but by gun-runners operating in commercial rather than political interests. The vast majority of licensed gun owners in South Africa are white. Whites were granted firearm licences more easily than blacks. It was customary during the apartheid era to demand that blacks, coloureds and Indians have training before they were granted firearm licences, although whites were not required to undergo such training. The number of licensed firearm owners has increased dramatically since 1976. At the end of 1996, the total number of licensed firearms in South Africa was 4,1 million.

Licences are easily available and enforcement is minimal. At present, you can get a licence if you are mentally stable (established in a ten-minute conversation, according to one police informant), have never been convicted of a serious (violent) crime in the last 10 years and are at least 16 years old. A number of informants maintained that there is a massive amount of police corruption in processing firearm licences, which extends deep into the Central Firearm Register. Increasing numbers of licensed firearms are ending up in criminal possession. In contemporary South Africa, widespread poverty and unemployment have contributed to violence as increasing numbers of citizens have come to rely on criminal violence as a means of livelihood.

Analysing gun violence as a social phenomenon involves more than exploring individual biographies, motives and meanings; it involves examining the diverse social organisations, cultural frameworks, social practices, group attachments and institutions built up around guns. Collectively, these constitute a robust 'gun culture'. Overall, this culture provides a social sanction to the possession of guns and much gun violence follows culturally defined repertoires of behaviour. The values, social practices and institutions which constitute this gun culture include what Raymond Williams calls 'consumerist militarism'. It involves the normalisation, legitimation and even glorification of war, weaponry, military force and violence through television, films, books, songs, dances, games, sports and toys. None of these are insignificant in the light of Mann's definition of militarism as 'a set of attitudes and social practices which regards war and the preparation for war as a normal and desirable social activity'.

All of these cultural forms constitute a kind of 'banal militarism' which operates near the surface of social life. Banal militarism is embedded in everyday activities; it works through prosaic routines and rituals to make war, weaponry and violence appear natural and inevitable. It is exemplified in war games such as paintball, which has become increasingly popular among white South Africans since 1985. At its core, paintball simulates the sequence of killing. One Johannesburg informant involved in this 'gun culture' spent much of his leisure time playing paintball, practising at shooting ranges and cleaning and 'stroking' (his word) the 12 guns he owned. This behaviour is chillingly reminiscent of that of the killer responsible for Britain's worst mass murder, the Dunblane school shooting of 16 children and their teacher in 1996.

This gun culture not only operates to glamorise war and weaponry, but to 'normalise' these social arrangements. Part of this 'normalisation' is the notion that private gun ownership is legitimate; a right, not a privilege. A key institution which promotes this notion is the South African Gun Owners' Association (SAGA). This is not as powerful as the National Rifle Association in the United States, but in 1995 SAGA organised petitions to the Constitutional Assembly stating that the Constitution should be amended to recognise the right to own firearms and to place a limitation on government's power to disarm the civilian population. SAGA maintains that 'the anti-gun lobby's emphasis shouldn't be on guns – it should be on people. Guns are to crime as cameras are to pornography but they don't ban cameras.'

The notion that private gun ownership is legitimate is linked to the notion that guns are an effective and necessary form of protection. The gun combines two contradictory images: it is a means of order and of violence; paradoxically it is believed to provide protection from violence through the potential threat of violence. A common theme articulated by many informants who had purchased guns for self-protection was a sense of being powerless, of being victims of social forces beyond their control. But the psychodynamic power of the gun as protection is largely illusionary. Legally owned weapons contribute to the problem of violent crime.

Bibliography

Alan S. *War, Economy and Society, 1939-1945*. Berkeley: University of California Press, 1977.

Backman, Jules. *War and Defense Economics*. New York: Rinehart, 1952.

Ballantine, Duncan S. *U.S. Naval Logistics in the Second World War*. Princeton: Princeton University Press, 1947.

Burnham, John. *Total War: The Economic Theory of a War Economy*. Boston: Meador Publishing Company, 1943.

Buzan, B.: *People, States and Fear: An Agenda for International Security Studies in the Post-Cold War Era,* Harverster Wheatsheaf, London, 1991)

Cohen, I. & Goodwin-Gil, G S. *Child Soldiers: A Study for the Henry Dunant Institute,* International Committee of the Red Cross and International Federation of Red Cross and Red Crescent Societies, 1993.

Greider, William. *Fortress America: The American Military and the Consequences of Peace*. New York, 1998.

Grimmett, Richard F.: *Conventional Arms Transfers to Developing Nations, 1993–2000*. Congressional Research Service Report to Congress. Washington, D.C., 2001.

Gurr, T.: *Minorities at Risk: A Global View of Ethno-political Conflicts,* United States Institute of Peace Press, Washington D.C, 1993.

Harkavy, Robert E. *The Arms Trade and International Systems*. Cambridge, Mass., 1975.

Harold G. *U.S. Economy in World War II*. New York: Columbia University Press, 1985.

Harold Glenn. *Fundamental Economic Issues in National Defense*. Washington, DC: Brookings Institution, 1941.

Hartung, William D. *And Weapons for All.* New York, 1994.

James L. *The Economic Impact of the Cold War: Sources and Readings.* New York, 1970.

Klare, M T. *Lethal Commerce: The Global Trade in Small Arms and Light Weapons,* American Academy of Arts & Sciences: Cambridge MA, 1994.

Klare, Michael T. *American Arms Supermarket.* New York, 1984.

Krause, Keith. *Arms and the State: Patterns of Military Production and Trade.* Cambridge, U.K., 1992.

Laurance, Edward J. *The International Arms Trade.* New York, 1992.

Lens, Sidney, *Military-Industrial Complex.* Philadelphia: Prigrim Press, 1970.

McGrath, R. *Landmines: Legacy of Conflict,* Oxfam Publication, 1994.

Michael D. Salomon, and Norman A. Graham. *The Reluctant Supplier: U.S. Decisionmaking for Arms Sales.* Cambridge, Mass., 1983.

Pierre, Andrew J. *The Global Politics of Arms Sales.* Princeton, N.J., 1982.

Robert E. Harkavy, eds. *Arms Transfers in the Modern World.* New York, 1979.

Robert H. *The Navy and Industrial Mobilization in World War II.* Princeton, N.J., 1951.

Sivard, R L.: *World Military and Social Expenditures,* World Priorities, Washington D.C, 1993.

Smith, C.: *The Diffusion of Small Arms and Light Weapons in Pakistan and Northern India,* Centre for Defence Studies, Brassey's, London, 1993.

Thayer, George. *The War Business.* New York, 1969.

Van de Goor, L.L.P.: *Conflict and Development: The Causes of Conflict in Developing Countries,* The Netherlands Institute of International Relations, The Hague, 1994.

Zwoll, Wayne van. *America's Great Gunmakers.* South Hackensack, N.J., 1992.

Index

□□□